THE THREE CIRCLES OF WAR

Related Titles from Potomac Books, Inc.

Iraq and the Evolution of American Strategy
—Steven Metz

Iraq in Transition: The Legacy of Dictatorship and the Prospects for Democracy
—Peter J. Munson

Losing the Golden Hour: An Insider's View of Iraq's Reconstruction
—James Stephenson

Public Opinion and International Intervention: Lessons from the Iraq War
—Richard Sobel, Peter Furia, and Bethany Barrett, editors

Wanting War: Why the Bush Administration Invaded Iraq
—Jeffrey Record

Through Veterans' Eyes: The Iraq and Afghanistan Experience
—Larry Minear

THE THREE CIRCLES OF WAR

Understanding the Dynamics of Conflict in Iraq

Edited by Heather S. Gregg, Hy S. Rothstein,
and John Arquilla

Potomac Books, Inc.
Washington, D.C.

Library of Congress Cataloging-in-Publication Data

The three circles of war : understanding the dynamics of conflict in Iraq / edited by Heather S. Gregg, Hy S. Rothstein, John Arquilla.
p. cm.
Includes bibliographical references and index.
ISBN 978-1-59797-499-8 (cloth : acid-free paper) — ISBN 978-1-59797-500-1 (pbk. : acid-free paper)
1. Iraq War, 2003- 2. Civil War—Iraq. 3. Insurgency—Iraq. 4. Internal security—Iraq. 5. Postwar reconstruction—Iraq. 6. Iraq—Strategic aspects. 7. Military planning—United States. I. Gregg, Heather S. II. Rothstein, Hy S. III. Arquilla, John.
DS79.76.T476 2010
956.7044'3—dc22

2010006050

Printed in the United States of America on acid-free paper that meets the American National Standards Institute Z39-48 Standard.

Potomac Books, Inc.
22841 Quicksilver Drive
Dulles, Virginia 20166

First Edition

10 9 8 7 6 5 4 3 2 1

To all veterans of the conflict in Iraq: for your courage, adaptability, and persistence in defending the people against the threats posed by the many forms of war manifested there, we humbly dedicate this book to you.

All proceeds from this book will go to the Wounded Warrior Project, which provides programs and services to severely injured service members.

Map No. 3835 Rev. 4 UNITED NATIONS
January 2004

Department of Peacekeeping Operations
Cartographic Section

Contents

Preface ix
Acknowledgments xi
Introduction: Analytical Framework—the Three Circles of War and Iraq, *John Arquilla, Heather S. Gregg,* and *Hy S. Rothstein* 1

Iraq's Culture

1. Identity Politics and the War in Iraq, *Glenn E. Robinson* 11

Stabilizing Iraq

2. Political Development in Iraq, *Heather S. Gregg* 25
3. An Economic View of Security and Reconstruction, *Raymond E. Franck, Jr.* 35
4. Lessons from Reconstructing Indigenous Security Forces in Iraq, *Hy S. Rothstein* 45

Understanding Our Adversaries

5. Insurgent and Terrorist Finances in Iraq, *Michael E. Freeman* 59
6. The Internet and the Iraq Conflict, *Dorothy E. Denning* 69
7. Intelligence and the Wars in Iraq, *Joshua Rovner* 79

Legal and Ethical Issues

8. Legal Dimensions, *Christopher M. Ford* 91
9. Ethics in the Three Circles of War, *Russell Muirhead, Jr.* 103

Measuring War and Victory

10. A System Dynamics Modeling Perspective of Iraq's Conflicts, *Tarek K. Abdel-Hamid* 117
11. Metrics in Iraq's Complex Conflict Environment, *Karen Guttieri* 137
12. System Modeling of U.S. Efforts as Applied to the War on Terrorism in Iraq and Iraq's Infrastructure Resiliency: The Indicators of Force Multipliers (INFORM) Model, *William P. Fox* 153

Shaping Perceptions and Military Strategy

13. Strategic Communications, *Robert Reilly* 167
14. Strategic Dimensions of the Iraq Conflict, *John Arquilla* and *Douglas A. Borer* 179

Conclusions

15. Considerations for Leaving Iraq, *Heather S. Gregg*, *Hy S. Rothstein*, and *John Arquilla* 193

Postscript 205
Appendix: Formal Modeling of Iraq Using Game Theory and Dynamic Systems, *William P. Fox* 209
Recommended Readings 237
Index 243
About the Editors and Contributors 253

Preface

The purpose of this investigation was to examine the conflict in Iraq in a comprehensive manner. Work on this project started in late 2007. Studies of ongoing events often have difficulty keeping pace with their evolving nature. The situation in Iraq has certainly changed dramatically since we began this investigation. However, the framework developed to guide this effort—which argues that Iraq has experienced three types of war: interstate conflict, insurgency, and civil war—not only took into account the dynamic Iraqi environment but also embraced it.

Once the three-war framework was established, the task of identifying the individual elements for a comprehensive inquiry began. Many of these elements were obvious, such as the need to investigate U.S. military strategy, and we sought the best scholars and experts available to address these issues. But the project also aimed to identify the not-so-obvious elements. Here we identified experts in a variety of disciplines, such as ethics and system dynamics, and gave them an opportunity to contribute to the project using the established framework as a guide. The result, we believe, is not only a comprehensive investigation of the conflict in Iraq but also an analysis that has a much broader application for future decisions about war and peace.

Acknowledgments

This book began as a research project funded by the Rapid Reaction Technology Office (RRTO) in the Pentagon. The authors, therefore, would like to thank RRTO and its director, Ben Riley, for sponsoring this work and allowing it to be made into a book.

The initial draft of the manuscript received a much-needed edit from John Guardiano, who helped tremendously in making the chapters more readable.

Finally, the authors wish to thank the students of the Naval Postgraduate School and particularly the students of the Defense Analysis Department for sharing their experiences in Iraq with the authors. Their lively discussions helped to inform the various chapters in this book.

Introduction
Analytical Framework—the Three Circles of War and Iraq

John Arquilla, Heather S. Gregg, and Hy S. Rothstein

Prior to the Cold War, the majority of armed conflicts—including, most notably, both world wars—were fought between states. The advent of nuclear weapons and the potential for catastrophic destruction made interstate war politically untenable. Since the Korean conflict, the overwhelming majority of armed conflicts waged during the Cold War were irregular wars fought *within* states, such as the insurgencies in Latin America, Africa, and Southeast Asia. This trend continued in the post–Cold War era, in which internal ethnic conflicts, such as the dissolution of Yugoslavia, the genocide in Rwanda, and the Chechen rebellion, were the dominant form of armed combat. In the post–September 11 era, internal wars have continued to dominate the security environment.

How does one characterize these various forms of warfare? What are the key characteristics of each type? International wars, civil wars, and insurgencies, while sharing some similarities, have distinct characteristics, and thus different strategies are needed to counter them. This chapter defines each of the three types of war, highlighting their unique causes and resolutions and describing the dynamics among the types. It also details the security landscape of Iraq, which contains elements of all three forms of war.

Interstate War

Interstate wars are the easiest to identify and define. At their most formal level, they involve the use of conventional military weapons and battlefield tactics between two or more states in open confrontation. The forces of each side are well defined and are the primary target of the opposing army. Interstate wars are instruments of statecraft. They can be waged defensively, in reaction to another state's aggression, or they can be fought offensively, when a state initiates an attack with political and military objectives, such as diminishing another state's war-fighting capabilities. Operation Iraqi Freedom, for example, began as an interstate war with the aim of eliminating the political and military threat posed by Saddam Hussein. Interstate wars typically end with one state successfully defeating the other militarily or through negotiated settlement.[1]

Interstate war, therefore, is defined as follows:

- Two or more states' governments employ military force against one another.
- The opposing forces primarily use conventional military weapons and battlefield tactics.[2]
- The forces on each side are well defined and are the primary target of the opposing army.
- The war ends either with one state defeating the other militarily or with a negotiated end to hostilities.

It is important to note that interstate wars, while primarily waged in conventional fashion by general-purpose military forces, often feature elements of irregular warfare as well, with the most familiar being the commando-style raid or coup de main. Interstate conflicts also sometimes feature irregular operations, such as partisan warfare and sabotage, that are observationally equivalent to insurgent activities. The revolt in the Arabian Desert during World War I is a good example of an irregular campaign that played a significant part in a more general interstate war.

Civil War

Civil war is perhaps the most common type of internal war. It involves a violent conflict between political entities within a country that are fighting over control of the state, one side's separatist goals, or some divisive government policy.[3] Civil wars typically cause the government to split along factional—including ethnic—lines, resulting in the presence of more than one polity within a state's borders and the government's loss of the monopoly on the use of force. In civil wars, all sides have similar power and tend to fight conventionally. If one side were significantly weaker, the fight would take on characteristics associated with insurgency, guerrilla warfare, or terrorism. Alternatively, if one side were so strong that it could seize power quickly with little bloodshed, the proper description would be a coup d'état. Civil wars usually end either when one faction defeats another militarily, compelling that side to rejoin the state, or when the state splits, forming two or more states.[4] For example, the U.S. Civil War began with the Southern confederation seceding from the Union, forming its own government, and declaring its independence. The war ended with the total defeat of the South and its forced reunification with the North. The civil war in Ethiopia (1974–91), by contrast, ended with the split of the state and the creation of Eritrea.

Civil wars share the following elements:

- Two or more political entities within a state use force to maintain or gain control of the government, territory, or both.
- More than one polity exists within a state's borders, each claiming to be the legitimate sovereign.
- The prior government loses the monopoly on the use of force.
- The fighting sides have well-defined forces.
- The war ends with one polity defeating the other and compelling the other faction to rejoin the state or with the state splitting and forming two or more states.

Civil wars can be waged in a conventional or irregular fashion or in some mixture of the two. The Spanish Civil War (1936–39) was fought almost entirely along conventional lines, while the contemporaneous internal war in China featured mostly irregular operations conducted by Mao Zedong's forces. Similarly, the unorthodox tactics of Francis Marion in the American Revolutionary War and of J. S. Mosby (among many others) during the U.S. Civil War reflect the often substantial presence of irregular operations in internal conflicts.

Insurgency

Insurgency is another form of internal conflict that gained prevalence in the twentieth century. Insurgency is a protracted political-military struggle whose proponents' goal may be the seizure of power through revolutionary takeover and replacement of the existing government. In some cases, however, their goal may be limited to extracting from the government specific political concessions that would be unobtainable through nonviolent means. Insurgents may also target occupying or colonial forces with the aim of compelling their withdrawal. Insurgents are thus forces outside the ruling authority with members who are typically unknown to government forces. They are politically and militarily weaker than the government they oppose and therefore must fight indirectly, using guerrilla warfare and terrorism. Additionally, insurgents target not only the government but also the population, which they mobilize through compelling causes to give them political, moral, and material support. The insurgency's center of gravity—the source of power that provides its moral or physical strength, its freedom of action, or its will to act—is the loyalty of a state's population, for which both the insurgents and the government are competing.[5]

Insurgency is waged by a combination of means, employing political, economic, informational, and military instruments. Insurgent activities include guerrilla warfare, terrorism, political mobilization, propaganda, and international activities, all designed to weaken government authority while increasing insurgent control and legitimacy.[6] Insurgencies typically do not end through a military victory but rather through political and informational means that either delegitimize the insurgents by separating them from the population or bring the insurgents into the political process by making them part of the government. The Farabundo Martí National Liberation Front (FMLN) in El Salvador, for example, waged an insurgency against the government in the 1980s that ended when the insurgents were allowed to run in elections, hold office, and effectively become part of the government.

The characteristics of insurgencies are as follows:

- An organized group uses force indirectly against the ruling authority with the aim of changing policies, overthrowing the government, or compelling foreign forces to withdraw.
- Its members are known to the population but not the ruling authority.
- The group has a cause or grievance, usually directed against the ruling authority, that gives it political and moral legitimacy.
- The government and the insurgents battle for the population's loyalty, which is the conflict's center of gravity.

- The conflict ends either when the insurgents are defeated militarily or delegitimized and lose popular support or when they enter the political process and become part of the government.

Whereas interstate wars tend to be waged in more conventional fashion and civil wars can unfold in either traditional or irregular ways, with insurgencies the unorthodox prevails. This point is particularly important when considering the current dynamics in the fight against transnational terrorism, in which the al Qaeda network is conducting a global insurgency —meaning that its "field operations" are almost entirely irregular.

The Three Circles of War in Comparison

In practice, few armed conflicts fall neatly into one type of war. Most feature at least two types of war, perhaps with one form dominating. For example, the U.S. Civil War had the potential for international involvement, particularly British intervention on the side of the Confederacy, but it was predominantly a civil war. Some conflicts have all three types of war. The Vietnam War, for example, was a civil war between the north and the south, an insurgency between the communist Vietcong and the southern government, and an international war, drawing large numbers of U.S. forces—along with a range of small allied contingents—to defend the government in the south. The Soviet Union, for its part, provided substantial material support to North Vietnam, rounding out the interstate dimension of that war. Conflicts can also feature different types of war at different times. The Israeli-Palestinian conflict is a case in point. The 1967 Six Day War was a classic interstate conflict, followed by a Palestinian-led irregular war of attrition aimed at compelling Israel to withdraw to the pre-1967 "green line." Beginning in 2005, the infighting between Palestinian Fatah and Hamas forces had begun to resemble a civil war, with two Palestinian governments—a Hamas government in Gaza and a Fatah government in Ramallah—fighting for legitimacy and control of the government.

The conflict in Iraq has gone through all three types of war. It began as an international war when the United States and allied forces invaded in March 2003. After deposing Saddam Hussein and his regime, U.S.-led forces soon faced an insurgency headed by Sunni factions—and including some al Qaeda elements—fighting Coalition troops and the Shia-dominated

Iraqi government and security forces. After the 2006 bombing of the Shia al-Askari Shrine (Golden Mosque)—perpetrated by the Sunni al Qaeda in Iraq—the conflict there took on the characteristics of a civil war, replete with reprisal attacks between Sunni and Shia militias, and caused the government to split along Sunni and Shia lines. The interstate dimension of the conflict in Iraq continues to loom with concerns about Iranian interference and about Turkish military incursions into northern Iraq that could be prompted by a perceived need to prevent Kurdish autonomy or independence.

It is important to observe that actions taken to counter one type of war may actually drive the conflict into another form of conflict. For example, the strategy that U.S. and multinational forces employed in Iraq helped to move the conflict from an interstate war to an insurgency. The Coalition Provisional Authority attempted to redress Shia grievances under Saddam Hussein by giving the Shia majority proportional representation in the government and in the emerging security forces. As the absolute majority in Iraq, the Shia were thus allowed to dominate the political and security apparatus, threatening the Sunni minority. The Sunni responded by forming an insurgency aimed at ousting foreign forces from Iraq and toppling the country's fledgling government. For nearly four years, however, the U.S. military remained largely constrained by an interstate warfare paradigm, albeit one that was now in the "occupation phase." By the time the U.S. military began to focus more on counterinsurgency strategies and tactics—such as the "outpost and outreach" program launched in early 2007—the conflict began to exhibit the characteristics of a civil war. Shia-dominated Iraqi security forces became implicated in death squad–like attacks against Sunni neighborhoods, further exacerbating tensions.

It appears that the U.S. strategy lagged behind the shifts in the Iraq conflict. We were still thinking largely in terms of interstate warfare through the first years of the insurgency and redirected ourselves toward counterinsurgency only after the conflict had moved from an insurgency to a fledgling civil war. Arguably, all three faces of war are still on display in Iraq but to varying degrees. Thus whatever policy prescriptions are developed, they will have to be crafted with all three types of war in mind. Steps taken to deal with the remnants of the still-existing insurgency, if not carefully calibrated, might empower factions in a renewed civil war. Likewise, efforts to conclude the civil war might run the risk of provoking foreign intervention (notably from Iran or Turkey).

The way ahead in Iraq is thus complex and perilous. Our goal in *The Three Circles of War* is to contribute to a deeper understanding of this conflict, and modern warfare in general, by examining the three faces of war and determining the ways in which they interact across various areas of endeavor. We hope that this analytic approach will prove useful beyond Iraq, as future crises and conflicts no doubt lie ahead and are likely to be fought in more than one realm.

Notes

1. Geoffrey Blainey, *The Causes of Wars*, 3rd ed. (New York: Free Press, 1988), 245–49.
2. The potential use of nuclear weapons in interstate war is acknowledged.
3. James D. Fearon, "Iraq's Civil War," *Foreign Affairs* 86, no. 2 (March–April 2007): 2–15.
4. One of the classic compendiums on civil wars and related phenomena is Harry Eckstein, ed., *Internal War: Problems and Approaches* (New York: Free Press, 1964), which contains perspectives on internal war from Gabriel Almond, Karl Deutsch, Seymour Martin Lipset, Talcott Parsons, Lucian Pye, Sidney Verba, and others.
5. See, for example, Ted Robert Gurr, *Why Men Rebel* (Princeton, NJ: Princeton University Press, 1970), 14; and David Galula, *Counterinsurgency Warfare: Theory and Practice* (New York: Frederick A. Praeger, 1964), 4.
6. See Department of the Army, *Field Manual 100-20: Military Operations in Low-Intensity Conflict* (Washington, DC: Department of the Army, December 1990); U.S. Department of State, Bureau of Political-Military Affairs, *Counterinsurgency for U.S. Government Policy Makers: A Work in Progress*, Publication 11456 (October 2007); and Department of the Army, *Field Manual 3-24: Counterinsurgency* (Washington, DC: Department of the Army, December 2006).

IRAQ'S CULTURE

1
Identity Politics and the War in Iraq

Glenn E. Robinson

It is by now clear that prior to the March 2003 invasion, the Department of Defense (DOD) failed to fully appreciate the social, cultural, and religious cleavages in Iraqi society. Had the nature of those cleavages and, even more important, the potential fluidity of identity politics in times of upheaval been recognized, DOD could have planned its postwar operations in a manner more likely to have achieved success. By way of taking stock, the purpose of this chapter is to review the major ethnic, religious, and tribal identity groups in Iraq and how each responded to its country's interstate war, civil war, and insurgency from 2003 to mid-2008.

Three overlapping lessons are apparent from this cursory review. First, the strength of identity claims on individuals will vary according to circumstances on the ground. Iraqi national identity was clearly a deeply felt sentiment during the 1980s and earlier, but it weakened in the 1990s primarily as a result of state policies. Similarly, tribal identity, on the wane since the 1960s, enjoyed a powerful resurgence in the 1990s and gained renewed vigor after the 2003 U.S.-led invasion. A second lesson is how central personal and familial security has become when one chooses a predominant identity group in Iraq. Whichever group can best guarantee such security will win one's loyalty. The Sadrists' dramatic rise in strength in the post-2003 period stems primarily from the leadership's ability to provide personal security to urban Shia in the face of other predatory groups as well as extending Sadrist influence and resources for their members through their own predation.

The extensive social services the Sadrists offered to their members, mostly urban slum dwellers, added considerably to their personal security.

A third lesson revolves around the centrality of the state in the constriction or unleashing of substate identity politics. When the Iraqi state was strong and could provide both security and resources to the general population, the politicization of substate identity groups was at relatively low levels. Conversely, when the state has been weak (or even nonexistent, as it was for a period), its best survival strategy has been to encourage the politicization of identity. Saddam Hussein's regime did so in the 1990s when it encouraged tribalism as a means of surviving. The Nouri al-Maliki government has done much the same thing in quietly promoting Shia ascendancy through state policy and institutions as a means of consolidating power.

Sunni Arabs

Although Sunni Arabs make up less than 25 percent of the Iraqi population, they have long dominated politics and the economy. The Sunni Arab urban elite was the favored group of the Ottoman Empire, which practiced indirect rule in the Baghdad, Basra, and Mosul provinces. After the defeat of the Ottomans in World War I, Britain ruled Iraq but maintained the preference for Sunni Arab rule. This inclination was most dramatically shown when London installed the Hashemite family as the monarchs of Iraq. The Sunni Arab—and aristocratic—Hashemites were called to rule over a country in which Sunni Arabs were certainly already a minority. The nationalist revolution of 1958 and the Baathist coup of 1968 brought significant political change to Iraq, but in both cases, the central position of Sunni Arabs in Iraq's power structure was maintained.[1] This long history of privilege has created among Sunni Arabs a sense that they are entitled to political power. Democracy, which would naturally advantage the Shia, who constitute a majority of the population, is not widely embraced by Sunni Arabs. Instead, their general preference is for cutting deals on political outcomes (for example, in a power-sharing arrangement) over allowing political processes to determine outcomes (for example, letting democracy decide).

Thus, the single most important driving force for Sunni Arabs in their engagement in all three circles of war has been a reaction to the loss of their "rightful" perquisites of power and their struggle to regain all or most of the power they lost in 2003.

Three different Sunni Arab groupings have been involved in the three circles of war in Iraq and have been by far the most important local participants in violence: Sunni Arab tribes located mostly in rural areas and smaller cities, detribalized urban Sunni Arabs, and al Qaeda in Iraq (AQI), consisting primarily of foreign fighters but until recently allied to tribal groups.

Tribes

Not all tribes in Iraq are Sunni Arab. Indeed, 75 percent of all Iraqis are tribalized, including most Shia and Kurds, and several tribes—including the Shammar, the largest tribal group in Iraq with 1.5 million members—are a mixture of Sunni and Shia.[2] Still, the Sunni Arab tribes have been most centrally involved in the brief interstate war between Iraq and the United States and in the anti-U.S. insurgency.

The most important subunit of Iraqi tribes is the *kham*, or extended family, defined as five generations of male heirs to a single great-great-grandfather. Blood duties, including revenge killings, are obligatory for members of the khams but not for the tribe more generally. The most important supratribal unit is the *qabila*, or tribal confederation. Most Iraqis can trace their origins to one of nine qabila that were in place before the seventeenth century. The most important Sunni Arab tribes and tribal confederations include the Dulaym, Ubaydi, 'Azza, Muntafiq, Shammar, and Jaburi (the latter two having Shia clans as well).

The importance of tribal identity was in sharp decline in Iraq in the 1960s. Indeed, when the Baath Party came to power in 1968, its Communiqué No. 1 denounced tribalism as a feudal structure that helped prevent the modernization of Iraq. The Baath Party committed itself to destroying tribalism in Iraq.[3] For the next twelve years, the Baathist regime took significant steps—both tangible, such as instituting land reform policies that confiscated the holdings of tribal sheikhs, and intangible, such as using the "bully pulpit" to degrade and denounce tribal mentalities—to undermine tribes in Iraq.

Iraq's regional aggressions reversed the regime's anti-tribal stance. Throughout its 1980–88 war with Iran, the regime emphasized tribal solidarity as a means of enhancing its survival. This process intensified sharply in the 1990s after Iraq's invasion of Kuwait and the United Nations placed subsequent sanctions on Iraq. In the face of serious threats to his regime's survival, Saddam turned increasingly to tribal rhetoric, recruited regime members from loyal tribes, and distributed resources to those same tribes. Members of Saddam's own al Bu Nasir tribe and its allies in the Tikrit region (including, incidentally, the Shia al-Ahbab tribe) became the linchpin of the regime during Saddam's rule, in spite of Baathist ideological goals to the contrary. When regime survival is at stake and a regime must choose between its ideological goals and staying in power, ideology is quickly sacrificed.[4]

Thus, on the eve of the 2003 invasion, Sunni tribes were a central cog in Iraq's power structure. They had everything to lose through the creation of a new political order, and, indeed, they did lose everything. The interstate war was brief, so the Sunni tribes played only a limited role in the events of March and April 2003. However, Sunni Arab tribes were the backbone of much of the insurgency against U.S. forces between 2003 and 2007. There is considerable evidence that in the insurgency these tribes, particularly in Anbar Province, allied with other Sunni groups, including AQI and former regime elements with whom they were closely tied. Funding for the tribal insurgency appears to have come in large part from sources in Saudi Arabia, which sought to assist their fellow Sunnis at a time of expanding Shia power. The Sunni Arab tribes were not significantly involved in the civil war with the Shia, however, leaving that job to AQI and some urban Sunni elements tied to the former regime.

Since mid-2007, Sunni Arab tribes have largely desisted from participating in the insurgency. This change in policy reflected a significant adjustment in U.S. counterinsurgency strategy: U.S. forces cut deals with the tribes instead of fighting them. Once the Americans promised to arm, train, and pay these tribes, the prospects for at least a partial resurgence of Sunni power through U.S. means became possible, and the tribes largely withdrew from the insurgency and renounced their marriage of convenience to AQI. Tribes are notorious for their lack of true affinity to radical ideological movements, and the Sunni tribes' view toward AQI was no different.

AQI

The jihadi movement in Iraq contains both nationalist jihadi elements and genuine al Qaeda–oriented elements.[5] AQI was not involved in the interstate war of 2003, and it has had only limited success in fighting U.S. forces in the insurgency. The main goal of AQI has been to fuel the civil war between the Sunnis and the Shia in Iraq. AQI, which is a Sunni jihadist movement, comprises both Iraqi and foreign fighters. Its goal of fomenting civil war is twofold: first, AQI wants to stir up the genuine ideological hatred of the Shia among the Sunni jihadists; and second, a civil war would essentially make Iraq ungovernable, would ultimately drive out the Americans, and would thus provide an opportunity for Sunni jihadi rule in the Arab heartland.

Urban Sunni Nationalists

Finally, among the Sunni Arabs are bands of nationalist Sunnis who are often tied to the ancien régime and generally located in Baghdad and a few other major urban areas. These groups appear to be the most active in the insurgency against U.S. forces. Their local militias have also engaged in some ethnic cleansing against the Shia living in predominantly Sunni neighborhoods.

Shia Arabs

Most Shia in Iraq derive from nomadic tribes that were settled in the nineteenth century.[6] While they are often lumped together with Iran's Shia—and they do share generally friendly relations, some familial ties, and close trade relations—their social roots are quite dissimilar. Briefly, Iraq's Shiism is more tribal and less urbane, and a follower's *marja* (the religious leader one chooses to emulate) is more authoritative. Iran's Shiism has a much longer tradition of urban cosmopolitanism and is less strictly tied to the marja tradition.[7]

The Iraqi Shia (virtually all of whom are Arabs) have a vastly different view of political order in Iraq than that of Sunni Arabs, but they also have a more fluid and complex internal dynamic that has yet to play out entirely. Although the Shia constitute a majority of the total population, they have never held political power in Iraq. Repression under the Baath Party became particularly intense after Iraq's defeat in Kuwait and the subsequent failed Shia uprising against Saddam's regime in 1991. In general, the Shia have supported ending the Baathist regime and implementing majority rule in Iraq. They are the chief beneficiaries of this change in political order. Their principal foreign patron, Iran, has also recognized the benefits of this change and has largely been supportive of it, if quietly so. Iran would like the Americans to withdraw from Iraq but to leave the American-constructed, new Shia order intact.

Thus, the dominant strategy for the Shia has been to back the creation of a new political order that rewards majority rule and to consolidate their strategic gains in Iraq with tactical local changes. In terms of the three circles of war, the Shia's overarching goal has meant their support for the interstate war that brought down the ancien régime, their broad opposition to the insurgency that seeks to overthrow the new order and its primary protectors, and a tit-for-tat strategy with regard to the low-grade civil war with Sunni Arabs. The consolidation of Shia gains on the ground has included a significant amount of ethnic cleansing of Sunni Arabs from Shia and mixed neighborhoods in urban areas, primarily Baghdad. That objective has largely been achieved, which helps explain the decrease in intercommunal urban violence beginning in 2007.

In addition, there is an internal competition for political supremacy between the two primary Shia groups—the relatively affluent Badrists and the urban poor Sadrists. The commanding position of the Badrists has compelled the Sadrists to adopt a minority strategy of shaking up the new political order enough to gain power themselves but not so much as to allow Sunni Arabs to reassert their traditional dominance.

Badrists

"Badr Brigades" refer specifically to the paramilitary forces of the Islamic Supreme Council of Iraq (ISCI), which were formerly known as the Supreme Council of the Islamic Revolution in Iraq. However, I am using the term "Badrists" to refer broadly to organized Shia followers of Grand Ayatollah Ali al-Sistani, in general, and Ayatollah 'Abd al-Aziz al-Hakim (now his successor, son Ammar al-Hakim), in particular. Hakim is the current leader of ISCI, having taken over for his deceased father and brother, who was murdered in 2003. The Badrists tend to be middle-class, mainstream Shia and are by far the largest and most important stream of political Shiism in Iraq today. Their armed components are also formidable. Elements of the Badr Brigades likely still exist as an independent force (although a policy of ridding Iraq of all militias is technically in place), but much of the Badr militia forces have been integrated into the police and military. Bayan Jabr, a former Badr Brigade commander himself, recruited the Badr Brigades into the security forces when he was the minister of interior in 2005. These forces often became death squads that carried out anti-Sunni attacks.

In addition, the large majority of the Iraqi Army and police forces are Shia, and most of them come out of the broader Badrist tradition. Through 2007, the United States had spent nearly $20 billion on rebuilding the Iraqi Security Forces (army, police, and paramilitary), whose personnel number over 500,000.[8] The overwhelming Shia composition of Iraq's state coercive forces feeds the Sunni Arab perception that the Iraqi state is a partisan entity acting solely in the interests of the Shia and not for those of the entire Iraqi nation. Badrists, often through the state, have been involved in anti-Sunni civil war activities but not in the insurgency.

ISCI and the Badrists have carried out a remarkable balancing act between their two major foreign supporters—the United States and Iran. ISCI was in exile in Iran from 1979 until 2003, and it continues to have close and friendly relations with Tehran. At the same time, Hakim—now his son—and his followers have close relations with the United States and have supported the U.S. project of majority rule in Iraq.

Sadrists

The Badrists are internally challenged by Moqtada al-Sadr and his followers from urban slums, primarily from the section of Baghdad known as Sadr City (named after Sadr's father-in-law, before the U.S. invasion in 2003). Sadrists do not have stark ideological differences with the ISCI/Badrists, although there is a small millenarian component to the Sadrists. Rather, they are separated by class and by personality. Sadr's following is among the poorest Iraqis, and there are indications that class jealousy does play a role in the often tense relations between the two primary Shia groups. But perhaps more important are Sadr's political ambitions. The heir to one of the most learned families of Shia thought and jurisprudence, this young cleric and firebrand is clearly ambitious. His level of training does not come close to Hakim's or Sistani's, so on traditional metrics of authority he must acknowledge their superiority. But in politics, such traditional metrics are not always definitive, and Sadr has rocked between being suitably deferential and shaking things up in a way that will better position him politically. He also runs a large social services network within Sadr City that helps cement his popular support.

Sadr's strategy for gaining political power is to extend his appeal beyond the Shia community. Staying only within the Shia would be a losing strategy because of his relatively low rank among Shia clerics. Thus, Sadr has appealed across sectarian lines to oppose the American occupation. He is the most popular Shia politician among Sunni Arabs.

The Sadrists have been involved in two of the three circles of war. They have been active in the civil war both through responding to Sunni and AQI attacks in kind and, more important, by undertaking extensive ethnic cleansing of Sunnis living in mixed neighborhoods of Baghdad. In addition, the Sadrists, through their Mahdi Army, have periodically engaged in anti-U.S. insurgent activity. The most serious rounds of fighting came in April and August 2004. In August 2007, with thirty seats in parliament to protect, and perhaps his own life as well, Sadr called for a cease-fire against U.S. troops. While fragile, the cease-fire has held to date.

Sadr is playing a high-stakes poker game. He has to show some deference to his religious superiors, who are also his rivals, but he must stir the pot at least a bit to create space for his own political ambitions to be realized. He wants to reach out to Sunni Arabs in his calls for opposition to the American occupation, but he can't go too far in that regard for fear of alienating his own base, which is decidedly anti-Sunni. Some violence promotes his agenda, but too much or ill-timed violence could backfire.

Kurds

Since the Kurds have not been active players in any of the three circles of war, this section is brief. Mostly, the Kurds have used their new political clout and protection from the United States to continue to build what is essentially an independent state in northern Iraq. They may overplay their hand when it comes to the Kirkuk question, so greater involvement in the simmering civil war cannot be ruled out in the future.

The Kurds are an ethnic group that comprises primarily Sunni Muslims but includes Shia, Jews, and Christians. The chief cleavage among the Kurds is political, and that political divide reflects a sociological difference. The Kurdistan Democratic Party (KDP) is closely associated with the Barzani family. The late Mullah Mustafa Barzani is an iconic figure among Kurds; his son, Massoud, currently leads the KDP. The KDP represents the still-tribalized segments of Kurdish society in the mountainous far north. The Patriotic Union of Kurdistan (PUK) represents largely detribalized Kurds who hail from the plains of Kurdistan, and its leader is the current president of Iraq, Jalal Talabani.

The KDP and PUK have had a love-hate relationship. Sometimes bitter rivals, such as during their 1994–96 near civil war, they have also cooperated when necessary to gain greater independence for Kurdistan. They ran a joint list in the 2005 Iraqi elections, for example.

There are other important currents within Kurdish society besides the KDP and PUK. The jihadi group Ansar al-Islam operates primarily in Kurdistan, and the Kurdistan Workers' Party (PKK) pushes for similar Kurdish autonomy against Turkey and Iran.

In Hindsight

Would events have played out differently if DOD had taken identity politics in Iraq seriously prior to the invasion? Had it done so, several major mistakes could have been avoided.

First, had the U.S. force in Iraq been triple in size (as Gen. Eric K. Shinseki had advised before the invasion and a Rand Corporation report published soon after the invasion[9]), many of the problems that gave rise to the insurgency could have been avoided—albeit at a huge cost. The chaos and looting in April, May, and June 2003 that first cast doubt on the American presence in the eyes of mainstream Iraqis could have been minimized, dampening support for calls to insurgency. Promptly establishing stability would have lent legitimacy to U.S. authority. Further, stability would have reduced the fodder available to Moqtada al-Sadr to rally his forces violently against the U.S. presence in early 2004 as the Sunni insurgency was gaining steam. A larger force would also have been better able to secure the U.S.-conquered areas, to prevent the large-scale theft of munitions that later armed the insurgency, and to mop up the Fedayeen Saddam forces, which started the insurgency.

Second, the United States treated Sunni Arabs (and especially their tribes) as a major enemy early on instead of trying to accommodate their interests. Sunni Arabs widely viewed the much-criticized moves to disband the army and marginalize all Baath Party members as frontal attacks on their community, since Sunnis dominated both these organizations. Given the inevitable displacement of Sunni power as a result of the invasion and the removal of the Baathist regime, some tension between Sunnis and U.S. forces was bound to occur. Still, a more nuanced approach toward this group would have greatly diminished early and strong support for the insurgency and would have denied AQI a strong foothold in Iraq. The United States eventually learned this lesson, and four years into the occupation, it switched to a policy of co-opting Sunni Arab tribes—instead of vilifying them—in order to stop their attacks on U.S. forces and end their ties with AQI.

Third, a more nuanced appreciation of the Shia in Iraq, their major cleavage, and their respective ties with Iran could have been used to bring about a more advantageous outcome. Indeed, quietly engaging Iran on what is an enormous shared interest in stability in Iraq could have gone a long way toward keeping the Sadrists in check.

Such measures, if employed, would not have made a significant difference in the outcome of the interstate war, but they would very likely have limited and perhaps even prevented the deadly insurgency. Moreover, without the insurgency, AQI would not have been in a strong position to provoke civil war between the Sunnis and the Shia, and the Shia would not have been given the opening to engage in ethnic cleansing of Sunnis in Baghdad's mixed neighborhoods.

Still, it is reasonable to presume that shifting power from the Sunnis to the Shia, as any majoritarian project must do, would ultimately have produced some form of communal tension—and perhaps civil war. Given the lack of communal agreement on the major issues of designing a new Iraqi state, a full-scale civil war may yet emerge. Had the war planners appreciated how identity politics might foment civil war in the aftermath of a U.S. invasion, the invasion itself might have been reconsidered.

Notes

1. The most comprehensive social and political history of this earlier period in Iraq is Hanna Batatu, *The Old Social Classes and the Revolutionary Movements of Iraq: A Study of Iraq's Old Landed and Commercial Classes and of Its Communists, Ba'thists, and Free Officers* (Princeton, NJ: Princeton University Press, 1978).
2. Hussein D. Hassan, "Iraq: Tribal Structure, Social, and Political Activities" (Washington, DC: Congressional Research Service Report for Congress, March 15, 2007).
3. For an excellent discussion of the evolution of tribalism in Iraq under the Baath Party, see Amatzia Baram, "Neo-Tribalism in Iraq: Saddam Husayn's Tribal Policies, 1991–1996," *International Journal of Middle Eastern Studies* 29, no. 1 (February 1997).
4. For a penetrating analysis of this Damoclean choice and the kinds of self-defeating politics it inspires, see Joel S. Migdal, *Strong Societies and Weak States: State-Society Relations and State Capabilities in the Third World* (Princeton, NJ: Princeton University Press, 1988). Migdal revisited many of the same themes in *State in Society: Study-*

ing How States and Societies Transform and Constitute One Another (New York: Cambridge University Press, 2001).

5. For a discussion of these differences, see Glenn E. Robinson, "Jihadi Information Strategy: Sources, Opportunities, and Vulnerabilities," in *Information Strategy and Warfare: A Guide to Theory and Practice*, ed. John Arquilla and Douglas A. Borer (New York: Routledge, 2007).
6. Yitzhak Nakash, *The Shi'is of Iraq* (Princeton, NJ: Princeton University Press, 1994).
7. A good discussion of these differences can be found in Juan Cole's *Sacred Space and Holy War: The Politics, Culture, and History of Shi'ite Islam* (London: I. B. Tauris, 2002).
8. Greg Bruno, "The Preparedness of Iraqi Security Forces" (New York: Council on Foreign Relations, 2008), http:// www.cfr.org/publication/14112/, accessed March 2, 2010.
9. James Dobbins et al., *America's Role in Nation-Building: From Germany to Iraq* (Santa Monica, CA: Rand, 2003), http://www.rand.org/pubs/monograph_reports/MR1753/.

STABILIZING IRAQ

2
Political Development in Iraq

Heather S. Gregg

This chapter outlines key events in Iraq's political transition following the U.S. invasion in 2003 and how these events affected Iraq's insurgency, its civil war, and its relationships with Coalition forces and with neighboring countries. Four key events have shaped post-invasion governance in Iraq: implementing de-Baathification, disbanding the Iraqi Army, drafting a constitution, and holding elections. The chapter argues that U.S. efforts to push for a quick democratic transition without first developing the necessary civic and political institutions led to voting along ethnic lines, which favored the Shia as the majority and the Kurds as the most politically mobilized, and alienated Sunnis from the political process. Sunni alienation from the political process in turn fueled Iraq's insurgency. Early elections also allowed hard-line Shia to hold and manipulate key ministries, which perpetuated civil war. Finally, the weakness of Iraqi governance has hindered the U.S. transition of authority and continues to make Iraq vulnerable to intervention from other foreign actors, particularly Iran, Syria, and Turkey.

The chapter concludes by suggesting steps that might help correct the problems of political instability in Iraq: building the key civic and political institutions necessary for functioning democracy and doing so while using institutions other than the political process, such as infrastructure development and the military. Correcting Iraq's governance problem will be a slow process requiring time and patience.

Four Key Events

The Coalition Provisional Authority (CPA) instituted its de-Baathification policy in Order Number 1 on May 16, 2003.[1] The purpose of de-Baathification was to prevent individuals loyal to Saddam Hussein's Baath Party from remaining in power and to punish those responsible for atrocities committed under Hussein's regime. De-Baathification had two critical negative effects for Iraq's political development and security. First, most of the civil servants in Iraq—those with experience in running government offices and the country's infrastructure—were affiliated with the Baath Party, a prerequisite for advancement in the government.[2] Purging the state of top-level Baath affiliates thus created a shortage of qualified workers to run the government and left an estimated fifteen thousand to thirty thousand civil servants unemployed.[3] Second, de-Baathification hit Sunni Arabs the hardest, which further alienated this group from the postwar political, economic, and reconstruction process and created ideal conditions for a Sunni insurgency.[4]

CPA Order Number 2 disbanded the Iraqi Army on May 23, 2003.[5] As with de-Baathification, the purpose of disbanding the army was to purge the country of Hussein's influence and punish those complicit in his crimes. Disbanding the army had three negative repercussions for political development and security in post-Hussein Iraq. First, it put roughly 350,000 Iraqi men out of work, disgruntling a significant portion of the population and very likely fueling the growing insurgency against Coalition troops.[6] Second, the CPA's decision underestimated the importance of the army as a symbol of Iraqi nationalism. Iraq's military was created in 1921, and prior to the 1991 Persian Gulf War, it was the fourth largest military in the world, standing as a testimony of the country's strength and perseverance. Thus, many Iraqis interpreted disbanding the military as an attack on Iraqi identity.[7] The loss of this national symbol had political consequences, notably the predominance of ethnic and sectarian identities instead of Iraqi identity in governance. Third, disbanding the Iraqi Army also alienated Sunnis, who made up the bulk of the officer corps. During the U.S. invasion in 2003, thousands of former Iraqi troops disbanded, most with their weapons, and then regrouped to form the Sunni-led insurgency against Coalition forces.[8]

A third key event that had problematic repercussions for Iraq's political development was the drafting of a national constitution, a document the

CPA believed would help mitigate contentious issues in Iraq—such as religious freedom, federalism, and the protection of minorities—and prevent radicalism and sectarianism from taking root in Iraq's political process.[9] Initially the CPA called for the appointed Iraqi Governing Council (IGC) to name a twenty-five-person team to draft the constitution. However, the highest-ranking Shia cleric in Iraq, the Grand Ayatollah Ali al-Sistani, issued a *fatwa* (religious edict) on June 28, 2003, calling for direct election of those responsible for drafting a constitution.[10] Various factions continued to debate the means by which the constitution should be drafted and what its content should be, stalling the process and preventing elections from taking place. The CPA and IGC eventually agreed to the drafting of a basic law, the Transitional Administrative Law, which was implemented on March 8, 2004, and eventually paved the way for the ratification of the constitution on October 15, 2005.

The process of drafting a constitution in Iraq revealed that it was difficult to get Iraqis to agree on large, contentious issues as a first step in the political process. Some of the key topics debated were the role of Islam in the new government, the creation of quotas for women in parliament, the rights to free speech and privacy, and the question of regional autonomy, specifically Kurdish autonomy.[11] The process also demonstrated that leaders of the majority group in Iraq—the Shia—held considerable sway over the methods of drafting the document, with al-Sistani effectively steering the process in the Shia's favor. Drafting the constitution early in the political process proved more divisive than unifying for Iraq.

The CPA's initial vision for political transition called for the creation of a transitional government by the end of May 2003 that would have power over "nonsensitive" government ministries, such as education and health care. It would be followed within six to twenty-four months by the formation of a "provisional government" that would have greater powers than those of its predecessor and be tasked with writing a constitution. The political transition would end with national elections for a permanent government.[12] However, with the insurgencies taking hold in the country and persistent friction between the interim government and the CPA, the timetable was accelerated.[13]

Iraq has had three general elections since the dissolution of the CPA on June 28, 2004. The first, held in January 2005, was for a 275-member transitional national assembly (tasked with writing the constitution and basic legislative functions), the governorate councils, and a 111-member council in the Kurdish region.[14] The Shia and Kurds dominated the election, winning 225 of the 275 assembly seats, while the Sunnis boycotted the election and won only five seats.[15] The election demonstrated the challenge of creating a representational government in a situation where parties formed along ethnic lines rather than around political interests. For example, the political party of the Shia secularist Ahmed Chalabi formed an alliance with the religiously motivated Shia Supreme Council for Islamic Revolution in Iraq (SCIRI); although their interests were mutually exclusive, the two parties joined forces on the basis of their Shia identity. Given the ethnic proportions of Iraq's population, alliances based on ethnic identity over political interests would inevitably result in the Shia dominating the political landscape—and that is precisely what occurred in the country's first two elections.

Iraq's second general election was held in December 2005 with the aim of electing a permanent 275-member Iraqi Council of Representatives. Given the problematic turnout of the January 2005 election, efforts were made to encourage Sunni voting and to balance ethnic and sectarian representation in the assembly through a complex system of seat allocations among Iraq's eighteen provinces.[16] The Shia once again dominated the elections, with the United Iraqi Alliance winning 128 of the seats, although this time the Sunni Iraqi Accord Front picked up 44 seats, giving Sunnis a voice in the central government.[17] Voting once again was divided along ethnic and sectarian lines, and the Shia United Iraqi Alliance added to its ranks the Sadrist movement, which won 29 of the Alliance's 128 seats.[18] The Shia also took several key ministries in the central government, most notably the Ministry of Interior, which has been held by a member of SCIRI (now renamed the Islamic Supreme Council of Iraq [ISCI]).[19] After six months of considerable struggle, the Iraqi Council of Representatives formed a government of the Shia United Iraqi Alliance, the Sunni Iraqi Accord Front, the Kurdistan Alliance, and the secular, cross-ethnic Iraqi National List, with the Shia Nouri al-Maliki as prime minister.[20]

Iraq's third elections were held in January 2009 for fourteen of the eighteen provinces in the country. Unlike the previous provincial elections, there were no major efforts to boycott the polls and security was good. The elections had an overall turnout of 51 percent of the voting population.[21] Results varied from province to province, but showed a trend toward a decreased popularity in ISCI and Sadrist Movement, with Prime Minister Nouri al-Maliki's Islamic Dawa Party holding or gaining ground in several provinces. Kurd and Sunni tensions in Kirkuk were not abated by the elections.[22] Overall, the elections showed some signs of improvement over the previous ones.

Rather than mitigate ethnic tensions in Iraq, the elections appear to have worsened them and to have helped foster insurgency, civil war, and conditions for interstate conflict. Early elections prompted voting along ethnic and sectarian lines, favoring the numerically superior Shia and the politically mobilized Kurds while discriminating against the numerically and politically weak Sunnis. This situation was particularly true in the January 2005 election, and although efforts were made to correct the weak representation of Sunnis in the government, the Shia and Kurds dominated the process again in the December 2005 election. Alienation of the Sunnis from the political process no doubt played the major role in inducing Sunni individuals and groups to take up arms against the government instead of working through the system to bring about political change.

Perhaps more important, sectarian voting in Iraq exacerbated an already volatile situation and fueled the potential for civil war. Sectarian fighting escalated after the February 2006 bombing of the Shia al-Askari Shrine (Golden Mosque) in Samarra, attributed to al Qaeda in Iraq (AQI), a Sunni organization. The Sunnis and the Shia engaged in tit-for-tat reprisal killings since the bombing, particularly in ethnically mixed areas and in Baghdad. It is believed that, following their appointment to the Ministry of Interior, the Shia used the national police forces as death squads against the Sunnis.[23] This dynamic has been particularly damaging for Iraq's fledgling national government. It suggests that the ruling party could turn the country's instruments of national power inward and stamp out its ethnic, sectarian, and political competition. Such a move would further weaken the legitimacy of the government and national unity and possibly create conditions for minority groups to secede.

Finally, Iraq's weak and divided government may also create conditions for external actors to meddle in Iraq's political process. In a September 2007 briefing to Congress, Gen. David Petraeus and Ambassador Ryan Crocker indicated that Iraq's security situation was improving but that its political progress had stalled.[24] Over the long haul, Iraq cannot stabilize without a functioning government, which also presents challenges for a complete drawdown of Coalition forces and the handing over of authority to Iraqis. Moreover, with a weak government and multiple forms of internal conflict, conditions are ripe for regional actors to meddle in the country's affairs. Within Iraq's borders, Iran continues to influence both the political process and the insurgency through aid and advisers, particularly to ISCI and the Sadrists.[25] Likewise, Turkey has initiated several incursions into northern Iraq in pursuit of Kurdistan Workers' Party (PKK) guerrillas.[26] International meddling in Iraq's affairs is likely to continue until the country can strengthen its political situation and defend its borders and territory.

Steps to Correct Political Instability

The United States faces several challenges in stabilizing Iraq's political landscape, particularly the ethnic and sectarian cleavages that have developed in Iraq's elections and government. According to democracy experts, a democratizing state should first develop, as one scholar put it, a "thick web of liberal institutions"—including a healthy civil society and an identity based in part on citizenship as opposed to tribal, ethnic, or religious loyalties—and *then* hold elections. Instead, Iraq's elections took place prior to the development of those critical institutions that undergird a healthy democracy. Once a transitioning democracy heads down the path of voting along ethnic and sectarian lines, it is difficult to use the political process to correct this trend, and the likely outcome is violence and possibly civil war.[27] The political process in Iraq, as we have seen, mirrors this prediction; these developments present several challenges for changing the course of Iraq's governance.

Any long-term solution to Iraq's governance requires the strengthening of its society and national identity. The United States, along with the international community, has several useful tools at its disposal to help in this process. For example, the U.S. government and military could use the training of Iraq's military and police force as an opportunity to build Iraqi identity and teach courses on good governance, responsible leadership, meritocracy, and the importance of rotating authority. The Iraqi Army once held a prominent position in the Iraqi national psyche. U.S. efforts to create a new Iraqi military could restore this institution as a national symbol of Iraq and teach its corps the values of service to one's country and responsible democratic leadership.

Another opportunity for the Iraqi government to strengthen society and weaken ethnic and sectarian rivalries is through the distribution of oil wealth. Rather than grant oil shares to every citizen in Iraq, which has been proposed,[28] oil dividends could be granted in lump sums to cities and provinces as development credits for infrastructure and other community needs. Thus, citizens would be compelled to organize and agree on how the capital would be invested to improve their communities and provinces.

U.S. and international aid agencies could also work to help strengthen Iraqi society by introducing and supporting a variety of volunteer organizations that would bring Iraqis together on the basis of various shared interests and thus bridge ethnic and sectarian divides. This outreach effort might include organizations like the Parent Teacher Association, such business groups as the Rotary Club or an appropriate equivalent, and labor unions. Even recreation and sports clubs could be valuable assets for strengthening Iraqi society and fostering a sense of national identity, or Iraqiness. 2007 national fervor over the Iraqi soccer team attests to this possibility.[29] In turn, building the foundation of civil society and organizing citizens around interests as opposed to ethnic or sectarian loyalties paves the way for governance based on interests over subnational identities and creates the necessary conditions for the people to hold their government accountable.

Near-term solutions to the problems of Iraqi governance are more challenging. Most would agree that maintaining security, including tamping down ethnic tensions and preventing foreign meddling, is a priority in Iraq. In the near term, a strong government with control of internal security is a necessity in order for society to stabilize and develop social capital and civic institutions. This requirement will most likely come at the expense of some liberal democratic practices, such as freedom of speech in campaigning, and a laissez-faire stance toward hard-line political parties. In the immediate near term, it may also require agreements or pacts among different leaders—ethnic, tribal, and religious—independent of the democratic process in order to achieve stability. Ironically, the premature push for democracy without the necessary civil institutions may actually necessitate undemocratic policies in the near term in order to get Iraq back on track toward democracy in the long run.

Notes

1. CPA Order Number 1 states: "On April 16, 2003, the Coalition Provisional Authority disestablished the Ba'ath Party of Iraq. . . . Full members of the Ba'ath Party . . . are hereby removed from their positions and banned from future employment in the public sector. . . . Those suspected of criminal conduct shall be investigated and, if deemed a threat to security or a flight risk, detained or placed under house arrest." See L. Paul Bremer, "Coalition Provisional Authority Order Number 1: De-Ba'athification of Iraqi Society," May 16, 2003, http://www.iraqcoalition.org/regulations/20030516_CPAORD_1_De-Ba_athification_of_Iraqi_Society_.pdf.
2. Alissa J. Rubin, "Coalition Revisits Purge of Baathists," *Los Angeles Times*, January 15, 2004; and Daniel Williams, "In Sunni Triangle, Loss of Privilege Breeds Bitterness," *Washington Post*, January 13, 2004.
3. Rubin, "Coalition Revisits Purge"; and Pamela Constable, "New Policy Unveiled for Ex-Baathists," *Washington Post*, January 12, 2004.
4. Rubin, "Coalition Revisits Purge."
5. CPA Order Number 2 states: "Any military or other rank, title, or status granted to a former employee . . . by the former Regime is hereby cancelled. . . . All conscripts are released from their service obligations." See L. Paul Bremer, "Coalition Provisional Authority Order Number 2: Dissolution of Entities," May 23, 2003, http://www.iraqcoalition.org/regulations/20030823_CPAORD_2_Dissolution_of_Entities_with_Annex_A.pdf. This decree also included Ahmed Chalabi's "Free Iraqi Fighters," a force of around seven hundred U.S.-trained militia. See Rajiv Chandrasekaran, "U.S. Sidelines Exiles Who Were to Govern Iraq," *Washington Post*, June 8, 2003.
6. Borzou Daragahi, "Disbanded Army Draws Praise, Condemnation," *Washington Times*, January 6, 2004.
7. Ibid.
8. International Crisis Group (ICG), "Iraq: Building a New Security Structure," Middle East Report no. 20 (Baghdad/Brussels: ICG, December 23, 2003), i.
9. Reuters, "A 'Federal System' with Leaders Chosen by the People," *New York Times*, April 16, 2003. These issues were elucidated in the April 15, 2003, meeting in Nasiriya, which produced the 13-Point Memorandum. See U.S. Central Command, "Visions of Freedom: 100 Iraqis Meet in Nasiriyah and Create Basis for New Government," April 15, 2003, http://www.state.gov/p/nea/rls/19714.htm (page now discontinued).
10. For a detailed account of the circumstances leading up to Sistani's fatwa and its effects on political development in Iraq, see Rajiv Chandrasekaran, "How Cleric Trumped U.S. Plan for Iraq," *Washington Post*, November 26, 2003.
11. International Crisis Group, "Iraq's Constitutional Challenge," Middle East Report no. 19 (Baghdad/Brussels: ICG, November 13, 2003), http://www.crisisgroup.org/home/index.cfm?id=2369&l=1; and Dexter Filkins, "Panel Starts to Draw Up Constitution for Short Run," *New York Times*, February 3, 2004.

12. Douglas Jehl, with Eric Schmitt, "U.S. Reported to Push for Iraqi Government, with Pentagon Prevailing," *New York Times*, April 30, 2003.
13. "Transfer 'Does Not Affect Troops,'" *BBC News*, November 16, 2003, http://news.bbc.co.uk/2/hi/middle_east/3274463.stm; and "Bremer: U.S. in Tough Fight in Iraq," *BBC News*, November 16, 2003, http://news.bbc.co.uk/2/hi/middle_east/3275485.stm.
14. "Q&A: Iraqi Election," *BBC News*, February 13, 2005, http://news.bbc.co.uk/2/hi/middle_east/3971635.stm; and Wikipedia, "Iraqi Parliamentary Election, January 2005," http://en.wikipedia.org/wiki/Iraqi_parliamentary_election,_January_2005.
15. Ibid. The Shia United Iraqi Alliance and the Shia Iraqi List won 140 and 40 seats, respectively, and the Democratic Patriotic Alliance of Kurdistan won 75 seats. Voter turnout in Kurdish areas was as high as 98 percent, whereas in the Sunni Anbar Province turnout was 2 percent.
16. Wikipedia, "Iraqi Parliamentary Election, December 2005." http://en.wikipedia.org/wiki/Iraqi_parliamentary_election,_December_2005.
17. Kurds dropped twenty-two seats to win fifty-three seats total in the national assembly. See Kenneth Katzman, "Iraq: Government Formation and Benchmarks" (Washington, DC: Congressional Research Service Report for Congress, October 25, 2007).
18. SCIRI won thirty-six seats, the most in the alliance. http://en.wikipedia.org/wiki/Iraqi_parliamentary_election,_December_2005.
19. International Crisis Group, "Shiite Politics in Iraq: The Role of the Supreme Council," Middle East Report no. 70 (Baghdad/Istanbul/Brussels: ICG, November 15, 2007), 13–15.
20. Wikipedia, "Iraqi Legislative Election, December 2005." http://en.wikipedia.org/wiki/Iraqi_parliamentary_election,_December_2005.
21. "Iraqi Shiite Party Denies Setback in Regional Vote," *New York Times*, February 2, 2009.
22. "Iraq Elections," *New York Times*, April 16, 2009, http://topics.nytimes.com/topics/news/international/countriesandterritories/iraq/elections/index.html, as of August 28, 2009.
23. International Crisis Group, "Shiite Politics in Iraq," 13–15; and Jon Lee Anderson, "Letter from Iraq: Inside the Surge," *New Yorker*, November 19, 2007.
24. Katzman, "Iraq: Government Formation and Benchmarks."
25. International Crisis Group, "Shiite Politics in Iraq."
26. Alexandra Zavis, "U.S. Practicing Balancing Act on Kurdish Question," *Los Angeles Times*, December 19, 2007.
27. Jack Snyder, *From Voting to Violence: Democratization and Nationalist Conflict* (New York: W. W. Norton, 2000), 15–43.
28. Charles J. Wolf, Jr., "Shareholders Don't Shoot Each Other," *Wall Street Journal*, November 23, 2005.
29. Kirk Semple, "Iraq's Escape Is Soccer, but Soccer Can't Escape War," *New York Times*, January 8, 2007.

3
An Economic View of Security and Reconstruction

Raymond E. Franck, Jr.

The purpose of this chapter is to assess the task of economic reconstruction within the complex conflict that prevails in Iraq. While the standard models of peacekeeping and nation building provide useful templates for economic reconstruction and recovery for economies like Iraq's, they do not necessarily consider the three circles of conflict that make the current situation so difficult or address in detail the dual problem of bringing about economic recovery and reconstituting the necessities for that recovery.

The chapter begins with a discussion of the need for order (the Hobbesian imperative) and how insurgent activity interacts with that need. It then outlines an orthodox ("Washington Consensus") view of what infrastructure is needed to facilitate economic activity within efficient markets. Next, it presents a proposed strategy of localities, or a bottom-up approach, to rebuilding the economy. The underlying rationale is that economic measures should follow closely on the restoration of a reasonable level of security, but within that system of complex conflict, the degree of security will vary widely by locality. Finally, the chapter offers a template for allocation rules for economic reconstruction and development resources.

The security problem in Iraq has greatly complicated the task of reconstitution and recovery. Even when the country had adequate security, the economic recovery task faced enormous challenges. The occupation following Operation Iraqi Freedom took place in an already wrecked economy. After the relative prosperity of the 1970s, Iraq waged the long war with Iran

(1980–88), launched the disastrous venture into Kuwait (1990), and endured more than a decade of economic sanctions. All these events drained away resources needed to maintain Iraq's infrastructure.

Moreover, the Coalition's failure to devote sufficient attention and resources to the problem of maintaining order in the months following the fall of Saddam Hussein's regime ensured that the economic infrastructure was subject to constant attack or subversion through illegal activities. Prominent among the major manifestations of this problem have been repeated attacks on the oil distribution system and the rise of a large-scale black market in refined products.

The Hobbesian Imperative: Security Comes First

It is a safe bet that Thomas Hobbes (1588–1679) would understand the basics of insurgency warfare. His best-known work, *Leviathan* (1651),[1] arose out of the English Civil War as well as from his earlier works. The basics of Hobbes's political philosophy are well known: the state of anarchy (life without order) is intolerable. It is the "war of every man against every man," in which the result for most is a life that is "solitary, poor, nasty, brutish and short."[2] In Hobbes's view, people form nations to escape this state of nature. The purpose of government is thus to provide the institutions and resources needed to maintain a state of security. Doing this job well—ensuring an orderly, peaceful society—confers legitimacy on that government.[3]

It is possible, however, to accept Hobbes's basic view and still arrive at different conclusions. The maintenance of order is a necessary, but not sufficient, condition for legitimacy. Also, more modern views of governance assert that the need for order is so fundamental that it is provided even if a government cannot do so.[4] Still another qualification comes from tribal forms of governance or some other social order based on kinship.[5] Thus, the disorder that followed the toppling of Saddam Hussein's regime was a significant impetus, among others, toward the formation of tribal and ethnic militias.

Within a Hobbesian perspective, the proximate goal of insurgents is to deny security to the populace through a number of means, including terrorism.[6] If the government's attempts to combat the insurgency cause the general population to be even less secure, so much the better for the insurgents. The government or counterinsurgents win if they either destroy the insurgency movement or restore and maintain security (even if they do not destroy the insurgency movement).

For the insurgents to win, they must either provide security when the established government cannot (a preferred mode of operations in the Maoist model of counterinsurgency warfare[7]) or cause the current government to give up the struggle. However, insurgents might also win by outlasting their opponents. There is good reason, for example, to believe this approach is how the insurgents prevailed over the French in Algeria.[8] After the previous government departs or dissolves, the insurgent movement provides a new order that allows the (acquiescent if not grateful) population to avoid the Hobbesian state of nature. Thus, the counterinsurgents win if they destroy the insurgent movement, or if they maintain order, or if they convince the general population that the insurgents intend to bring on the Hobbesian state of nature, against which the counterinsurgent force is its best defense.[9]

Creating a Climate for Economic Success: A Washington Consensus View

One current orthodox view of long-term growth and prosperity embraces free markets and free trade (both domestically and internationally). The most common set of prescriptions resulting from this perspective is frequently referred to as the "Washington Consensus."[10] Among other things, the Washington Consensus holds that the proper role of government is to facilitate economic activity, not to control it. More specifically, this policy means providing the infrastructure—physical and social—that protects and promotes economic activity. The social infrastructure includes well-defined and transferable property rights, enforcement of contracts, and the rule of law in general. It also concerns environments conducive to the trust that lowers transaction costs in commercial relationships. Finally, it arguably involves a safety net that provides a measure of protection against the vagaries and misfortunes of economic affairs.

The infrastructure covers various security and enforcement services that protect citizens from force and fraud. That is, security and economic matters are inextricably related. It also involves reliably functional physical assets that promote economic activity, such as roads, waterways, airports, air traffic control systems, navigation aids, oil pipelines, communications aids, water supply, sewerage, and distribution of electrical power.

The Washington Consensus also assigns a role to national policy. Government should, for example, maintain macroeconomic stability and avoid as much as possible too much inflation and too much unemployment. For developing countries, this strategy implies, among other things, a stable currency and a stable climate for markets to function.

A Proposal for Consideration: A Strategy of Localities

The problem of economic reconstruction and recovery in Iraq is complicated by an environment of complex warfare with at least three circles of conflict characterizing Iraq's current situation. National economic recovery has been enormously exacerbated by an incipient civil war with at least three major factions: Kurdish, Shia, and Sunni.[11] The magnitude of the task also makes recovery more difficult. The effects of three decades of warfare, neglect, and civil disorder have severely damaged Iraq's physical infrastructure. Likewise, an even longer period of Saddam Hussein's repression damaged the social infrastructure.

Yet another complication comes from the sui generis nature of the task at hand. There is an interesting and valuable literature available on economic reconstruction and recovery as part of the general problem of peacekeeping and nation building. However, while the "lessons learned" aspects of the Iraq War (that is, how we can do it better next time) have been widely discussed, less attention has been given to what we can do after our original strategy proved insufficient to the task. A related point is that the situation in Iraq is not one generally envisioned by the standard nation-building paradigm. Instead of being a case of economic reconstruction as part of "winning the peace," it has been a matter of rebuilding the economy in a time of war.

However, providing security and maintaining order are complementary missions to economic recovery. In a standard nation-building scenario, restoring the economy is a means of securing a general peace. In Iraq for the foreseeable future, peace is likely to be found only in localized situations; nonetheless, economic recovery is an effective means of keeping a locality peaceful. That is, the economic and security issues are inextricably interrelated.

The preferred end state for a reconstructed Iraqi locality has several significant features. First, the area is sufficiently secure for commercial activity. Second, local police (and paramilitary forces) have the wherewithal to maintain order and protect the local infrastructure, such as roads and utilities. Third, the local population does not engage in hostile actions against any outside groups. Fourth, the local population is willing and able to conduct limited defense against hostile incursions from either outside militias or insurgents. Finally, the local population actively supplies intelligence to Iraqi and Coalition authorities.

A standard approach to attaining that outcome would tie economic reconstruction to areas in which security has been restored. The first stage would see the imposition of security by military forces (U.S., Iraqi, or both); the second would reestablish the means for local security, preferably with local police forces; and the third would reconstruct an economic infrastructure in both its social and physical dimensions. However, the magnitude of the task suggests that there may be strong advantages to the use of careful, targeted resource allocation.

Allocating Economic Reconstruction Resources: Which Projects to Back?

While a strategy for reconstruction in an environment of complex warfare should be informed by local circumstances, a number of matters are inherently centralized. For example, there should be a national plan for some classes of physical infrastructure, such as long-haul transport systems and oil pipelines. Also, allocating necessarily finite resources for reconstruction is inherently a task for centralized decision making. And, since the magnitude of needs and claims exceeds available resources, some method of sorting out the best opportunities is needed.[12]

One method for accomplishing this task is suggested by Peter Schuck and Richard Zeckhauser's optimal targeting of potential aid recipients.[13] While intended for use with domestic social welfare programs, the basics of this model are applicable for prioritizing local reconstruction project proposals in Iraq. The idea is to sort among proposals or recipients on the basis of "bad draws," "bad bets," and "bad apples."[14] Bad draws are areas in need of assistance—that is, impoverished areas—while "good draws" are localities that are relatively prosperous. Bad bets are areas in which projects are unlikely to succeed; "good bets" are the opposite. Bad apples in the context of Iraq are populations that are likely to be either aggressive against their neighbors (engaging in civil conflict) or supportive of outside insurgents or terrorists, whereas "good apples" are populations that are more likely to engage in peaceful pursuits and to cooperate with security forces.

In distributing limited resources, the basic idea is to target areas that are, ideally, bad draws, good bets, and good apples. To illustrate, a Kurdish area with access to oil revenues would likely be a good draw, good bet, and good apple. An impoverished Shia area with an active militia and jihadist leadership would likely rate as a bad draw, bad bet, and bad apple. A Sunni tribe that is tired of insurgencies and terrorism is likely to be a bad draw, good bet, and good apple.[15]

Basically, the return on committed resources is a function of the types of draw, bet, and apple—the characteristics of the area in question—as well as the usual characteristics of the project being considered. That is,

$$\text{Return}_{ij} = F(\text{draw}_i, \text{bet}_i, \text{apple}_i; \underline{Y}_{ij}),$$

where Return_{ij} is the expected return for the j-th project proposed for the i-th area; draw_i, bet_i, and apple_i are characteristics of the i-th area; and $\underline{Y}_{ij}$ is a vector composed of the characteristics of the j-th project in the i-th area. Overall, the equation states that the return on the j-th candidate project in the i-th area is a function (F) of the characteristics of the project ($\underline{Y}_{ij}$), and the characteristics of the area itself. The fundamental insight from this equation is that standard methods of project evaluation (or cost-benefit analysis) should include the nature of the local area in estimating project return.

Suppose a project under consideration is the restoration of reliable electrical supply. The return for the project is higher (other things equal) for areas that are bad draws, good bets, and good apples. A good-draw area would likely feature a fairly good electrical grid already in place or the means to restore electrical distribution with resources already at hand.[16] A good-bet area would be characterized by, among other things, a security situation that makes the new electrical grid unlikely to be seriously damaged by insurgent operations. An area that rates as a good apple is likely to use this infrastructure improvement to facilitate economic activity, making the area more prosperous. A bad-apple area might use the improvements to daily life to strengthen a local leadership whose major objective is promoting sectarian violence (as in Sadr City, perhaps).

A representation of how one might sort out which projects to fund is provided in figure 3.1.[17] The notional representation provided assumes evaluation of the same project (for example, a reliable electrical power grid) in a given area. It also assumes that all areas under consideration are rated bad draws. Then the decision of which projects to fund depends on the characteristics of the areas in question and the resources available.

Proposed projects with sufficient combinations of good-apple and good-bet ratings would be funded under this scheme. If available resources increase, then the boundary between funded and unfunded projects would shift down and to the left.

Concluding Thoughts

Several operational considerations must be kept in mind in conjunction with the scheme presented above. First and foremost, local situations and local knowledge are paramount. Programs must conform to facts on the ground, and careful consideration of the local situation must inform the prioritization of projects. In an environment of complex warfare, the situation (including the state of security) will vary considerably among localities.

Figure 3.1. Determining resource allocation

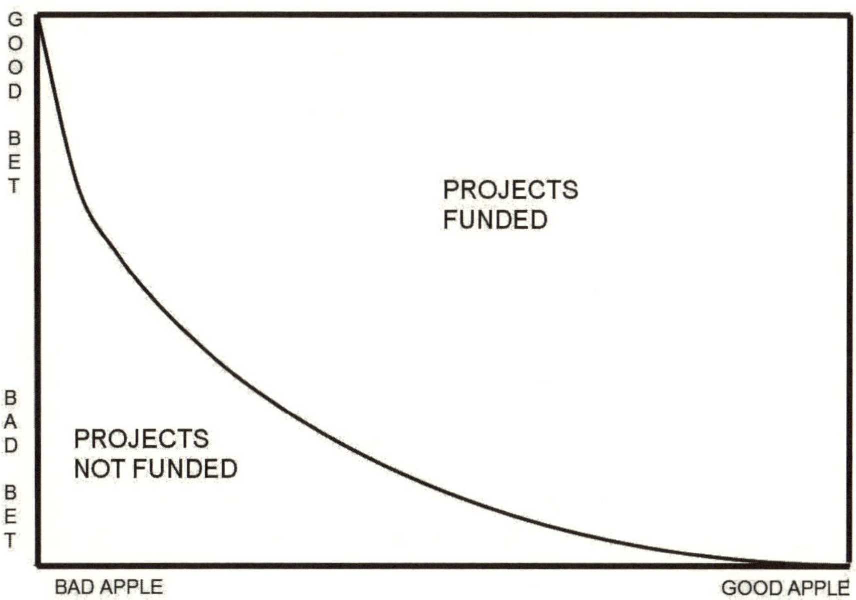

Second, waiting for comprehensive security to be established before starting a comprehensive program of reconstruction would mean that reconstruction is unlikely ever to begin. Planning for reconstruction must extensively delegate decision-making authority to those familiar with the (ever-changing) conditions in the various localities.

Third, economic reconstruction must be tied closely to local security. Given the magnitude of the reconstruction task and the rather thin presence of Coalition troops in Iraq, it is useful not only to choose reconstruction projects carefully but also to do so with a view to consolidating security gains. This conclusion implies, among other things, that the reconstruction efforts will employ strategies that are flexible enough to take full advantage of local security gains.

Finally, as indicated above, assessments of local conditions should be thoroughly embedded in project evaluations. This work implies, among other things, extensions to standard cost-benefit methodology from the outset of the evaluation process.

Notes

1. Thomas Hobbes, *Leviathan*, ed. Michael Oakeshott (Oxford, UK: Blackwell, 1960).
2. Ibid., especially 82.
3. Ibid., especially 84–97, 219–24. This assertion is true even for governments other than the monarchy Hobbes had in mind.
4. Avinash K. Dixit raises the possibility of alternative governance means for economic activity if (for example) a government should fail to fully function. See Dixit's *Lawlessness and Economics: Alternative Modes of Governance* (Princeton, NJ: Princeton University Press, 2004); his views are nicely summarized in chapter 1, especially pages 1–7. Sudhir Venkatesh discusses order within a criminal organization—that is, governance in the absence of governmental authority—in *Gang Leader for a Day: A Rogue Sociologist Takes to the Streets* (New York: Penguin, 2008). Steven D. Levitt also has an excellent report on Venkatesh's work, in Steven D. Levitt and Stephen J. Dubner, *Freakonomics: A Rogue Economist Explores the Hidden Side of Everything* (New York: HarperCollins, 2005), 89–114.
5. That is, Dawkins's "selfish gene" may prevent or ameliorate Hobbes's state of nature. (The "selfish gene model views human self interest as including one's gene pools. Thus kinship provides allies, and the Hobbesian state of nature is not entirely a war of all against all.) See Richard Dawkins, *The Selfish Gene* (New York: Oxford University Press, 1978), especially 71–94. First published 1976.
6. Alistair Horne, *A Savage War of Peace: Algeria 1954–1962* (New York: New York Review of Books, 2006; originally published 1977), especially 105–127.
7. Mao Tse-Tung, *On the Protracted War* (Beijing: Foreign Language Press, 1960), especially 41-50.

8. Horne, *A Savage War of Peace*, especially 314–29.
9. The insurgents in Iraq have been remarkably cooperative in this regard, especially al Qaeda in Iraq. They have become increasingly identified as murderers of the faithful. Concerns appeared in the Ayman al-Zawahiri epistle to Abu Musab al-Zarqawi. See Office of the Director of National Intelligence, "Letter to al-Zarqawi [from al-Zawahiri]," news release no. 205, October 11, 2005. Along these lines, Andrea Elliott raises the issue of how killing Muslims could affect foreign fighter recruiting in "Where Boys Grow Up to Be Jihadis," *New York Times Magazine*, November 25, 2007.
10. Economist John Williamson coined the term in 1989 in the context of strategies Latin American countries were to pursue during the financial crisis of the 1980s. See John Williamson, "A Short History of the Washington Consensus," paper presented at the Center for International Relations and Development Studies (CIDOB) conference From the Washington Consensus Towards a new Global Governance, Barcelona, September 24–25, 2004, http://www.iie.com/publications/papers/williamson0904-2.pdf.
11. Not to mention, for example, the hostilities between the Iraqi government and the Sadr militia in the spring of 2008 that had elements of an intra-Shiite conflict.
12. In fact, given the magnitude of the task relative to the resources available (at least in the near term) and with security forces being fairly thin on the ground, the good use of resources and the synchronization of reconstruction programs with security operations are critical.
13. Peter H. Schuck and Richard J. Zeckhauser, *Targeting in Social Programs: Avoiding Bad Bets, Removing Bad Apples* (Washington, DC: Brookings Institution Press, 2006).
14. For a summary, see ibid., 9–27.
15. A caveat might be in order here. Since stereotypes in Iraq are not terribly helpful, these examples are offered merely as illustrative and are not definitive characterizations of regions or groups.
16. In standard cost-benefit terminology, the counterfactual for the project in a good-bet area is for the electrical system to be restored without outside aid. The return to the electrical grid project (relative to the counterfactual) is accordingly lower. Anthony Boardman discusses counterfactuals both concisely and well in Boardman et al., *Cost-Benefit Analysis: Concepts and Practice*, 3rd ed. (Upper Saddle River, NJ: Prentice Hall, 2006), chapter 1, especially page 817. Adapted from Schuck and Zeckhauser, *Targeting in Social Programs*, especially chapter 7.
17. Adapted from Schuck and Zeckhauser, *Targeting in Social Programs*, especially chapter 7.

4
Lessons from Reconstructing Indigenous Security Forces in Iraq

Hy S. Rothstein

There is little doubt that potential U.S. enemies have observed developments in Iraq as well as the domestic debate in the United States about the war since the invasion in March 2003. As Nora Bensahel has noted, given the quick initial U.S. victory over Iraqi forces and then the bogging down of the U.S. military mission in counterinsurgency, it would not be unreasonable for potential adversaries to conclude that the United States is significantly less proficient at countering an insurgency than it is at defeating a conventional foe.[1] Regardless, the United States will continue to respond to threats to its interests; there is no evidence to the contrary. That said, future U.S. interventions may again create insurgencies, attract transregional terrorists, and unleash sectarian violence, just as it occurred in Iraq. In fact, one could argue that the larger and more intrusive the U.S. intervention, the greater the attraction for forces opposed to U.S. action and the resultant change in the status quo. Our experience in Iraq has clearly shown us the high cost of defeating a well-established insurgency. Preventing insurgencies from arising in the first place is a better course. How can the United States minimize the likelihood of an insurgency as it intervenes abroad to defend its global interests?

In this chapter, no attempt is made to review the erroneous prewar assumptions and missed opportunities that led (or at least contributed) to the insurgency and sectarian violence in Iraq. The purpose of the chapter, rather, is to draw from the experience in Iraq in an attempt to learn something new about reconstructing indigenous security forces. To be fair, it is doubtful that better planning would have completely preempted the violence that followed the collapse of the Iraqi regime. U.S.-dominated interventions and the presence of U.S. forces, especially in Muslim countries, will be a magnet for groups with anti-U.S. agendas.[2] But let there be no doubt that proper planning and skillful execution can dramatically reduce the chances that an insurgency will develop beyond the nascent stages and infect an entire society. Furthermore, any plan for U.S. intervention must devote adequate attention and resources to maintaining public order in the aftermath of combat operations. Maintaining order is crucial to impeding insurgencies from developing in the first place, and reconstructing indigenous security forces quickly is key to maintaining public order.[3]

Iraqi Security Forces: An Assessment

In September 2007, Gen. James L. Jones, USMC (Ret.), led an independent commission to evaluate the state of Iraqi security forces (ISF). The commission reported that the Iraqi armed forces are increasingly effective and can assume greater responsibility for security, but they are far from being able to meet Iraq's security requirements. The commission's assessment of Iraq's police forces was much less optimistic, concluding that the police could not yet meaningfully contribute to Iraq's security.[4] The commission, however, may have sidestepped a more critical aspect of ISF capabilities and potential. In a critique of the commission's findings, Anthony H. Cordesman noted that the report "does not address the degree to which all elements of the Iraqi Security Forces from the Prime Minister's office down have links to Shi'ite efforts to retain and expand power and carry out sectarian cleansing in mixed areas."[5] Cordesman continues:

> The report badly understates the sectarian and ethnic divisions in the Army, and does not address just how important providing a larger share of real power sharing with the Sunnis will have to be to make accommodations/conciliation work. The assessment of the transfer of responsibility is dangerously flawed both by this omission and the failure to examine the reality of Iraq's ongoing divisions into Arab Shi'ite, Kurdish, and Arab Sunni dominated zones, and the power of Shi'ite and Kurdish factions within the Army.[6]

Cordesman's assessment helps explain why heavy Coalition investment in recruiting, training, advising, and equipping the ISF has not had a more positive impact. His comments also explain why institution building and reform in Iraq have been so elusive. Cordesman may have identified the principal flaw in the capacity-building effort in Iraq that must be addressed: unless we find a way to mitigate the sectarian divisions—divisions that have deep ethnic, historical, and cultural roots—our current plans may only delay the inevitable civil war.

Uneven Policy Toward Iraqi Militias

Both the Iraqi and U.S. governments have responded to militias in an inconsistent manner, further frustrating the overall effort to achieve stability and security. The Kurdish area of northern Iraq has been stable and secure because of a policy that encourages local militias to undertake the burden of maintaining local security. The United States simply finds the Peshmerga (Kurdish militia) to be a "good" militia, and the Iraqi government has learned to tolerate the pseudo-state status of the Kurdish region. Meanwhile, the rise in importance of Sunni militias was a response to their new minority status and the fear that the new majority Shia government would marginalize the Sunnis. The Sunnis were logically more susceptible to insurgent mobilization. As a result, both the U.S. and Iraqi authorities assumed that these militias, populated by Iraqis who once supported Saddam Hussein, could not be trusted; therefore, they were unwilling to enlist Sunni militias to assist in securing the state. Finally, Shia militias organized quickly after the fall of the Baath Party in 2003 to fill the security vacuum that the Coalition forces were unable or unwilling to fill. The extreme lawlessness in local neighborhoods was, in part, a catalyst for the formation of Shia militias. These forces quickly gained legitimacy because they were the only forces capable of protecting local citizens. Shia militias, and in particular Moqtada al-Sadr's Mahdi Army, also reestablished essential services that the Coalition could not adequately provide to Iraqi citizens. The relative legitimacy of Shia militias and their ties to the Iraqi government give them a semiofficial status.[7]

The Origins and Development of Iraqi Security Forces

Conventional wisdom holds that the formation of a capable national Iraqi security structure will allow U.S. forces to withdraw from Iraq. With this in mind, Gen. George W. Casey, Jr., former commander of the Multi-National Force–Iraq (MNF-I), opted to accelerate the formation of the Iraqi Army in early 2005. Competent ISF would not be perceived as occupiers, would have access to better local intelligence than Coalition forces would have, and as a result would be able to take over the majority of counterinsurgent operations and thus undercut the motivation behind the insurgency. General Casey was so convinced of the efficacy of this approach that he ordered Coalition forces to shift their focus from hunting insurgents to training Iraqis. Accordingly, U.S. adviser teams were embedded with every Iraqi Army battalion, brigade, and division.[8]

It was clear from the outset that the ISF were meant to be an integrated national force that resembled the ethnic makeup of Iraq. The disastrous experience in 2004 with the Sunni National Guard's Fallujah Brigade convinced the U.S. leadership that an all-Sunni unit would be trouble.[9] This decision also sat well with the Shia-dominated Iraqi government. It was felt that ethnically pure units would undermine the development of the Iraqi state and that pure Sunni units would cooperate with insurgents. Therefore, units would be filled with Kurdish, Shia, and Sunni personnel. The integration, however, never occurred as envisioned. Although a few units did have Sunni officers, the vast majority of the men were Shia.[10]

Assessments of ISF capabilities in late 2006 were not good. The ten Iraqi divisions that were projected were considered too few to put down the insurgency. Observers argued that the United States had failed to provide sufficient training, equipment, and skilled advisers. Gen. John Abizaid, the former commander of U.S. Central Command, in his testimony before the U.S. Senate, said: "In discussions with our commanders and Iraqi leaders it is clear that they believe Iraqi forces can take more control faster, provided we invest more manpower and resources into the coalition military transition teams, speed the delivery of logistics and mobility enablers, and embrace an aggressive Iraqi-led effort to disarm illegal militias."[11] Winning in Iraq was directly tied to both qualitative and quantitative improvements in the ISF. U.S. investments to enable these improvements were key to any reasonable exit strategy.

A Capable Iraqi Army Emerges

Contrary to some reports, Coalition efforts to build a capable Iraqi Army seemed to be paying off. By late 2005, Iraqi forces were providing almost half of the manpower in Anbar Province for counterinsurgency operations. By early 2006, three Iraqi brigades were conducting operations independently. More importantly, the Iraqis were demonstrating strong combat proficiency in basic maneuvering and assaulting insurgent positions as well as in more complex tasks, such as calling in close air support. The insurgents were never able to rout an Iraqi Army unit. Iraqi soldiers at remote outposts stood and fought against well-coordinated, repetitive insurgent attacks. When intelligence was available, the Iraqi units successfully mounted operations to capture or kill insurgents. In fact, many advisers rated selected Iraqi brigades as more proficient than some U.S. units. Iraqi units had clearly demonstrated combat proficiency despite shortfalls in equipment, training, and advisers.[12]

Increased ISF Competence Leads to Increased Insurgent Attacks

Unfortunately, strong combat performance by the Iraqi Army had little to do with the level of insurgent activity. In fact, insurgent attacks increased even while the Iraqis were capably executing counterinsurgency operations.[13] Most disconcerting, al Qaeda continued to operate, demonstrating that competent Iraqi units could not manage the insurgency even with U.S. assistance. Therefore, it is reasonable to assume that the Iraqi Army could not defeat the insurgency without the presence of U.S. forces.[14]

One would assume that the best performing Iraqi units would eventually face fewer attacks within their areas of operation—after all, the Iraqis successfully took the fight to the insurgents—but it was not the case. Therefore, there is little reason to believe that better training, better advising, and more equipment are the answers to the problem. Some suggest that the problem was simply insufficient numbers of Iraqi forces to crush the insurgency. While this line of reasoning is appealing, there is reason to doubt that greater numbers would have been decisive. In fact, reinforcing Iraqi Army units in Ramadi and Haditha in 2006 had disappointing results. Insurgent attacks increased. Even when Ramadi was saturated with Iraqi patrols, insurgent activity did not subside. Therefore, insufficient forces do not adequately explain the continued insurgent attacks in the face of increasingly competent Iraqi forces.[15]

Sunnis View ISF as a Large Shia Militia

The reason a competent Iraqi Army continued to suffer insurgent attacks was that the population sympathized with the insurgency and rejected the Iraqi Army as a symbol of the government in Baghdad. The insurgents thus continued to have the intelligence advantage over the army. Any prospect of defeating an insurgency requires the government, first and foremost, to find the enemy. The importance of superior intelligence is clearly articulated in the U.S. Army's current counterinsurgency manual:

> Without good intelligence, counterinsurgents are like blind boxers wasting energy flailing at unseen opponents and perhaps causing unintended harm. With good intelligence, counterinsurgents are like surgeons cutting out cancerous tissue while keeping other vital organs intact. Effective operations are shaped by timely, specific, and reliable intelligence, gathered and analyzed at the lowest possible level and disseminated throughout the force.[16]

The reason the insurgents continued to attack was that they could move freely among the population. In fact, many provided shelter and support to the insurgents. Many joined the insurgency. Popular support for the insurgents was exacerbated by Sunni hatred for the Shia-dominated army. Shia power, demonstrated after the February 2006 bombing of the al-Askari Shrine (Golden Mosque), magnified the Sunni perception of a Shia intention to oppress them. Polling throughout 2006 clearly indicated that the majority of Iraqis viewed the government as illegitimate. As far as the Sunnis were concerned, the Iraqi military was nothing more than an oversized Shia militia bent on dominating the Sunnis. No Iraqi unit could ever gain the support of a significant portion of the local population.[17]

Al Anbar: All Politics and Insurgencies Are Local

If the Shia identity of the Iraqi Army was an impediment to reducing levels of violence, one might expect that a Sunni-dominated unit would have more success. This experience is, in fact, what happened to one Iraqi brigade that had a substantial number of Sunnis in its ranks. The 3rd Brigade, 7th Iraqi Division (3-7 Brigade) occupied Al Qa'im in early 2006. Immediately prior to the brigade's arrival, a large-scale Coalition operation had taken place that successfully cleared insurgents from the area. Although the brigade was too small a force to have independently cleared the area, it was big enough to prevent the insurgents from infiltrating back into the city. The brigade faced few insurgent attacks despite being severely undermanned. In fact, its casualty rate was approximately 75 percent less than the Iraqi Army suffered in Fallujah, a town of similar size, population, and political geography. Most interesting is that the presence of this under-trained and undermanned brigade resulted in significantly reduced insurgent attacks. This fact undermines the notion that increased training and numbers are critical to the Iraqi Army's ability to defeat the insurgency.[18]

The success of the 3-7 Iraqi Brigade was directly related to its relationship with the Albu Mahal tribe, the most powerful tribe in the area. As many as 40 percent of the brigade's men came from that tribe, and it disliked the heavy-handed tactics al Qaeda used to control the population. Unfortunately, al Qaeda had more muscle than the tribesmen and battled to win control of the city in 2005. Once Coalition forces pushed al Qaeda out of Al Qa'im and the 3-7 Brigade moved in, the Albu Mahal readily provided their fellow tribesmen with information on al Qaeda operatives, safe houses, ammunition caches, and bomb-making facilities. Fortunately, the Iraqi Ministry of Defense recognized the benefits of these relationships and allowed Albu Mahal tribesmen to serve in the 3-7 Brigade notwithstanding the rule that prohibited local Sunnis from filling the ranks of units in Al Anbar.[19]

The importance of homegrown security forces should have been more obvious, considering the threat. Still, the Shia-led government rightfully feared the creation of armed groups that rivaled its own security forces. Shia resistance to a Sunni-dominated militia was reinforced by the American notion that a fully integrated force, or an army that was a melting pot, would serve Iraq well. However, the obvious advantage of exploiting local capabilities could not be ignored in the face of mounting violence. While the Iraqi government remains opposed to Sunni-dominated militias, it accepts the formation of local police forces. Accordingly, General Casey declared 2006 as the "year of the police." The police performed reasonably well because of support from local sheikhs and imams who encouraged the young men to volunteer and the people to provide information. Still, rising sectarian violence drove many Sunnis to feel that aligning with al Qaeda was the best means of defense against the Shia military forces. Unfortunately, in the end, insurgents outnumbered local police forces.[20]

The Three Circles of War in Iraq

The building of local security capacity is key to defeating insurgents. Episodic successes in Iraq confirmed this fundamental tenet of counterinsurgency doctrine. The 2007 "Sunni Awakening," in which former insurgents became allies, supports this point. Local Sunni fighters were integral to the lull in violence that accompanied the U.S. troop surge. With financial support from the Pentagon, the nearly eighty thousand Sunni fighters are operating relatively independently of the Iraqi government.[21] While competent local forces are necessary to thwart insurgents, they raise the risk that after the various towns feel safe from al Qaeda, these forces will be a competing armed interest group operating against the Shia central government and will thus increase the potential for civil war. The possibility also exists that these local forces may turn their guns on U.S. troops again.

In many ways, the U.S.-backed Sunni groups reinforce the sectarian wedge between Iraqi political factions. Accordingly, Iraqi minister of defense, Abdul-Qadir al-Obaidi, explicitly stated that these groups will eventually be dismantled. Prime Minister Nouri al-Maliki has expressed similar sentiments. Sunni leaders, in response, have stated that there is zero chance that they will ever voluntarily disband their groups in the Concerned Local Citizens program. Perhaps a reasonable solution can be found. If not, a showdown is looming on the horizon.[22]

Finally, the Jones Report indirectly suggests shortfalls in the capability of Iraqi forces to defend the country against external threats. Cordesman's critique of the report more precisely states, "The report does not really address the lack of any clear U.S. plan to look beyond counterinsurgency and to eventually create forces capable of independently defending the country."[23] The inability of the Iraqi military to defend the country against state actors in what is arguably the most volatile region in the world is obvious. Overemphasizing the counterinsurgency fight comes at the expense of developing a capability to deter and defend Iraq against external threats. The Iraqi people need a military that they can rally around when a regional competitor again threatens their country.

Conclusion

Iraq offers insights that may be relevant elsewhere about minimizing the likelihood of an insurgency as the United States intervenes abroad to defend its global interests. It is clear that a Shia-dominated army cannot quell the insurgency in Iraq. Unless a way is found to mitigate the sectarian divisions—divisions that have deep ethnic, historical, and cultural roots—current plans are only likely to delay the inevitable civil war. If the United States withdrew from Iraq today, it is probable that the level of violence would dramatically increase. A Shia army coupled with government efforts to eliminate local Sunni forces is a recipe for protracted internal conflict. If the Shia government succeeded through overwhelming force, the stage would still be set for a bloody civil war.[24]

Enhanced training, better equipment, and more advisers will improve the effectiveness and efficiency of Iraqi units but will not reduce insurgent violence, the measure that counts. The identity of the Iraqi Army would remain Shia. Sunnis would not join this force. Security efforts should focus on building local forces—essentially sanctioning Sunni militias—and Baghdad must reward these forces for eliminating insurgents from their respective jurisdictions.

A qualitative improvement in U.S. advisers might help, along with a change in their mission focus. The advisory effort in the 1980s in El Salvador provides a possible model. Advisers in El Salvador were predominantly seasoned Special Forces majors who possessed competent language skills and a deep understanding of the country's local politics, culture, and history. The initial tactical training of the Salvadoran military eventually evolved into a more relevant strategic role for the U.S. advisers. The advisers played a key part in modifying the army's behavior from that of abusing the population to one of protecting it. In fact, negotiations that led to the 1992 peace accords that ended the civil war required U.S. advisers to remain with their Salvadoran units. The insurgents demanded this condition because the advisers' presence resulted in an overall lower level of violence and increased respect for human rights. U.S. advisers influenced Salvadoran leaders through their ability to persuade, their partial control of a tangible incentive structure, and their ability to meter the flow of resources to Salvadoran military units. Placing greater emphasis on local forces does not mean deserting the Iraqi Army. However, it would mean undermining the formation of a national democracy, and nonelected local imams and sheikhs could have more authority than would elected officials. Shifting emphasis could also move Iraq a step closer to dividing into Shia, Sunni, and Kurdish areas. It is hard to argue that the goal of moving Iraq's political development forward would not be adversely affected.[25]

Whether the greater risk is a Shia-dominated army or an able Sunni militia is unclear. However, we already have a good idea of the link between a Shia-dominated army and stability and security at the local level. The government in Baghdad can develop an incentive structure to help manage local Sunni security forces that would militate against local rogue armed groups.

Washington and Baghdad have a choice: either support local, single-identity security forces to eliminate the insurgency and maintain local order but risk civil war down the road, or refocus on an integrated and ultimately Shia-dominated national force and ensure continued sectarian violence supported by al Qaeda now. The Iraqi government may actually gain better control over Iraq by supporting the existence of permanent Sunni militias.

Notes

1. Nora Bensahel, "Preventing Insurgencies After Major Combat Operations," *Defence Studies* 6, no. 3 (September 2006): 278–79.
2. Ibid., 283.
3. Indigenous security forces in Iraq are comprised of the Iraqi military (army, Special Forces, navy, and air force), which operates under the authority of the Ministry of Defense; the local and national Iraqi police, which operate under the Ministry of Interior; and other forces authorized by the government of Iraq.
4. *The Report of the Independent Commission on the Security Forces of Iraq*, September 6, 2007, 12, http://www.csis.org/component/option,com_csis_progj/task,view/id,1028/ (page now discontinued).
5. Anthony H. Cordesman, "The Independent Commission on the Security Forces of Iraq: A Critique" (Washington, DC: Center for Strategic and International Studies, September 6, 2007), 2, http://www.csis.org/media/csis/pubs/070906_isfcommissioncritique.pdf.
6. Ibid., 4.
7. See James J. Smith, "U.S. Post-Conflict Integration Policy of Militias in Iraq," thesis, Naval Postgraduate School, Monterey, California, March 2008, 24, 25, 31, 42–44; and Jon Lee Anderson, "Letter from Iraq: Inside the Surge," *New Yorker*, November 19, 2007.
8. Carter Malkasian, *Will Iraqization Work?* (Alexandria, VA: Center for Naval Analysis, 2007), 6.
9. In 2004 the Fallujah Brigade performed poorly. The troops were inadequately trained, were either intimidated by or sympathetic to the insurgents, and refused to cooperate with the Iraqi government.
10. Malkasian, *Will Iraqization Work?* 6.

11. Gen. John Abizaid, Testimony to Senate Armed Services Committee, 109th Cong., 2nd sess., November 15, 2006, http://armed-services.senate.gov/statemnt/2006/November/Abizaid%2010-15-06.pdf. Also see the statement by Gen. Martin Dempsey, U.S. Army, former commanding general of the Multi-National Transition Command–Iraq, given to the House Armed Services Subcommittee on Oversight and Investigations on Iraqi Security Forces, June 12, 2007, http://armedservices.house.gov/pdfs/OI061207/Dempsey_Testimony061207.pdf.
12. Malkasian, *Will Iraqization Work?* 8–11.
13. Michael E. O'Hanlon and Ian Livingston, "Iraq Index: Tracking Reconstruction and Security in Post-Saddam Iraq" (Washington, DC: Brookings Institution, Saban Center for Middle East Policy, ongoing).
14. Malkasian, *Will Iraqization Work?* 12.
15. Ibid., 13.
16. Department of the Army, *Field Manual 3-24: Counterinsurgency* (Washington, DC: Headquarters, Department of the Army, December 2006).
17. Malkasian, *Will Iraqization Work?* 14.
18. Ibid., 16.
19. Ibid.
20. Ibid., 18, 20, 21.
21. John Hendren, "'Sunni Awakening': Insurgents Are Now Allies," *ABC News*, December 23, 2007, http://abcnews.go.com/print?id=4045471.
22. Kevin Drum, "Sunni Awakening Update," December 23, 2007, http://www.cbsnews.com/stories/2007/12/23/politics/animal/main3642703.shtml.
23. Cordesman, "The Independent Commission," 4.
24. Malkasian, *Will Iraqization Work?* 23.
25. Ibid., 24.

UNDERSTANDING OUR ADVERSARIES

5

Insurgent and Terrorist Finances in Iraq

Michael E. Freeman

All insurgencies and terrorist campaigns need money to sustain themselves. This chapter explores how insurgent and terrorist groups in Iraq raise and spend their funds. It also discusses the ways in which the issues of terrorist and insurgent financing are complicated by the particular dynamics of the struggle in Iraq, namely, the simultaneous and overlapping elements of an insurgency, a civil war, and an interstate conflict.

Sources and Expenditures

The insurgent groups in Iraq—comprising Sunnis, Shia, Kurds, nationalists, Marxists, and others—collectively raise between $70 million and $200 million per year to finance their activities, according to a leaked classified National Intelligence Estimate (NIE) report.[1] (To put this amount in perspective, the Provisional Irish Republican Army was thought to have an annual budget of $15 million, al Qaeda raised about $30 million per year prior to 2001, and Hezbollah receives somewhere between $100 million and $200 million per year, around half of it from Iran.[2]) Most of these funds are probably spent on travel, food, lodging, payments to the families of dead insurgents, and bribes, while some money goes into the personal coffers of the insurgent leaders.[3] Spending on munitions is minimal because stockpiles of weapons are fairly plentiful in Iraq. Payments to the foot soldiers for conducting attacks are fairly low. The price to have someone plant an improvised explosive device has reportedly dropped from around $100 to

$40,[4] and payments for more elaborate attacks cost somewhere between $100 and $2,000.[5]

As one might expect, it is difficult to compute precise figures for insurgent funding. Sourcing methods are complex, distributed, adaptive, and opaque to outside analysts and possibly to the insurgents themselves. The numbers provided below are necessarily estimates and should be considered with some caution.

Insurgent funding comes from a multitude of sources, among them oil smuggling, kidnapping and ransom, counterfeiting, charitable donations, ordinary crime, legal activities, and state sponsorship.[6] Oil smuggling accounts for $25 million–$100 million of revenue per year, according to the leaked NIE report. With higher estimates, Iraqi oil and finance ministers claim that 10–30 percent of the $4 billion–$5 billion in oil imports are smuggled out for resale and that insurgents receive about half of those profits (at least approximately $200 million).[7] From the Baiji refinery alone, Iraq's largest, 70 percent of its $2 billion in fuel production went to the black market in 2007, and at least 33 percent of its production was still being diverted to black markets in 2008.[8] At one point, al Qaeda in Iraq (AQI) is estimated to have received $50,000 to $100,000 a day in smuggled profits from the Baiji refinery.[9]

Kidnapping and ransom activities reportedly account for approximately $36 million per year, with $30 million of that amount allegedly paid by the French and Italian governments in 2005.[10] Although some kidnappers are simply criminals who ransom their victims for economic gains, others sell their hostages to insurgent groups that then collect the ransom for themselves. This method of fund-raising has a particularly destabilizing effect: it undermines support for the Iraqi government, which is seen as incapable of protecting its citizens.[11]

Unknown amounts are also raised through extortion.[12] Some reports claim that hundreds of thousands of dollars have been extorted from U.S. rebuilding funds in Anbar Province alone. In some cases, insurgents demand that contractors and transporters pay up to half the value of their contract in return for their safety, and often they seize the goods being transported by the contractors.[13] In Mosul, insurgents extort "5 to 20 percent of the value of contracts local businessmen get from the government."[14]

Charities have provided an unknown amount of funding to the insurgents. According to Caleb Temple, formerly the operations director for the Defense Intelligence Agency's Joint Intelligence Task Force for Combating Terrorism, mosques in Iraq as well as in Iran and the Gulf states collect funds for the insurgents. Sometimes the imams are "openly sympathetic" to the insurgents while in other cases the insurgents pay the imams to allow them to raise money in their mosques.[15] According to official counts, however, few charities or nongovernmental organizations (NGOs) support the insurgency. The leaked NIE report found that only ten to fifteen of the four thousand NGOs in Iraq back the insurgents.[16] The extent of this foreign support is debated. A U.S. defense official claimed in 2004 that money was raised in Saudi Arabia, funneled through charities, and then passed through Syria into Iraq.[17] National security expert Anthony H. Cordesman disputes these claims, however, noting that little evidence has been produced to support them.[18]

Legal transactions are also used to generate funds for insurgent financing. According to interviews with Iraqi officials, there are reports of insurgent groups financing their activities by simply selling off the members' assets. In one reported example, an insurgent financier raised cash for an operation by selling off some furniture. There are also descriptions of insurgents using trade to move funds into and around the country. Instead of trying to smuggle cash, which is still the norm, groups can buy and ship merchandise and resell it at another location. Iraqi officials noted that they witnessed insurgent-affiliated businessmen selling cars and shirts to raise cash in a particular region or neighborhood.[19]

Some allege that outside states are providing support to insurgents.[20] In particular, Iran is believed to be providing money, training, and supplies to the main Shia insurgent group, the Mahdi Army led by Moqtada al-Sadr.[21] According to a classified report leaked to the *New York Times*, "Iran's Islamic Revolutionary Corps-Quds Force is providing professionally built EFPs [explosively formed penetrators (or projectiles)] and components to Iraqi Shia militants."[22] American officials have also claimed that Iranian-sponsored Hezbollah trained a thousand to two thousand fighters from the Mahdi Army and other groups in Lebanon.[23] In Gen. David Petraeus's September 2007 report to Congress, this Hezbollah unit is identified as Department 2800 and works closely with the Quds Force to train Shia militants.[24]

Trends

According to the leaked National Intelligence Estimate report, "The pattern of insurgent financing changed after the first 18 months of the war, from the Hussein loyalists who financed it in 2003, to 'foreign fighters and couriers' smuggling cash in bulk across Iraq's porous borders in 2004, to the present reliance on a complex array of indigenous sources."[25] This trend has ramifications that go beyond simply the source of financing. In fact, it shows that the nature of the insurgency itself has changed.

When the insurgency was dominated by such former regime elements as the Fedayeen Saddam, the Republican Guard, the Mukhabarat (secret police), the Baath Party, the military, and others loyal to the Hussein regime, their funding came mostly from former regime officials who had absconded with funds before the regime fell and funneled them back into Iraq from outside its borders.[26] Qusay Hussein, one of Saddam's sons, took out $1 billion in cash as the invasion was in progress.[27] Other former regime elements fled to Syria, Jordan, Saudi Arabia, Iran, and the United Arab Emirates and "established financial bases to fund the insurgency."[28] In 2004, U.S. officials thought that "about a half-billion dollars that once belonged to the former Iraqi government, along with funds from individuals and religious groups in Saudi Arabia, [was] being funneled through Syria and used to fund insurgents."[29] These former regime loyalists were dealt a blow when a U.S.-led effort froze $3.6 billion of assets. This loss, coupled with the increasing realization that the Baathists would not return to power, especially after Saddam Hussein's capture and execution, led to a decline in this segment of the insurgency.[30] Many of the former regime elements have since shifted their allegiance to Islamist and nationalist causes.[31]

While the insurgency was for a time led by former regime elements and Iraqi nationalists, Sunni religious extremists now dominate it. The particularly Sunni nature of the insurgency is reflected in an ABC News poll from March 2007 in which 51 percent of Iraqis said "that violence against U.S. forces is acceptable," whereas among Sunnis the proportion exceeded 90 percent.[32] Supporting this trend, by 2005, approximately 90 percent of the insurgents were Iraqi Sunni Arabs, not former regime elements.[33] Generally, these groups receive some portion of their funding from wealthy Gulf state donors and some from donations collected at mosques. The rest is obtained through extortion, smuggling, and other criminal activities.

Foreign fighters and couriers bringing cash to radical Sunni groups, such as AQI, were also prominent sources of funding for the insurgents.[34] However, the influx of foreign fighters has slowed for several reasons: Iraqi tribes have turned against them; U.S. and Iraqi efforts have made it difficult for them to operate in Iraq; and other governments, such as those of Saudi Arabia and Morocco, have put pressure on the smuggling networks.[35] As a consequence, AQI and other groups increasingly rely on criminal activities, such as extortion and kidnapping, to raise funds. Overall, the insurgency is "now self-sustaining financially" and does not rely on outside sources of funding for its continued operations.[36]

Vulnerabilities and Countermeasures

How vulnerable are insurgency finances to disruption? What countermeasures can be implemented to exploit their vulnerabilities? One element of insurgency financing that may be vulnerable is an increasing reliance on criminal activity, which is often unpopular among the insurgents' own constituency, as a source of funds.[37] The predatory nature of criminal fundraising activities—extortion, kidnapping and ransom, smuggling, and drug dealing—has already cost insurgent groups in terms of legitimacy and local support. AQI's "coercive fundraising backfired" in Sinjar, for example.[38] AQI was aware of its image problem and issued its own announcement disavowing illegal activities and those who engaged in them.[39] In sum, terrorists do not want to be seen as criminals, and criminals do not want to be seen as terrorists—and the Iraqi government can do a better job of exploiting this dynamic.

Insurgent finances can also be curtailed by improving the overall level of security in Iraq. As governance spreads and becomes more pervasive, the conditions that enable criminal activity of any kind will be reduced, and the larger black market economy will shrink.[40] Although improving security may not be explicitly intended to curb insurgency funding, as general security increases, smuggling, extortion, kidnapping, and other criminal activities may diminish.[41]

The external sponsorship of the insurgent groups provides its own set of challenges. Dissuading or deterring Iran from its support of Shia militants will require the full range of diplomatic, military, economic, legal, and financial tools in the U.S. arsenal. Moreover, insurgent financing is just one issue that must be appropriately prioritized in the U.S.-Iranian relationship. For instance, it may need to take a back seat to negotiations over Iranian political support for the government of Iraq, Iranian involvement in Afghanistan, Iranian-Israeli relations, and Iranian support for Hezbollah. Countering insurgent support from charities and individuals in Saudi Arabia and other Gulf states is also problematic. This issue has been an ongoing source of tension between the United States and Saudi Arabia, not just in relation to Iraq, but also in the larger effort in the war on terrorism.[42] While Saudi officials claim that they are taking measures to curb the flow of funds from the kingdom to terrorist organizations, it remains an issue.[43]

For any type of financing countermeasure, there are several confounding issues. First, the Iraqi government may not be up to the task. The classified NIE report "paints an almost despairing picture of the Iraqi government's ability, or willingness, to take steps to tamp down the insurgency's financing."[44] Without the resources to improve Iraqi capabilities, and with continued corruption undermining the willingness of leaders to target insurgent financing, little will be accomplished.[45] Second, even if the government had the capabilities and the will, the insurgents have an inherent advantage because of the nature of the insurgency, which is "opaque and complex."[46] The insurgents are decentralized and secretive, making any assessment of where they get their financing or how they move and spend their resources difficult. Critics of the NIE report note that U.S. officials are "just guessing . . . they really have no idea [because] they've been very unsuccessful in penetrating these organizations."[47] In addition, insurgents finance their operations from diverse sources, they are highly adaptive to pressures and constraints, and they have proven to be regenerative after apparent Coalition successes.[48] All of this evidence points to the conclusion that efforts to counter insurgent financing may have only limited or marginal effects and that addressing the funding, by itself, will be unlikely to defeat the insurgents.

Insurgent Financing Within the Three Circles of Conflict

The insurgency-related violence in Iraq is now primarily self-financing. Groups fighting the Coalition forces or the Iraqi government finance their operations with oil smuggling, kidnapping and ransom, extortion, counterfeiting, charitable donations, ordinary crime, and even legal businesses. Some support comes from charities in Saudi Arabia and other Gulf states and from Iran. However, financial assistance from the Gulf is no longer a primary source of income, and the support from Iran is more about logistics, weapons, and training than about financing. The increasing self-reliance of the insurgent groups is not surprising. For any terrorist or insurgent group, state funding is a double-edged sword: it provides access to large amounts of funds, but it also limits the group's freedom of maneuver. Outside financiers may demand that a group do more or do less than it would do otherwise; moreover, they also might choose to end their support for political reasons, leaving the insurgents in the lurch.

While financing the fighting in Iraq now takes place primarily within the insurgents' circle, it does have implications for, and overlaps with, the civil war and interstate conflict circles, especially as the conflict may shift in its nature.

In the interstate conflict circle, there have been allegations of support from Iran, Saudi Arabia, and other Gulf states as well as from individuals coming to Iraq as foreign fighters. While support from the Gulf states has become less important, the Iranian supply of weapons and training of insurgents have become a matter of increasing concern to the United States and an additional source of tension between the two countries. Further, it could be used (legitimately or not) as a casus belli for a U.S.-Iranian conflict.

The interstate dimension also comes into play because the United States itself is an international actor that became involved in Iraq out of its own concerns with the war on terrorism and al Qaeda. The U.S. interest in curtailing terrorist financing may not always align with the interests of other states, the Iraqi government, local sects and tribes, international institutions, and NGOs. In engaging with Sunni tribal leaders, for example, the United States will have to decide whether they should be treated as terrorists who must be defeated, as sectarian leaders who must be brought into the government to avoid a civil war, or as insurgents who challenge the Iraqi government's legitimacy and its capacity to win the hearts and minds of the population.

A final concern where the insurgent and interstate circles overlap is the possibility that there may be surplus funds in Iraq that insurgents may be moving to finance groups outside Iraq. While the NIE report noted this possibility, most experts found it unlikely because, except for AQI, all the Iraqi insurgent groups maintain a "single-minded regional focus."[49]

In terms of the overlap between the insurgency and civil war, the shift to sectarian violence had and will continue to have several implications. In the future, Iraq might provide an arena for Iran and Saudi Arabia to wage a low-scale proxy war.[50] In that case, Iran and Saudi Arabia would provide funds and training for Shia and Sunni groups while maintaining their distance and refraining from any overt involvement in Iraq, much as the Soviet Union and the United States waged proxy wars during the Cold War. In other words, if tensions between Saudi Arabia and Iran rise, we may see increased funding going to local Iraqi groups that are loyal to their opposing outside sponsors and inflaming the conflict into more of a civil war. Alternatively, if the sectarian element of the conflict grows in importance as a result of internal Iraqi dynamics, Shia and Sunni leaders in Iraq might pressure outside governments for assistance that Iran and Saudi Arabia might otherwise be reluctant to give. Also, if the fighting shifts to a more sectarian conflict, it may lead to groups seeking different avenues of funding. For example, coercive techniques, like extortion, or involvement with corruption and drugs may be less effective for resistance groups as they come to rely more on popular support for their cause. Conversely, if the sectarian nature of the conflict is somehow mitigated (through politics, national identity formation, and so on), we may see less of an impetus for states and individuals from other countries to support their sectarian brethren in Iraq by financing their militant wings.

In sum, the violence in Iraq is financed from multiple sources. The conflict is currently located primarily within the insurgent circle, with most of the insurgency being self-financed by groups within Iraq. However, international actors—the United States, Iran, and Saudi Arabia—are all involved in Iraq, often with opposing goals. Should the conflict shift to more of a civil war, the dynamics of the struggle's financing would become more complex by involving the insurgent, sectarian, and interstate elements in the conflict.

Notes

1. John F. Burns and Kirk Semple, "U.S. Finds Insurgency Has Funds to Sustain Itself," *New York Times*, November 26, 2006.
2. See Jeanne Giraldo and Harold Trinkunas, eds., *Terrorism Financing and State Responses: A Comparative Perspective* (Stanford, CA: Stanford University Press, 2007).

3. Testimony of Caleb Temple, director (operations), Joint Intelligence Task Force for Combating Terrorism, Defense Intelligence Agency, before the House Armed Services Committee hearing on the financing of the Iraqi insurgency, July 28, 2005; and Jacob Shapiro, "Bureaucratic Terrorists: Al-Qa'ida in Iraq's Management and Finances," in *Bombers, Bank Accounts, and Bleedout: Al-Qa'ida's Road In and Out of Iraq*, ed. Brian Fishman (West Point, NY: Combating Terrorism Center at West Point, Harmony Project, 2008), 74.
4. Evan Thomas and John Barry, "A New Way of War," *Newsweek*, August 20, 2007.
5. Robert E. Looney, "The Business of Insurgency: The Expansion of Iraq's Shadow Economy," *National Interest* 81 (Fall 2005): 2.
6. Burns and Semple, "U.S. Finds Insurgency Has Funds."
7. Robert Worth and James Glanz, "Oil Dollars Fund the Insurgency, Iraq and U.S. Say," *New York Times*, February 5, 2006; Burns and Semple, "U.S. Finds Insurgency Has Funds"; and Richard Oppel, Jr., "Iraq's Insurgency Runs on Stolen Oil Profits," *New York Times*, March 16, 2008.
8. Oppel, "Iraq's Insurgency."
9. Ibid.
10. Burns and Semple, "U.S. Finds Insurgency Has Funds."
11. Looney, "The Business of Insurgency," 4.
12. Testimony of Caleb Temple.
13. Hannah Allam, "Insurgents Extort U.S. Aid, Iraqis Say," *Columbus Dispatch*, August 8, 2007.
14. Oppel, "Iraq's Insurgency."
15. Testimony of Caleb Temple.
16. Burns and Semple, "U.S. Finds Insurgency Has Funds."
17. John Lumpkin, "Insurgents Infiltrating Iraq Have Cash," *USA Today*, October 21, 2004.
18. Ibid.
19. Personal interviews, Baghdad, March 2008.
20. International Crisis Group (ICG), "Iran in Iraq: How Much Influence?" Middle East Report no. 38 (Amman/Brussels: ICG, March 21, 2005), is generally skeptical of these claims.
21. For more on the Mahdi Army and al-Sadr, see the International Crisis Group's reports, "Iraq's Muqtada al-Sadr: Spoiler or Stabiliser?" Middle East Report no. 55 (Amman/Brussels: ICG, July 11, 2006); and "Iraq's Civil War, the Sadrists, and the Surge," Middle East Report no. 72 (Baghdad/Damascus/Brussels: ICG, February 7, 2008).
22. Quoted in Michael R. Gordon, "Deadliest Bomb in Iraq Is Made by Iran, U.S. Says," *New York Times*, February 10, 2007.
23. Michael R. Gordon and Dexter Filkins, "Hezbollah Said to Help Shiite Army in Iraq," *New York Times*, November 28, 2006.
24. Mark Hosenball, "Rise of a Secret Unit," *Newsweek*, October 1, 2007.
25. Burns and Semple, "U.S. Finds Insurgency Has Funds."
26. Thomas Ricks, "Rebels Aided by Allies in Syria," *Washington Post*, December 8, 2004.
27. Burns and Semple, "U.S. Finds Insurgency Has Funds."
28. Testimony of Caleb Temple.

29. "U.S.: Saddam Regime Funds Financing Iraq Insurgency," *CNN.com*, October 22, 2004, http://www.cnn.com/2004/WORLD/meast/10/22/iraq.main/.
30. Burns and Semple, "U.S. Finds Insurgency Has Funds."
31. Wikipedia, "Iraqi Insurgency," http://en.wikipedia.org/wiki/Iraqi_insurgency.
32. As cited in "Poll: Iraqis Pessimistic on War's Outcome," *MSNBC.com*, March 19, 2007.
33. "Report: Saudis Bring Money, Fighters to Iraq's Insurgency," *FOXNews.com*, September 20, 2005.
34. See Fishman, ed., *Bombers, Bank Accounts, and Bleedout*. The Associated Press (AP), in its news article "Al-Qaeda Turns More to Extortion, Abductions to Fund Fight, U.S. Says," *San Diego Union-Tribune*, July 30, 2008, notes that foreign fighters provided up to 70 percent of AQI's budget in one sector.
35. AP, "Al-Qaeda Turns More to Extortion."
36. Burns and Semple, "U.S. Finds Insurgency Has Funds."
37. The AP article "Al-Qaeda Turns More to Extortion" notes that AQI's "funding scheme could drive an even deeper wedge between the terrorist organization and the Iraqi tribes."
38. Ibid.
39. Ibid., 72.
40. See Looney, "The Business of Insurgency."
41. On the other hand, the AP article "Al-Qaeda Turns More to Extortion" notes that as Iraq becomes wealthier and more stable, it will have more affluent citizens who would make lucrative targets for extortion and kidnapping.
42. Alfred B. Prados and Christopher M. Blanchard, "Saudi Arabia: Terrorist Financing Issues" (Washington, DC: Congressional Research Service, March 1, 2005).
43. Embassy of Saudi Arabia, "Initiatives and Actions Taken by the Kingdom of Saudi Arabia to Combat Terrorism," December 2006, http://www.saudiembassy.net/ReportLink/KSA%20WOT%20Report%20Dec06.pdf (page now discontinued).
44. Burns and Semple, "U.S. Finds Insurgency Has Funds."
45. Looney points out that Iraq is the most corrupt country in the Middle East and is ranked 129th out of 145 countries globally; see "The Business of Insurgency," 2.
46. Burns and Semple, "U.S. Finds Insurgency Has Funds."
47. W. Patrick Lang, quoted in Burns and Semple, "U.S. Finds Insurgency Has Funds."
48. Testimony of Caleb Temple.
49. Burns and Semple, "U.S. Finds Insurgency Has Funds."
50. See International Crisis Group, "The Next Iraqi War? Sectarianism and Civil Conflict," Middle East Report no. 52 (Amman/Baghdad/Brussels: ICG, February 27, 2006).

6
The Internet and the Iraq Conflict

Dorothy E. Denning

"On blogs and Web sites, by e-mail and video, the Iraq war is fought on the Internet."

—*Associated Press, Baghdad, March 16, 2008*

In recent years, the Internet has come to play a part in every major conflict—for example, in Kosovo in 1999; in the ongoing Israeli-Palestinian conflict, particularly since the second intifada in 2000; and now in Iraq. While the Internet's role in the Iraq conflict may seem insignificant compared with events on the ground, it cannot be ignored. At the very least, it has affected support for the war and for al Qaeda's insurgency, both within Iraq and globally.

This chapter examines how the Internet has been used in the Iraq conflict. Its use is manifest in a range of activities, from disseminating information to launching cyber attacks. The chapter describes who is engaging in these activities and some of the effects these activities have had. It also considers how the Internet might be used more effectively to counter al Qaeda in Iraq (AQI) and the al Qaeda–global Salafi jihad's social movement. First, however, the chapter briefly summarizes the state of the Internet.

The Internet

According to Internet World Stats, approximately 1.3 billion people, or about 20 percent of the world's population, were connected to the Internet as of

December 2007.[1] Connectivity varies by region, with North America having the highest penetration rate at 71 percent and Africa the lowest at 5 percent. The Middle East, at 17 percent, is a little below average, but some countries in the region, including Iraq, are well below average. Indeed, the data for Iraq show only thirty-six thousand users, or 0.1 percent of the population connected. This estimate was made in October 2005, however; the number has likely increased, especially considering that the Internet population in the Middle East as a whole grew by 920 percent from 2000 to 2007. In addition, the data for Iraq might not take into account all of the Iraqis who access the Internet through cyber cafés. In 2004, Baghdad alone was reported to have 150 such cafés.[2]

With such a low penetration rate in Iraq, it might seem that the Internet would have little impact on Iraqis. Yet, this supposition is not the case. One reason is that information can jump media. For example, information that is distributed through the Internet can be picked up by Iraqi television, radio, and print news media and then be passed along to the Iraqi public. In addition, Iraqis who are connected to the Internet can share information they acquire online with friends and family through face-to-face conversations.

Another reason Iraqis are not immune to Internet activities is that information disseminated on the Internet can influence the decisions and actions of anyone exposed to it, and the consequences, in turn, can impact the Iraqi population. This information could originate from Iraqis, Coalition forces, reporters and visitors in Iraq, foreign militants in Iraq, and other parties with Internet access. AQI, for example, uses the Internet to help bring foreign fighters to Iraq, where they then kill Iraqis as well as Coalition forces.

With that background, the following sections examine specific ways in which the Internet has been employed in the Iraq conflict. The discussion focuses on activities related to the initial U.S.-Iraq interstate war and the ongoing occupation as well as to al Qaeda's global insurgency and operations in Iraq, as the international dimension of all these conflicts has been well suited to, and heavily supported by, the Internet. Sunni insurgent groups in Iraq have also used the Internet to support their efforts to rid Iraq of Coalition forces and, in some instances, to spread hatred toward Iraqi Shia.[3] The latter illustrates how the Internet has also played a role in Iraq's sectarian strife.

The U.S.-Iraq Interstate War

Even before the war began in March 2003, the U.S. government launched an e-mail campaign to persuade Iraqi military leaders not to use weapons of mass destruction. According to reports, the Department of Defense sent thousands of e-mail messages that January, promising to protect those who cooperated and their families but threatening to treat as war criminals those who "took part in the use of these ugly weapons." In response, the Iraqi government blocked e-mail access to its state-controlled e-mail service in order to keep the messages from circulating.[4]

Hackers took a different approach in their attempts to influence U.S. government officials and posted messages on hacked websites. In September 2002, the cyber intelligence and security firm mi2g reported that the Unix Security Guards—a pro-Islamic group of hackers from Egypt, Morocco, Kuwait, and Indonesia—alone had recently carried out 155 digital attacks, leaving behind messages such as "Long live Palestine & take your dirty hands off Iraq!"[5] Web attacks escalated after the onset of the war, with an estimated twenty thousand defacements, both for and against the war, between mid-March and mid-April 2003.[6] There is no evidence that any of these attacks had an impact on policymakers, however.

These examples illustrate two ways in which the Internet has been used to attempt to influence government officials—direct messaging and Web attacks. Antiwar activists have also used the Internet to organize and coordinate both online and offline actions, including petitions and letter-writing campaigns, street demonstrations and marches, boycotts, and denial-of-service attacks against websites. For example, the protest organization A.N.S.W.E.R. (Act Now to Stop War and End Racism), which was formed in the wake of the September 11, 2001, terrorist attacks, used its website before the invasion for an antiwar referendum and to promote street demonstrations in the United States against war in Iraq. The website has continued to support antiwar actions.[7]

By far the greatest use of the Internet in the Iraq conflict has been for disseminating information, such as news, opinions, instructions, decrees, and exhortations. Information is disseminated through websites, forums, blogs, e-mail, and other online media in a variety of formats, including text, images, audio, and video. Much of the information is intended to influence a target audience and gain its members' support, but even Web content that is not intended to exert influence and draw support has the potential of doing so.

Blogs have played an especially interesting role. During the early "shock and awe" days of the U.S.-led Iraq War, when the primary sources of news were U.S. military officers, the Iraqi minister of information (Mohammed Said al-Sahhaf, known as "Baghdad Bob"), and reporters embedded with U.S. forces, a blogger in Baghdad began writing about what he saw and experienced. Salam Pax's blog, "Where Is Raed?" attracted a substantial readership, offering information and a perspective that were compelling and not available elsewhere. Since then, hundreds of Iraqi bloggers have contributed to the inside story from Iraq. U.S. military personnel also began blogging from Iraq, offering some of the best coverage of the Iraq conflict.

Using the Internet to tell the Iraq narrative may have contributed to the pervasive antiwar sentiment in the United States and elsewhere. Although any causal link would be difficult to establish, the widespread distribution of images and video clips showing the horrors of war and incidents such as the mistreatment of prisoners at the Abu Ghraib prison, plus countless essays and reports challenging the reasons for invading Iraq and the conduct of the war itself, reflected poorly on the war.

Al Qaeda's Global Insurgency and Operations in Iraq

Al Qaeda, as well as the global social movement inspired by it, has made extensive use of the Internet to distribute information, attract and recruit new members and supporters, finance operations, engage in cyber attacks, and maintain communications among its members.[8] Thousands of jihadi websites have supported the movement, carrying audio and video statements by Osama bin Laden, Ayman al-Zawahiri, and other al Qaeda leaders; horrific videos of beheadings, suicide explosions, and other acts of terrorism; calls for jihad; and training in such areas as weapons (explosives, AK-47s, surface-to-air missiles, and poisons), hacking, intelligence, and operations security. In 2007, al Qaeda's al-Sahab media company alone released seventy-four videos, or on average about one every three days.[9] These high-quality products are often posted in multiple languages, including Arabic and English, and in multiple formats, such as Windows Media, MPEG-4, Flash, and a format for mobile devices. By using the Internet, al Qaeda has bypassed the mainstream media and taken its messages directly to an international audience. Further, major media such as CNN and Al Jazeera also broadcast its products, so al Qaeda's audience is not limited to Internet users.

Abu Musab al-Zarqawi, leader of al Qaeda in Iraq until his death in June 2006, used the Internet to post gruesome videos of AQI's terrorist operations and to immortalize the organization's suicide bombers.[10] He started a monthly Internet magazine, offering religious justifications for jihad and advice on how to conduct it, and he posted films of his bomb-making classes so that his expertise would not be lost. In the summer of 2005, AQI averaged nine online postings per day. Two years later, in July 2007, its rate of posting was still high, with 201 for the month, or six to seven per day.[11] AQI used several online media production and distribution entities, including the Al-Fajr Media Center, the Global Islamic Media Front, and the Al-Furqan Media Institute. These entities serve to "brand" jihadist media and post them on the Internet. AQI postings have since dramatically declined, with only thirty-four in February 2008.[12] The slowdown is likely a result of stepped-up efforts against AQI that resulted in the capture or death of thirty-nine AQI members responsible for producing and disseminating materials on the Internet.

Much of al Qaeda's Internet activity is interactive, taking place in open and closed Web forums and groups. Marc Sageman observes that while websites have been instrumental in the al Qaeda movement's distribution of documents and other materials, it is through the interactive forums that relationships are built, bonding takes place, and beliefs are hardened. "It is the forums," he writes, "not the images of the passive websites, which are crucial in the process of radicalization. People change their minds through discussion with friends, not by simply reading impersonal stories."[13] Sageman believes that the forums are to the current generation of jihadists what the mosques were to the previous generation. They play a much larger role in al Qaeda's efforts to recruit jihadists than do the passive websites, where visitors are already predisposed to the views that are promulgated. Moreover, it is in conversation that commitments are made, plans are hatched, and actions are put into motion. In today's networked world, these conversations can as easily be conducted online as in person.

Internet forums have facilitated AQI's recruitment of foreign jihadists to Iraq. One forum, for example, offered instructions to jihadists transiting Syria on their way to Iraq.[14] Another held a live interview with a militant in

Iraq who answered questions about the progress of the conflict in Iraq and how to emigrate and join the fighting.[15]

Jihadists have also used Internet forums to facilitate cyber attacks. The al-Jinan forum, for example, has been used to plan, organize, and support electronic jihad against websites deemed anti-Islamic.[16] The objective is to "inflict maximum human, financial and morale damage on the enemy by using the Internet." Visitors to the forum can download the Electronic Jihad software tool, which automates distributed denial-of-service attacks against target websites. The forum lists websites attacked and their impact and gives awards to the most effective participants.

Cyber attacks are also used to finance and support al Qaeda's operations. The Moroccan-born British resident Younes Tsouli, whose online identity was "Irhabi [Terrorist] 007," hid al Qaeda files and communications on websites he penetrated. His seventy-four-page manual "The Encyclopedia of Hacking the Zionist and Crusader Websites" provides hacking instructions and a list of vulnerable websites.[17] Tsouli also used stolen identities and credit card numbers to pay for Web hosting services. To acquire card numbers, he and his cohorts planted keystroke loggers on their websites and sent out bogus e-mails with links to websites requesting financial information. His websites also featured materials from Zarqawi and AQI.[18]

Countering al Qaeda

Much has been written about how to counter al Qaeda and its global social movement. Especially recommended are Marc Sageman's book and reports by J. Rami Roz, Robert Martinage, and Frank Ciluffo and others.[19] The following four strategies explicitly target al Qaeda's Internet presence: intelligence collection, denial, subversion, and engagement.

Intelligence Collection

The first strategy, intelligence collection, entails monitoring al Qaeda's Internet forums and message exchanges and developing actionable intelligence regarding al Qaeda members and their social networks, safe houses and other facilities where members gather and weapons are produced, proposals and plans for terrorist acts, financial sources and transactions, and other relevant information. Information gleaned from such surveillance can be used to arrest members, confiscate weapons, and thwart plots. Law enforcement and intelligence agencies already engage in such monitoring, and it has been valuable in the fight against al Qaeda. As noted earlier, the effect of "capture or kill" operations against AQI have had the added benefit of curtailing the organization's media campaign.

Denial

The second strategy, denial, is more controversial. The goal is to take actions that deny al Qaeda access to the Internet, for example, by shutting down its e-mail and instant messaging accounts, websites, and forums. The premise is that with al Qaeda barred from the Internet, it will be unable to post materials and engage with potential recruits. In addition, communications among jihadists will be severely hampered, making it more difficult for them to plan and organize actions. While these results can be beneficial, the approach also has problems and limitations. One is that it is easy to establish new Internet accounts and reinstate websites and forums in new locations, so removal at best only impairs al Qaeda's efficiency. Moreover, because jihadists can access the Internet from an Internet café or any other place with Internet access, the targeting of particular access points—say, at a known safe house or a particular cyber café—will not go far in denying them access.

In addition to removing Internet accounts and websites, denial can be approached by censoring certain Internet traffic. For example, AQI might be denied access to the Internet by monitoring all Internet communications coming into and out of Iraq and blocking anything that appeared to be related to al Qaeda. However, it would be extremely difficult to develop filters that would distinguish al Qaeda traffic from other traffic, especially given al Qaeda's practice of using code words to hide the meaning of messages. In addition, the jihadists have their own encryption tool, a software program called Mujahideen Secrets, for concealing the content of files and messages. The software is based on strong, well-vetted ciphers, including the Advanced Encryption Standard (AES) and the RSA (Rivest, Shamir, Adleman) algorithm. On top of that, there are software tools that bypass Internet filters. The net effect is that filtering would not be foolproof, and it would almost certainly suppress legitimate traffic, which would be a violation of human rights.

Another problem with denial is that much of the content on jihadi websites is permissible under principles of free speech. Hence, removal is impossible without compromising human rights, especially if materials are posted for informational purposes on non-jihadi sites. Denial also has adverse effects on intelligence collection, potentially eliminating valuable sources of information as jihadists move further underground on the Internet or if they move to conduct their operations entirely offline. Finally, denial requires complete and successful international cooperation, since jihadi Internet accounts and websites can be hosted all over the world. Such cooperation can be difficult to achieve. Still, the effort in making al Qaeda less efficient and keeping it on the run has merit, so denial may be appropriate when there is a clear violation of the law and when this strategy has potential gains. Indeed, it is already a practice of Internet service providers to remove websites that directly advocate violence and that provide support to known terrorist organizations.

Subversion

The third strategy, subversion, is also controversial. It involves infiltrating al Qaeda forums, disrupting the organization's operations, and using deception to subvert its objectives, for example, by injecting misinformation into a forum discussion in order to erode trust in an al Qaeda leader or undermine a planned terrorist operation. This strategy is risky, as operations can have unintended consequences and backfire. Also, if not coordinated with intelligence operations, it can undermine collection efforts and lead to false conclusions. However, the strategy should not be dismissed outright, as deceptive techniques can be effective.

Engagement

The fourth strategy, engagement, takes a more positive approach. The idea is to converse with jihadists and potential recruits, challenging basic premises and beliefs through dialogue and writings. The goal is to draw people out of the movement and deter potential recruits from joining. If indeed it is through conversations in Web forums that potential recruits are radicalized and become committed to the jihad, then alternative conversations might lead them in the opposite direction. Saudi Arabia's online Al-Sakinah ("Tranquility") campaign illustrates this effect. Muslim scholars and sheikhs with expertise on Islam, aided by experts in sociology and psychology, enter extremist Web forums, engage with participants, and encourage them to renounce their extremist ideas. According to reports, the campaign has been successful. About seven hundred individuals, including high-ranking members of al Qaeda, have recanted their beliefs.[20]

For engagement to succeed, speakers must be able to develop rapport and trust with their target populations. Ideally, they should come from the same ethnicity, religion, and culture, as in the Saudi Tranquility campaign. In general, people are more influenced by people who share their backgrounds than they are by those who do not.

Of these four strategies, the first three require that al Qaeda operatives and their Internet sites be accurately identified. Otherwise, innocent persons could be swept up in counterterrorist operations. This unintended consequence could be particularly harmful with denial- and subversion-based strategies, adding to the problems already associated with these approaches.

Although all four strategies have value, intelligence collection appears to be the most promising strategy, followed by engagement. Denial and subversion may be used but only under conditions where there are clear benefits and controllable risks. A strategy that focuses primarily on getting jihadists off the Internet is likely to severely undermine intelligence collection against al Qaeda while compromising the civil liberties of innocent persons caught in the sweep. Moreover, it is not likely to work.

Notes

1. Internet World Stats, http://www.internetworldstats.com (accessed March 20, 2008).
2. Initiative for an Open Arab Internet, "Implacable Adversaries: Arab Governments and the Internet," *Openarab.net,* "Iraq" page, http://www.openarab.net/en/node/356 (accessed July 23, 2008).
3. Daniel Kimmage and Kathleen Ridolfo, *Iraqi Insurgent Media: The War of Images and Ideas* (Washington, DC: Radio Free Europe/Radio Liberty, June 2007).
4. Dan Caterinicchia, "DOD Confirms Iraq E-Mail Campaign," *Federal Computer Week,* January 16, 2003.
5. mi2g, "Digital Conflict over Iraq Has Begun," September 10, 2002.
6. Peter Rojas, "The Paranoia that Paid Off," *Guardian,* April 24, 2003.
7. This information is based on the author's own observations of A.N.S.W.E.R.'s website at http://www.internationalanswer.org/ since early 2003.
8. Much has been written on this issue. See, for example, Gabriel Weimann, *Terror on the Internet: The New Arena, the New Challenges* (Washington, DC: U.S. Institute of Peace Press, 2006).

9. "Al-Qaeda Recruiting Computer-Savvy Techs," *Sydney Morning Herald,* March 12, 2008.
10. Susan B. Glasser and Steve Coll, "The Web as Weapon: Zarqawi Intertwines Acts on Ground with Propaganda Campaign on the Internet," *Washington Post,* August 9, 2005.
11. Daniel Kimmage, "The Al-Qaeda Media Nexus: The Virtual Network Behind the Message" (Washington, DC: Radio Free Europe/Radio Liberty, March 2008).
12. Randy Fabi, "U.S. Military Says Hits Al Qaeda Propaganda Units," *Reuters,* March 22, 2008.
13. Mark Sageman, *Leaderless Jihad: Terror Networks in the Twenty-First Century* (Philadelphia: University of Pennsylvania Press, 2008), 116.
14. Stephen Ulph, "Islamist Website Issues Travel Warning for Syrian Mujahideen Crossing into Iraq," *Terrorism Focus* 2, no. 7 (March 31, 2005).
15. Shane Drennan and Andrew Black, "Jihad Online: The Changing Role of the Internet," *Jane's* (online), July 19, 2007.
16. Abdul Hameed Bakier, "Forum Users Improve Electronic Jihad Technology," *Terrorism Focus* 4, no. 20 (June 26, 2007).
17. "Hacking Manual by Jailed Jihadi Appears on Web," *Terrorism Focus* 5, no. 9 (March 4, 2008).
18. Brian Krebs, "Terrorism's Hook into Your Inbox," *Washington Post,* July 5, 2007; and Laura Mansfield, "Me and Terrorist 007," *LauraMansfield.com,* March 1, 2006, http://www.lauramansfield.com/j/007.asp (accessed March 27, 2008).
19. Sageman, *Leaderless Jihad*; J. Rami Mroz, "Countering Violent Extremism: Videopower and Cyberspace," Policy Paper 1/2008 (New York: EastWest Institute, February 2008); Robert C. Martinage, "The Global War on Terrorism: An Assessment" (Washington, DC: Center for Strategic and Budgetary Assessments, 2008); and Frank Cilluffo et al., *NETworked Radicalization: A Counter Strategy* (Washington, DC: George Washington University Homeland Security Policy Institute; Charlottesville, VA: University of Virginia Critical Incident Analysis Group, 2007).
20. Y. Yehoshua, "Reeducation of Extremists in Saudi Arabia," Inquiry and Analysis Series Report no. 260 (Washington, DC: Middle East Media Research Institute, January 18, 2006); and Cilluffo et al., *NETworked Radicalization.*

7
Intelligence and the Wars in Iraq

Joshua Rovner

The war in Iraq began with a rapid conventional invasion that quickly deposed Saddam Hussein's regime. Later, it morphed into an insurgency against the new government and a vicious ethno-sectarian civil war. Policymakers, intelligence officials, and military leaders were slow to recognize the changing character of the war. Why? A set of related problems caused the delay. The first problem was the poor quality of available intelligence before and after the conventional phase of Operation Iraqi Freedom. Ambiguous and unreliable information affected the quality of analysis in each period of the conflict. The second problem was dysfunctional intelligence-policy relations, which exacerbated the basic information problem by encouraging intelligence agencies to focus on a small subset of issues, especially nuclear weapons and terrorism, at the expense of others, such as Iraqi society, politics, and ethnography. The breakdown in intelligence-policy relations also enabled the military's institutional preference for conventional operations. This led to an under-resourced intelligence effort and further neglect of important kinds of information that may have helped it anticipate the insurgency and adapt to the civil war.

Intelligence-Policy Dysfunction Before the War

Intelligence estimates concerning Iraq had two defining characteristics before mid-2002. First, they concluded that Iraq possessed a small amount of chemical and biological agent left over from the 1980s and that Saddam

Hussein wanted to add to that stockpile and reconstitute Iraq's nuclear weapons infrastructure. Second, they were clear about the limits of actual data on Iraqi capabilities. The paucity of human intelligence, along with the dual-use dilemma, forced analysts to base their conclusions on assumptions about Iraqi intentions. This premise was no basis for firm conclusions about Iraqi capabilities, a point that was repeatedly stressed in estimates.[1] However, these caveats were noticeably absent in statements from key policymakers, who offered increasingly ominous and unequivocal public assessments of the threat.[2]

As the summer progressed, the administration urged intelligence agencies to bring their estimates in line with official statements. Pressure on the intelligence community was both subtle and blunt. Indirect pressure took the form of repeated and gratuitous questioning on single issues, leaving analysts with the impression that policymakers were waiting for predetermined answers. Direct politicization came later, when high-level policymakers actively enlisted the intelligence community to help make the case against Iraq. The immediate effect of politicization was a noticeable change in the content and tone of estimates. Gone were the previous caveats about the lack of reliable information concerning Iraqi capabilities, as well as the previous indications of disputes among analysts over the interpretation of the meager evidence at hand. What was left was an image of consensus in the intelligence community that Iraq already possessed substantial chemical and biological capabilities and was on the verge of going nuclear.[3]

These conclusions persuaded military officials to begin planning for an adversary armed with chemical and biological weapons because they were concerned about vulnerable infantry and that unconventional weapons could offset U.S. advantages in training and technology. Military intelligence (MI) analysts spent far less time considering the post-invasion phase. Under extraordinary time pressure to prepare for a major conventional war with a small invasion force, they did not have the opportunity to think deeply either about the possibility of insurgency or civil war or about how American troops would respond. While the Central Intelligence Agency (CIA), Defense Intelligence Agency (DIA), and the National Intelligence Council (NIC) spent some time on the problem of sectarian violence, military planners had to deal with more pressing issues.[4] The thrust of the overall intelligence effort did not shift from hunting for unconventional weapons until six months after the end of major combat operations.[5]

The politicization of estimates before the war reinforced mutual mistrust between intelligence and policy officials. Policymakers who expected more public support from the intelligence community harbored suspicions that analysts were ideologically opposed to the administration's foreign policy. Richard Perle spoke for neoconservatives in the White House when he declared that the CIA's analysis "isn't worth the paper it's printed on."[6] Intelligence warnings about the possibility of postwar instability, including two noteworthy estimates from the NIC in January 2003, had no observable impact on the administration.[7]

Meanwhile, disillusioned analysts felt that they were being abused for political purposes. Retired intelligence officials spoke out against the Bush administration, and their actions probably reinforced the policymakers' belief that they were never on board in the first place. Poisoned intelligence-policy relations made it difficult for intelligence officials to overcome lingering hostility from the White House. Eighteen months after the invasion, the president shrugged off a pessimistic CIA estimate on trends in Iraq, arguing that the agency was "just guessing as to what the conditions might be like."[8]

Conventional Intelligence and Irregular War

Deteriorating intelligence-policy relations in Washington also emboldened military officers who thought of Iraq in terms of conventional war.[9] The administration was confident about winning with a small invasion force in part because it believed that reconstruction and state building would be relatively easy. Ignoring intelligence on potential ethno-sectarian flash points, it assumed that Iraqis would welcome U.S. forces as liberators and that Iraqi oil exports would fund the reconstruction. Postwar planning was minimal and ad hoc.

Because the administration downplayed warnings from the intelligence community, it had no reason to tell planners to prepare for irregular war. This oversight encouraged military leaders to think in familiar conventional terms, even after the insurgency began in the summer of 2003. Military leaders paid lip service to Iraqi culture and society, concentrating instead on locating and targeting "former regime elements." Even Gen. John Abizaid, who had a reputation for less doctrinaire thinking, minimized the size of the insurgency and called for "better and more timely intelligence to crush those responsible for roadside bombings, ambushes, and mortar attacks."[10]

Lost was the kind of deeper reassessment that might have revealed underlying conditions that gave rise to the insurgency in the first place.

Limited understanding of Iraqi society hindered the military's ability to adapt to changing circumstances. Useful intelligence would have included assessments of Iraqi social networks, political parties, inter- and intra-tribal relations, and kinship ties. But encouraging this kind of analysis was difficult in the early years of the war, when some officers mocked briefings on Iraqi society and culture as "sensitivity training."[11] MI analysts may have been unwilling to push back against this bias because of the traditional stigma associated with the intelligence military occupational specialty (MOS).[12] As a result, analysts were not prepared to grapple with the complexity of a growing insurgency, and combat officers did not effectively use intelligence assets.[13]

The focus on conventional operations affected intelligence in other ways. Killing or capturing high-value individuals offered measurable results but did not necessarily contribute to progress in counterinsurgency (COIN). Meanwhile, analysts were tasked with fusing a mountain of intelligence from multiple sources in order to fix targets, leaving them little opportunity or incentive to leave the large bases at Fallujah, Ramadi, and al Asad. Analysts sequestered in headquarters were unlikely to make accurate judgments about public sentiment. Conventionally minded officers sought to increase the amount of actionable intelligence through large sweeps beginning in the late summer of 2003, but MI analysts were not prepared to absorb a flood of new data from interrogations. These reports could be misleading or meaningless unless they were cataloged, cross-referenced, and checked against other sources.[14]

The continuing belief in conventional operations may have also led to what Colin F. Jackson calls the "learning trap" in counterinsurgency.[15] Officers with deeply held professional military norms conflated sequential tactical successes with strategic victory in COIN, paradoxically becoming more confident even as the overall situation worsened. Positive assessments following a string of offensive operations more than two years after the insurgency began to suggest that the learning trap contributed to the delay in recognizing the change in the war's character. Rapid conventional sweeps, such as Operation Kennesaw Dragon (November 2005) and Operation Swarmer (March 2006), were celebrated as victories even though they did not provide lasting security to civilians and did little actual damage to insurgents.[16]

Not all officers fell into the learning trap; moreover, the failure to quell the insurgency caused some military leaders to reassess the use of intelligence. Maj. Gen. Peter Chiarelli, then the commanding general of the 1st Cavalry Division in Baghdad, wrote that it had become "rapidly apparent that we needed to develop a keen understanding of demographics as well as the cultural intricacies that drive the civilian population."[17] In mid-2005 the U.S. Army began work on the Human Terrain System (HTS), an initiative designed to give brigade commanders more comprehensive knowledge about local economics, society, culture, and ethnography. The project recruited civilian social scientists to work in forward-deployed brigade and regimental staffs.[18] Other efforts represented bottom-up attempts to break down information barriers among intelligence collectors, analysts, and operators in the field. A number of "impatient and hard-pressed U.S. military officers in northern Iraq took matters into their own hands by creating arrangements whereby intelligence and military organizations share horizontally, including with local counterparts."[19]

Escalating violence in 2006, including a substantial amount of ethnic cleansing in mixed areas, forced the administration to undertake a strategic reassessment. Policymakers became more receptive to intelligence during this period. Deputy National Security Adviser Meghan O'Sullivan, previously of the State Department's Bureau of Intelligence and Research (INR), concluded in a July memo that the violence "had a momentum of its own." When asked by the president for her assessment of the daily life of Iraqi civilians, O'Sullivan responded bluntly, "It's hell, Mr. President."[20]

Late in the year the White House appointed Robert Gates as secretary of defense and Gen. David Petraeus as commander of the Multi-National Force–Iraq (MNF-I). Gates's long experience in the intelligence community and in the National Security Council (NSC) gave him a sophisticated view of intelligence-policy relations, and his appointment suggested that intelligence would play a larger role in strategic decision making.[21] Similarly, Petraeus's promotion signified a change in how the military would employ intelligence in Iraq. Petraeus was an early champion of waging a counterinsurgency in Iraq instead of viewing the war through a conventional lens. Shifting the strategic approach meant investing more heavily in collection efforts and refocusing analysis on the underlying social and political questions at the root of the insurgency.[22]

With new leadership in place, the military began to reshape its intelligence effort. It began by adding resources. The Marine Corps doubled and in some cases tripled the size of battalion intelligence sections in Iraq.[23] Army maneuver battalion and brigade intelligence sections also doubled in size. Brigade Combat Teams (BCTs) began to include specialized MI companies with organic human intelligence (HUMINT), signals intelligence (SIGINT), unmanned aerial vehicle imagery, and analysis platoons. The Army also began forming intelligence battalions as the core of new "multifunctional battlefield surveillance brigades" with the explicit purpose of operating in complex environments such as Iraq.[24]

The authors of the intelligence chapter in the new counterinsurgency field manual recommended other changes. HUMINT and SIGINT specialists, they argued, should be attached to tactical units. More analysts should be included at the battalion and company levels in order to coordinate with collectors and bring them in closer contact with the population. Intelligence fusion centers should exist at all echelons for the same reasons. Social and cultural intelligence training should be mandatory. Finally, they recommended a longer transition period during unit rotations to preserve hard-won institutional knowledge.[25]

These recommendations led to noticeable changes. The expansion of programs such as HTS indicated that cultural and ethnographic analyses were becoming routine, as were more systematic efforts to understand detainees' morale and motivation.[26] Other efforts sought to improve soldiers' ability to act as front-line intelligence collectors, improving the quality and reliability of tactical HUMINT. Some of these efforts incorporated new technologies, such as the Tactical Ground Reporting System, a map-centric software package that allowed patrol leaders to upload and review information in a common database in order to generate a fine-grained and constantly updated picture of local intelligence.[27] Other changes helped make it possible to exploit favorable trends at the strategic level. Increased attention to social and cultural intelligence, for example, allowed U.S. officials to recognize the growing intra-Sunni split in 2006, creating opportunities for new alliances with tribal leaders in common cause against al Qaeda in Iraq (AQI).[28] The subsequent creation of tactical fusion cells, combining assets from across the intelligence community with special forces, made it possible to isolate AQI and more effectively target its leaders. According to recent reporting, these fusion centers are a picture of interagency cooperation and intelligence-policy harmony that would have been unthinkable in the early years of the war.[29]

Summary and Recommendations

This chapter described how intelligence-policy dysfunction affected the conduct of intelligence in all three phases of the war in Iraq.[30] The early breakdown in relations created lasting antipathy between intelligence producers and consumers that slowed the recognition of the insurgency and civil war. It also inhibited operations because it enabled military leaders to indulge their preference for conventional war fighting. A period of intense sectarian violence led to changes in intelligence collection and analysis that appear to have improved performance. Sustaining these gains requires continued efforts to refine intelligence practices. It also requires more attention to how political and military leaders use intelligence.

There is no simple solution for the kind of myopia that inhibited intelligence in Iraq. Some problems are intractable. Domestic politics sometimes create an incentive to use intelligence for public advocacy, and politicization will still be possible as long as leaders believe that intelligence can be a potent tool of persuasion.[31] Cognitive barriers also make it hard for analysts, policymakers, and military leaders to absorb intelligence that cuts against their existing preferences and beliefs.[32]

But politics and psychology do not preclude marginal improvement to intelligence performance and intelligence-policy relations. More comprehensive training, for example, will help intelligence officers prepare for a broader assortment of security challenges. The recent expansion of the intelligence community should provide an opportunity for time-strapped analysts to step away from daily tasks and explore the specific characteristics of intelligence in different types of conflict. To this end, the intelligence community should also ease security standards so that it can recruit new hires with experience in regions wracked by insurgency and civil war. An overbearing security regime will exclude these individuals, leading to a homogenous workforce and risking intellectual sclerosis.[33]

Intelligence-policy relations will benefit by ending the practice of declassifying current estimates on controversial issues. The public expectation that intelligence will play a role in the policy debate increases the incentive to politicize estimates. Reestablishing the norm of secrecy will go some distance toward encouraging frank discussions between policymakers and intelligence officials and preventing the kind of breakdown that occurred before the war in Iraq.[34] In addition, political and military leaders should be briefed on the purposes and limits of intelligence so they do not harbor unrealistic expectations about what it can provide, and intelligence officers should be educated on their consumers' practical requirements.

Notes

1. Joshua Rovner, "Intelligence-Policy Relations and the Problem of Politicization," (Ph.D. diss., Massachusetts Institute of Technology, 2008), 283–89, 293–95.
2. Representative examples are found in Vernon Loeb and Thomas E. Ricks, "Al Qaeda Active, Rumsfeld Says," *Washington Post*, June 4, 2002; and "The Vice President Delivers Remarks to the National Association of Home Builders," the White House, June 6, 2002, http://georgewbush-whitehouse.archives.gov/vicepresident/news-speeches/speeches/vp20020606.html.
3. For an extended discussion of prewar politicization, see Rovner, "Intelligence-Policy Relations," 272–367.
4. Michael R. Gordon and Gen. Bernard E. Trainor, *Cobra II: The Inside Story of the Invasion and Occupation of Iraq* (New York: Pantheon Books, 2006), 138–63; and U.S. Congress, Senate Select Committee on Intelligence, "Report on Prewar Intelligence Assessments About Postwar Iraq," 110th Cong., 1st sess., May 2007, 93–106.
5. Bruce Hoffman, *Insurgency and Counterinsurgency in Iraq*, Rand Occasional Paper (Santa Monica, CA: Rand, June 2004), 10.
6. Spencer Ackerman and John B. Judis, "The First Casualty," *New Republic*, June 30, 2003, 14–25, at 17.
7. Intelligence Community Assessment (ICA) 2003-03, *Regional Consequences of Regime Change in Iraq*; and ICA 2003-04, *Principal Challenges in Post-Saddam Iraq*. Declassified versions were released in Senate Select Committee on Intelligence, "Report on Prewar Intelligence Assessments About Postwar Iraq," 110th Cong., 1st sess., pp. 13–91. Richard Best argues that these estimates alerted the administration to the difficulties in postwar reconstruction and might have convinced it to delay handing over power to Iraqis. His argument would be more persuasive if the administration had appointed experts in nation building to work in the Coalition Provisional Authority (CPA). Instead, hiring decisions in the CPA appear to have been based on political ideology. See Richard A. Best, Jr., "What the Intelligence Community Got Right About Iraq," *Intelligence and National Security* 23, no. 3 (June 2008): 289–302; and Rajiv Chandrasekaran, "Ties to GOP Trumped Know-How Among Staff Sent to Rebuild Iraq," *Washington Post*, September 17, 2006.
8. Office of the Press Secretary, the White House, "President Bush Meets with Prime Minister Allawi in New York Tuesday: Remarks by President Bush and Prime Minister Allawi of the Interim Government of Iraq," September 21, 2004, http://georgewbush-whitehouse.archives.gov/news/releases/2004/09/20040921-9.html.

9. To be clear, the U.S. military is not monolithic in its approach to war, and significant doctrinal differences exist among and within the services. The argument here is that policy guidance strengthened advocates of conventional planning and marginalized challengers to the prevailing wisdom.
10. Eric Schmitt and David E. Sanger, "Guerrillas Posing More Danger, Says U.S.," *New York Times*, November 14, 2003.
11. James L. Higgins, Michelle L. Trusso, and Alfred B. Connable, "Marine Corps Intelligence," *Marine Corps Gazette* 89, no. 12 (December 2005): 23–24.
12. A number of articles in professional journals suggest that intelligence in support of conventional operations took precedence as late as 2006. Examples include Dan Zeytoonian, "Intelligent Design: COIN Operations and Intelligence Collection and Analysis," *Military Review* 86, no. 5 (September–October 2006): 188–95; F. J. Bing West, "American Military Performance in Iraq," *Military Review* 86, no. 5 (September–October 2006): 2–7; Fred Renzi, "Networks: Terra Incognita and the Case for Ethnographic Intelligence," *Military Review* 86, no. 5 (September–October 2006): 16–22; Matthew Collins, "Beyond the Van Riper Plan: How Are We Growing Intelligence Officers?" *Marine Corps Gazette* 90, no. 10 (August 2006); and John P. Coles, "Incorporating Cultural Intelligence into Joint Doctrine," *IO Sphere* (Spring 2006): 7–13. Informal conversations with MI officers suggest that the stigma associated with intelligence still exists but has weakened.
13. These were the conclusions of a report from the Center for Army Lessons Learned at Fort Leavenworth, as reported in Thomas E. Ricks, *Fiasco: The American Military Adventure in Iraq* (New York: Penguin, 2006), 193–95. For other critical assessments of intelligence in this period, see Ahmed S. Hashim, *Insurgency and Counterinsurgency in Iraq* (Ithaca, NY: Cornell University Press, 2006), 319–22; and Hoffman, *Insurgency and Counterinsurgency in Iraq*, 9–16.
14. This problem also plagued intelligence efforts in Vietnam. See Orrin DeForest and David Chanoff, *Slow Burn: The Rise and Bitter Fall of Intelligence in Vietnam* (New York: Simon & Schuster, 1990).
15. Colin F. Jackson, "Defeat in Victory: Organizational Learning Dysfunction in Counterinsurgency" (Ph.D. diss., Massachusetts Institute of Technology, 2008), chap. 2.
16. Austin Long, "Doctrine of Eternal Recurrence: The U.S. Military and Counterinsurgency Doctrine, 1960–1973 and 2003–2006," Rand Counterinsurgency Study, Paper 6 (Santa Monica, CA: Rand, 2008).
17. Peter Chiarelli and Patrick R. Michaelis, "Winning the Peace: The Requirement for Full-Spectrum Operations," *Military Review* 85, no. 4 (July–August 2005): 13–17.
18. Jacob Kipp et al., "The Human Terrain System: A CORDS for the 21st Century," *Military Review* 86, no. 5 (September–October 2006): 8–15.
19. David C. Gompert et al., *War by Other Means: Building Complete and Balanced Capabilities for Counterinsurgency* (Santa Monica, CA: Rand, 2006), 132.
20. Bob Woodward, "Doubt, Distrust, Delay," *Washington Post*, September 7, 2008.
21. For a sample of his views about intelligence and policy, see Robert M. Gates, "Guarding Against Politicization," *Studies in Intelligence* 36, no. 5 (1992): 5–13.
22. Petraeus oversaw the production of *Field Manual 3-24: Counterinsurgency* (Washing-

ton, DC: Department of the Army, 2006), which stressed the primacy of intelligence. See chap. 3, "Intelligence and Counterinsurgency."

23. Kyle Teamey and Jonathan Sweet, "Organizing Intelligence for Counterinsurgency," *Military Review* 86, no. 5 (September–October 2006): 24–29, at 25.
24. John F. Kimmons, "Transforming Army Intelligence," *Military Review* 86, no. 6 (November–December 2006): 69–72.
25. Teamey and Sweet, "Organizing Intelligence."
26. Walter Pincus, "U.S. Working to Reshape Iraqi Detainees," *Washington Post*, September 19, 2007.
27. David Talbot, "A Technology Surges," *MIT Technology Review* (March–April 2008).
28. Austin Long, "The Anbar Awakening," *Survival* 50, no. 2, (April–May 2008): 67–94.
29. Joby Warrick and Robin Wright, "U.S. Teams Weaken Insurgency in Iraq," *Washington Post*, September 6, 2008.
30. It is certainly not a comprehensive history of intelligence in Iraq. Other issues deserving specific attention include the evolution of regional intelligence-sharing arrangements; the growing interservice friction over control of intelligence, surveillance, and reconnaissance (ISR) assets; and the controversies over interrogation as a tool in COIN.
31. Glenn P. Hastedt, "Public Intelligence: Leaks as Policy Instruments—the Case of the Iraq War," *Intelligence and National Security* 20, no. 3 (September 2005): 419-39; and Lawrence Freedman, "War in Iraq: Selling the Threat," *Survival* 26, no. 2 (Summer 2004): 7–50.
32. Robert Jervis, *Perception and Misperception in International Politics* (Princeton, NJ: Princeton University Press, 1976); and Richards J. Heuer, Jr., *Psychology of Intelligence Analysis* (Washington, DC: Center for the Study of Intelligence, 1999).
33. See also Joshua Rovner, "The Perils of Shallow Theory: Intelligence Reform and the 9/11 Commission," with Austin Long, *International Journal of Intelligence and Counterintelligence* 18, no. 4 (Winter 2005–2006): 609–637, at 628–29.
34. The director of national intelligence (DNI) issued a moratorium on releasing estimates in October 2007. One month later, however, the office of the DNI posted key judgments from the National Intelligence Estimate (NIE) on Iranian nuclear activities on its website. Pamela Hess, "Spy Chief to Restrict Intel Estimates," *Washington Post*, October 26, 2007.

LEGAL AND ETHICAL ISSUES

8
Legal Dimensions

Christopher M. Ford

Classifying a given conflict as an interstate war, an insurgency, or a civil war can provide valuable context for commanders at all levels. However, while these concepts are militarily and politically distinct, they have little bearing on the legal obligations of the combat forces. Under both international and domestic law, the obligations of the U.S. military remain largely consistent regardless of the military or political nature of the conflict. To the extent that obligations change during the course of hostilities, they do not fall neatly into the three circles.

Using Iraq as a case study, this chapter examines U.S. military obligations during interstate war and in various circumstances that may follow: insurgency, civil unrest, peace, and so on. Broadly stated, a panoply of international obligations was invoked when the United States commenced hostilities with Iraq. These obligations changed with the fall of Saddam Hussein's Baathist government and then again with the transfer of authority to the current Iraqi government. Each of these three legal "way points" is addressed in turn, within the larger context of the "law of war."[1]

The idea that armed forces have legal obligations during hostilities has a long tradition. The modern development of the law of war came with the publication of the *Instructions for the Government of Armies of the United States in the Field* (General Order No. 100), which President Abraham Lincoln commissioned and Francis Lieber drafted in 1863.[2] This document, popularly known as the Lieber Code, was the first modern codification of a fixed set of rules applicable to all combatants. Later it served as a foundation for the current legal paradigm, which was established by the Hague Regulations (1907) and the Geneva Conventions (1949). Both of these treaties were ratified and thus became part of the "supreme law of the land."[3] The obligations they contain have in turn been applied to U.S. military forces through executive orders, Department of Defense directives, Department of Defense Standing Rules of Engagement, and army field manuals, such as *FM 27-10: The Law of Land Warfare*, *FM 3-24: Counterinsurgency*, and *FM 2-22.3: Human Intelligence Collector Operations*.

The law of war is broadly applicable. It applies equally to all forms of warfare, including interstate, civil, and insurgent. Army policy, citing the Geneva Conventions, holds that:

> the customary law of war applies to all cases of declared war or any other armed conflict which may arise between the United States and other nations, even if the state of war is not recognized by one of them. The customary law is also applicable to all cases of occupation of foreign territory by the exercise of armed force, even if the occupation meets with no armed resistance.[4]

The law of war applies "from the first acts of hostilities or unresisted occupation."[5] Department of Defense policy holds that the law of war applies "during all armed conflicts, however such conflicts are characterized."[6] In the context of Iraq, the law of war applied at the start of operations, even before the commencement of hostilities on March 19, 2003, when U.S. and Coalition forces began air strikes.

Interstate War

Application of Force

Any application of force must comply with the basic tenets of the law of war. These requirements are well known, frequently trained by units and Judge Advocates, and incorporated in the rules of engagement for each conflict.[7] Briefly, the law of war comprises four tenets: military necessity, unnecessary suffering, distinction, and proportionality. Perhaps most critical among these legally is distinction, that is, the requirement that military forces distinguish between combatants and noncombatants.

In an interstate war, there are three categories of persons: lawful combatants, unlawful combatants, and noncombatants. A lawful combatant is a member of the regular armed forces of a state, militia, organized resistance movement, or any other organization whose members wear a fixed insignia, carry arms openly, and abide by the law of war.[8] An individual may also be a lawful combatant if he or she is participating in a *levée en masse* (literally, massed uprising), which occurs when "[i]nhabitants of a non-occupied territory, who on the approach of the enemy spontaneously take up arms to resist the invading forces. . . ."[9] Lawful combatants can be targeted once they have been identified.

An unlawful combatant is an individual who is participating in combat activities but does not meet the definition of a lawful combatant. Generally, unlawful combatants should be treated as criminal suspects and detained when possible. Where they engage in a hostile act or present a hostile force, commanders and troops should act in self-defense, including, as necessary and appropriate, using hostile force. As with lawful combatants, unlawful combatants may also be targeted.

A noncombatant can be one of two categories of persons—civilians or persons entitled to special protection. A civilian is a person who is not taking part in hostilities, including "members of the armed forces who have laid down their arms and those placed [out of combat] by sickness, wounds, detention, or any other cause."[10] If civilians "directly participate" in hostilities, they lose their protection and can be targeted.[11] Persons entitled to special protection are those who may be participating in hostilities but fall under one of the following categories: shipwrecked personnel, parachutists in distress, medical personnel, religious personnel, and members of the civil defense.[12] These individuals may not be targeted.

Interactions with the Populace

Detention

When lawful combatants are captured, they are categorized as "prisoners of war" and are entitled to combatant immunity, that is, immunity for their *lawful* military actions (likewise, they may be prosecuted for violations of the law of war). In cases where an individual claims to be a prisoner of war but does not appear to meet the criteria, the Geneva Conventions provide for a procedure to determine their status.[13] If the individual is found to be an unlawful combatant, he or she can be detained during the conduct of hostilities and, as discussed below, during the subsequent occupation. Because the actions of unlawful combatants are essentially criminal acts, these individuals can be prosecuted for these acts in the local national courts in accordance with their rules and laws.[14] They can also be prosecuted by military tribunals. Although they are unlawful combatants, they are still entitled to humane treatment.[15]

What constitutes "humane treatment" has been an issue of some debate, particularly in the context of interrogation policies in the war on terrorism. The general consensus is that customary international law and Common Article 3 of the Geneva Conventions (so called because it is common to all four conventions) provide the minimum standard for humane treatment. The point of debate on this issue concerns the applicability of Common Article 3 in the context of the war on terrorism. The Bush administration argued that the article is inapplicable because it was designed to apply to internal conflicts (that is, according to the conventions, to conflicts "not of an international character") and not to international conflicts, such as the war on terrorism.[16] The U.S. Supreme Court addressed the issue in *Hamdan v. Rumsfeld* and held that the protections contained in Common Article 3 apply at all times. In fact, the court quoted from the commentary to the convention, which notes that the article "has the merit of being simple and clear. . . . Its observance does not depend upon preliminary discussions on the nature of the conflict."[17] The Department of Defense has since acknowledged the court's holding.

Generally stated, Common Article 3, in combination with customary international law, prohibits genocide, slavery, murder, torture, violence to life or limb, taking of hostages, punishment without fair trial, prolonged arbitrary detention, failure to care for the sick and wounded, systematic racial discrimination, and a consistent pattern of gross violations of internationally recognized human rights.[18]

Obligations to the Populace

In an interstate war, fighting forces are obligated at a minimum to adhere to the principles of the law of war. Beyond this stipulation, a hostile force has no other obligations until it becomes an occupying force, as discussed in the next section.

Insurgency and Civil War

Application of Force

Where the United States finds itself in the midst of a civil war in another country, its ability to target hostile forces is the same as in an interstate conflict: it can target lawful combatants and noncombatant civilians who directly participate in hostilities. The same rules apply in an insurgency; however, in this case, the application of force is complicated by the fact that insurgents do not wear uniforms, have an insignia, and so on. Unlawful combatants can be targeted if they can be positively identified, but making this determination is quite difficult in a counterinsurgency. Further, more often than not, counterinsurgent troops are forced to rely on principles of self-defense.

Interactions with the Populace

Detention

As noted, in a counterinsurgency virtually all captured individuals will be unlawful combatants. As such, they are not entitled to combatant immunity, and they can be prosecuted for their actions in either a military or a civilian tribunal. If the hostile force is an occupying force (discussed below), it has additional powers of detention.

An occupying power can restrict the movement of the occupied population but only when doing so is necessary to ensure security.[19] Critically, this provision allows the occupying power to detain individuals without charge who are deemed to pose a threat to security. The detention can continue until either their threat dissipates or the occupation ends. More broadly, an occupying power may impose measures such as curfews and border restrictions where necessary to ensure internal security. However, the Geneva Conventions specifically prohibit "[i]ndividual or mass forcible transfers . . . regardless of their motive."[20] Nevertheless, there is an exception for "total or partial evacuation of a given area if the security of the population or imperative military reasons so demand."[21] Such movements should be within the country, and the displaced individuals should be returned as soon as possible. While such persons are displaced, the displacing power must provide for their "hygiene, health, safety and nutrition."[22]

Obligations to the Populace

A hostile force that is present during an insurgency or civil war does not incur any additional responsibilities toward the local national population. The hostile force is only obligated to abide by the principles of the law of war. Significant obligations ensue, however, when the hostile force becomes an occupying force. A territory is considered occupied under international law when it "is actually placed under the authority of the hostile army. . . . The occupation extends only to the territory where such authority has been established and can be exercised."[23] According to the U.S. Army's *Field Manual 27-10* (paragraph 355), an occupation occurs when the hostile force displaces the invaded territory's government and substitutes its authority for that of the displaced government. Although occupying forces historically have often proclaimed their occupation, this declaration is not a requirement.[24]

In Iraq, there is no definitive point at which U.S. forces became an occupying power. Nor could it be argued that U.S. forces ever occupied the entire country. In the context of international law, the United States and its allies became occupying powers near the end of April 2003, when major combat operations ended and the U.S.-led Office for Reconstruction and Humanitarian Assistance assumed political control of the country. At various times in various locations, the Coalition has lost "control" over portions of Iraq. For instance, Fallujah was arguably not under U.S. control from April 2004 through the conclusion of Operation Phantom Fury in late November 2004. During this time, the obligations of an occupying force did not apply in this uncontrolled area, although the basic tenets of the law of war still applied.

In areas under the occupying power's control, the occupying power is obligated to assume responsibility for the territory. The occupier does not assume sovereignty over the country; rather, during occupation, sovereignty is suspended, with the occupying power simply exercising control over the country. Thus, it cannot act as the "official" government of the country and bind it to an international treaty, for instance. Hence, in Iraq the occupying powers established the Coalition Provisional Authority (CPA)—provisional in that it was never designed to be the sovereign government of Iraq but rather a caretaker government until a sovereign Iraqi government could be established.

What obligations ensue? The basic requirement reads as follows: "[the occupying power] shall take all measures in his power to restore and ensure, as far as possible, public order and safety, while respecting, unless absolutely prevented, the laws in force in the country."[25] Simply put, the occupying power should provide security and take all possible measures to ensure that ordinary life continues—for example, that public transportation runs, garbage is collected, energy is generated, crime is policed, medical facilities are operational, schools are in session, and so on. There is no legal obligation either to make the country "better" than it was before the occupation or to repair damage caused during the armed conflict beyond the extent necessary to maintain public order and safety. Nevertheless, public policy or military needs may mandate actions that are not strictly required by the law.

The inhabitants of an occupied territory are obligated, at a minimum, to refrain from engaging in hostilities.[26] At the same time, the occupier must respect and retain the occupied nation's laws to the greatest extent possible. *Field Manual 27-10* states: "In restoring public order and safety, the occupant will continue in force the ordinary civil and penal (criminal) laws of the occupied territory. . . . These laws will be administered by the local officials as far as practicable" (paragraph 370). Thus, an individual charged with violating a criminal law should be tried according to the local national laws in the local national court system.[27] The local police force can be used to enforce the nation's laws, which, with a few exceptions, the occupier is required to keep intact. *Field Manual 27-10* provides such an exception to allow for suspension where the laws "constitute a threat to [the occupying power's] security or an obstacle to application of the [Geneva] Convention" (paragraph 369). The United States exercised this power when the CPA continued the use of the Iraqi Penal Code of 1969 minus a handful of provisions relating to political crimes.[28]

Practically, an occupation ends when the occupying power ceases to exert actual control over the territory. Legally, the issue is more complex. The Geneva Conventions hold that an occupation ends one year after the start of the occupation.[29] As one legal commentator has noted, this quirk is "somewhat unfortunate" and creates a complex legal situation in which the full body of international occupation law applies during the first twelve months of occupation, and thereafter more limited provisions of international law apply.[30] Interestingly, Additional Protocol I to the Geneva Conventions dispenses with the one-year time limit and holds that the conventions apply until the occupation is terminated.[31]

Confusing this issue further, the United States has not ratified Additional Protocol I, although as a matter of policy it has abided by most provisions.

There is no legal obligation requiring an occupation to continue until public order and safety have been established. So, in short, even though international law compels the occupying power to establish public order and safety, it does not compel it to remain until this task has been achieved.

When, then, does an occupation end for U.S. military forces? The best practice would be to consider the occupation (and all related obligations) in force until the U.S. occupying authority relinquishes actual control over the territory in question. Absent other authority, the former occupying authority can no longer promulgate laws, control indigenous security forces, or otherwise govern the state. Furthermore, the former occupying forces cannot unilaterally conduct military operations in the country or detain individuals deemed a threat to security. Such actions would have to be taken in cooperation with the host government.

When the U.S.-led Coalition invaded Iraq in March 2003, it was operating under several United Nations (UN) Security Council resolutions.[32] Once the war ended, the CPA was established pursuant to Security Council Resolution 1483, adopted on May 22, 2003. The CPA transferred "full governing authority" to the Iraqi Interim Government and dissolved itself on June 30, 2004.[33] The Security Council resolution that terminated the CPA (Resolution 1546, adopted on June 8, 2004) also empowered the U.S.-led multinational force to "take all necessary measures to contribute to the maintenance of security and stability in Iraq . . . including by preventing and deterring terrorism."[34] The resolution also required that "the mandate for the multinational force shall be reviewed at the request of the Government of Iraq or twelve months from the date of this resolution."[35]

The Security Council has reaffirmed this mandate several times and most recently on December 18, 2007, in Resolution 1790. It extended the mandate through December 31, 2008, but noted that the mandate "shall be reviewed at the request of the Government of Iraq or no later than 15 June 2008, and declares that it will terminate this mandate earlier if requested by the Government of Iraq."[36] Once the mandate is terminated, the continued presence and activities of Coalition military forces will be at the invitation of the sovereign Iraqi government. As a "guest force," the only obligations on U.S. forces are the basic provisions in the adherence to the law of war, customary international law, and Common Article 3 and a more general responsibility to act in accordance with the mandate provided by the host nation.

Conclusion

Broadly stated, military obligations under international law fall into three situation-based paradigms: interstate war, occupation, and the post-occupation period. Regardless of the nature of the conflict, a multitude of international and domestic legal obligations are universally applicable—for example, the fundamental concepts contained in the law of war, customary international law, and Common Article 3 of the Geneva Conventions. Additional obligations apply during an occupation. As in the case of Iraq, UN mandates may supplement these responsibilities. While complex, these obligations essentially require the occupying power to maintain security in the occupied territory until it terminates the occupation. When the occupier leaves, the occupation and all attendant obligations end. In cases where the occupier legally terminates its occupation—that is, restores sovereignty—but physically remains in the occupied country, this circumstance triggers the third paradigm, in which the formerly occupying forces are either acting under an international mandate or operating as a "guest force" at the behest of the host country.

Notes

1. For ease of discussion, throughout this chapter the term "law of war" is used to describe "[t]hat part of international law that regulates the conduct of armed hostilities. . . . The law of war encompasses all international law for the conduct of hostilities binding on the United States or its individual citizens." U.S. Department of Defense Directive 5100.77, December 9, 1998.
2. *Instructions for the Government of Armies of the United States in the Field,* prepared by Francis Lieber, LL.D. (originally issued as General Orders No. 100, War Department, Adjutant General's Office, Washington, DC, April 24, 1863), http://Avalon.law.yale.edu/19th_century/lieber.asp.
3. U.S. Constitution, art. VI, sec. 2.
4. Department of the Army, *Field Manual 27-10: The Law of Land Warfare* (Washington, DC: Department of the Army, July 18, 1956), para. 8(a).
5. Frédéric de Mulinen, *Handbook on the Law of War for Armed Forces* (Geneva: International Committee of the Red Cross, 1987), 7, citations omitted.
6. U.S. Department of Defense Directive 2311.01E, para. 4.1 (May 9, 2006). See also Chairman of the Joint Chiefs of Staff Instruction 5810.01, para. 5a: the United States "will apply law of war principles during all operations that are categorized as Military Operations Other Than War." Although the general applicability of the law of war is clear in U.S. military policy, there is some debate about the continued relevance of the Geneva Conventions. It has been argued that because the conventions were drafted in the wake of World War II in the context of an interstate model of warfare,

they are of limited relevance to the asymmetric warfare that has characterized recent conflicts. See, for example, Derek Jinks, "The Applicability of the Geneva Conventions to the 'Global War on Terrorism,'" *Virginia Journal of International Law* 46, no. 1 (Fall 2005): 165–96. This debate, however, is beyond the scope of this chapter.

7. Commanders draft the rules of engagement as a tool to regulate the use of force, taking into account political, military, and legal considerations. The legal aspect of the rules of engagement is taken from the law of war, as discussed in this chapter, and is largely fixed—that is, the same rules of law apply regardless of the type of conflict. It should be noted that the rules of engagement are drafted for each conflict at the most strategic level. At that level, the rules provide broad limitations that reflect national, strategic-level concerns. Commanders at lower echelons may make modifications to reflect specific concerns or objectives.
8. *Operational Law Handbook* (Charlottesville, VA: International and Operational Law Department, Judge Advocate General's Legal Center and School, 2008), citing the Geneva Convention Relative to the Treatment of Prisoners of War, art. 4, August 12, 1949 (hereafter Geneva III), and Geneva Convention for the Amelioration of the Condition of the Wounded and Sick in Armed Forces in the Field, art. 13, August 12, 1949 (hereafter Geneva I).
10. Geneva Convention Relative to the Protection of Civilian Persons in Time of War, art. 5, August 12, 1949 (hereafter Geneva IV).
11. Yoram Dinstein, *The Conduct of Hostilities Under the Law of International Armed Conflict* (Cambridge, UK: Cambridge University Press, 2004), 27.
12. Ibid., 141–49.
13. Geneva IV, art. 5.
14. Geneva IV, art. 64.
15. Geneva IV, art. 5.
16. The government asserted, and a three-judge panel of the U.S. Court of Appeals for the District of Columbia Circuit agreed, that Common Article 3 does not apply to Salim Ahmed Hamdan because the conflict with al Qaeda, being "international in scope," does not qualify as a "conflict not of an international character." *Hamdan v. Rumsfeld*, 126 S.Ct. 2749, 2795 (2006).
17. *Hamdan v. Rumsfeld*, 126 S.Ct. 2749 (2006), quoting Geneva III, Commentary, 35.
18. *Operational Law Handbook*, 46–47.
19. Geneva IV, art. 48, 49.
20. Geneva IV, art. 49.
21. Ibid.
22. Ibid.
23. Annex to the Convention Respecting the Laws and Customs of War on Land: Regulation Concerning the Laws and Customs of War on Land (hereafter Hague Regulation), October 18, 1907, art. 42.
24. David A. Wallace, "The Law of Occupation and Post–Armed Conflict Governance: Considerations for Future Conflicts," *Military Review*, November–December 2007.
25. Hague Regulation, art. 43.
26. Geneva IV, art. 5.

27. From *Field Manual 27-10*, para. 370: "Crimes not of a military nature and not affecting the occupant's security are normally left to the jurisdiction of the local courts."
28. L. Paul Bremer, Coalition Provisional Authority Order Number 7: Penal Code, June 10, 2003.
29. Geneva IV, art. 6.
30. Hans-Peter Gasser, "Protection of the Civilian Population," in *The Handbook of Humanitarian Law in Armed Conflicts*, ed. Dieter Fleck (New York: Oxford University Press, 1995), 251.
31. Protocol Additional to the Geneva Conventions of 12 August 1949, and relating to the Protection of Victims of International Armed Conflicts (Additional Protocol I), June 8, 1977, art. 3(b); see also Michael J. Matheson, "The United States Position on the Relation of Customary International Law to the 1977 Protocols Additional to the 1949 Geneva Conventions," 2 AM. U. J. INT'L L. & POL'Y (1987): 419–420, http://www.auilr.org/pdf/2/2-2-2.pdf. The United States objects to Articles 1(4), 35(3), 39(2), 47, 55, and 56, ibid; Howard S. Levie, "The 1977 Protocol I and the United States," 38 ST. LOUIS U. L. J. 469 (1993–1994).
32. The U.S. Department of State cited seventeen UN resolutions in a background paper on Iraq at the outset of Operation Iraqi Freedom. Of particular note are UN Security Council resolutions 678 (November 29, 1990), 687 (April 3, 1991), and 1441 (November 8, 2002).
33. L. Paul Bremer, Coalition Provisional Authority Order Number 100, June 28, 2004.
34. UN Security Council Resolution 1546, June 8, 2004.
35. Ibid.
36. UN Security Council Resolution 1790, December 31, 2007, para. 2.

9
Ethics in the Three Circles of War

Russell Muirhead, Jr.

The most common view of the relation between ethics and war may be that there is no relation: once war starts, ethics stop. Effectiveness is the only metric that does—and should—guide decisions and actions in war. In war, as in love, all is fair. Yet, throughout history, soldiers have often engaged in moral analysis, moral evaluation, and moral decision. Morality and ethics are not imposed on the business of war by philosophers, priests, and outside meddlers; they arise on their own in the judgments, evaluations, and decisions of fighting men and women. Ordinary moral niceties may be sacrificed to the necessities of fighting, but warriors do not like to think of themselves as murderers or of the countries they serve as nothing but "gangs of criminals on a large scale."[1] For this reason, justice and morality do not lose their relevance but, on the contrary, attain a special urgency in times of war.

No one has made this argument more emphatically or more persuasively in recent decades than Michael Walzer, whose book *Just and Unjust Wars* collects the arguments, evaluations, and judgments that arise in the context of fighting wars and arranges them into several general and practicable precepts.[2] The first fundamental claim that Walzer offers is that the ethics of war include two independent subjects: the cause of war and the manner of fighting. A just war may be fought unjustly, and an unjust war may be fought justly. The justice of war (*jus ad bellum*) and justice in war (*jus in bello*) are separate matters.[3] This distinction—and every ethical consideration raised in this chapter—stems from two basic ethical ideas: it is wrong to kill innocent human beings, and it is justifiable to kill others in self-defense. These ideas underlie the ethics of war and are at the root of the inevitable ethical judgments that men and women make in the course of fighting wars.

The Ethics of Interstate War

To assess the morality of interstate war, it is worth recalling what a state is for—to protect the lives, liberties, and common life of the individuals who live within its boundaries. A state has no ethical basis unless, at a minimum, it protects its members from elemental harms, such as premature and violent death. To accomplish this end, states claim a monopoly on the use of force. They can deprive subjects of their lives, property, and liberty, and no other association or individual can. In the best or most decent examples, states have a "legitimate" monopoly on the use of force. In other words, the population broadly approves of the state's monopoly on coercive power because the state effectively defends the basic claims of the individuals residing in it.

Yet states do go to war, endangering and sacrificing the very lives they are meant to secure. This paradox that afflicts the modern state is one reason why decent states or legitimate states do not go to war except in self-defense: lives are endangered or sacrificed only for the sake of, in turn, saving vastly more lives. It is also for this reason that aggressive wars of aggrandizement are never just.[4] The only exceptions to the prohibition on aggressive war are, first, a preemptive attack to foreclose a truly imminent act of aggression and, second, an intervention in a foreign conflict for the sake of assisting another country (or warring parties within a country in the case of civil war) that is responding to aggression.[5]

Aggressor states that fight wars of aggrandizement betray their responsibility to their own subjects by exposing them to attack, as they ignore the rights of foreigners by attacking them. But the individuals within aggressor states do not forfeit their elemental rights by virtue of suffering the accident of belonging to a state fighting an unjust war. Aggression is undertaken by the state and not by all the individuals within the state. Thus individuals within aggressor states who are not fighting or posing a threat can be viewed as innocents and deserve noncombatant immunity. Civilians who belong to or reside in the enemy nation are not justifiable targets, even if it is reasonably thought that they are indirectly contributing to the war effort or are sympathetic to its aims or that demoralizing the citizenry through attack will contribute to victory. The only exception concerns the killing of noncombatants who are not direct targets (they are, as it were, bystanders, and constitute what in military parlance is "collateral damage"), and this exception applies only so long as noncombatant deaths are proportional to the strategic goals being pursued. Even soldiers fighting for aggressor states are often (if not always) coerced to do the fighting; thus, soldiers, once they are captured or surrender, deserve to have their basic rights respected as prisoners of war.

Ethics of Interventions: Tyranny and Civil War

What of states that fight in self-defense against combatants who are not themselves affiliated with a state—who are, for instance, pirates or terrorists? In contrast to the conscripts of foreign armies, terrorists and pirates cannot fully be seen as "moral equals" (in the respect that they retain the right not to be killed) for at least two reasons: they freely choose to make war, and by virtue of their disguise and deceit (symbolized by the absence of a uniform and a fixed insignia), they defy the war convention.[6] Those who murder innocents and attack under the cover of civilian garb have no claim to the immunities and protections of prisoner-of-war status. It may be prudent under certain circumstances to accord them such status (to solicit the good opinion of mankind, for instance), but there is no unconditional moral duty to do so.

All now realize that unless its power declines precipitously, the United States is more likely to find itself fighting pirates—or today's equivalent, terrorists—than it will fight foreign armies. Today's wars originate not only from the rogue actions of aggressor states but also from the absence of any power base sufficiently effective and popular to obtain a monopoly on the legitimate use of force. Such "failed states" are in a condition of actual or latent civil war, depending on the real level of violent conflict.[7] In a fluid situation where there are multiple parties to the conflict and no single party has an advantage, it is not merely a civil war but also anarchy. In some important respects, anarchy is worse than tyranny, for it exposes even more individuals to violence, insecurity, and the real threat of premature violent death.

This fact bears urgently on the present war in Iraq. To be sure, the United States is not in any obvious respects the moral equivalent of the Iraqi state: among other considerations, it lacks legitimacy in Iraq, and by its own design, there is alongside the U.S. presence a sovereign and elected Iraqi government (striving for legitimacy). But neither the sovereign Iraqi government nor the electoral system can succeed or continue to exist without U.S. support. No alternative source of legitimate order exists that is fully independent of the U.S. military (acting in support of the elected Iraqi government). Because the United States brought about this situation—the absence of any alternative source of order—by invading Iraq and removing the prior government, an ethical obligation to provide the conditions for order has accrued to the United States.

The moral duty to provide order for the Iraqis is complicated by other, sometimes competing, moral duties. On the one hand, the United States has a duty to be responsive to the settled opinions of Americans as expressed in elections. If Americans demand that the country withdraw its support and involvement in Iraq, there will be a powerful incentive to forget our moral obligation with respect to the Iraqis. On the other hand, the United States has a duty to be responsive to the fledging Iraqi government. If the factions controlling the Iraqi government demand that America withdraw its troops, there will be a powerful reason to neglect our moral duty with respect to the Iraqis as a whole. So long as Americans and Iraqis support some kind of U.S. involvement in Iraq, the central ethical standard to consider will remain the establishment of political order and the minimization of grave harm.

Consider, for instance, the following three hypothetical probabilities for events in Iraq over the next five years.

Scenario A

If the United States commits 400,000 to 500,000 troops and annual outlays exceeding $250 billion and executes the best available military and political strategies competently, assume the following hypothetical outcome probabilities:

- an 80 percent chance that a stable, relatively responsive, and rights-respecting Iraqi government that should last twenty-five to fifty years or longer will result;
- a 10 percent chance that Iraq will devolve into violent and intense civil war (with over 50,000 deaths) over the next five years; and

- a 10 percent chance that after five years, things will be going much as they have during the past two to three years, with latent civil conflict among rival factions, a fragile and weak central state that itself is poised to become a rival faction in civil conflict, conditions too dangerous to permit effective rebuilding and a flourishing civil society, and the absence of any foundational settlement on the allocation of political powers or state revenues.

Scenario B

If the United States commits 80,000 to 140,000 troops and annual outlays between $100 billion and $150 billion and pursues the most effective military and political strategies with reasonable competence, assume the following hypothetical outcome probabilities:

- a 10 percent chance that after five years a stable, relatively responsive, and rights-respecting Iraqi government that should last twenty-five to fifty years or longer will result;
- a 10 percent chance that within five years Iraq will devolve into violent and intense civil war that will last either two to five years, until the United States and other third parties broker a power-sharing agreement and enforce it with upward of 400,000 troops, *or* five to fifteen years, until one party wins a clear victory, but in the process secessionist aims, terrorism, and refugees by the millions spill over into neighboring countries and destabilize the region;[8] and
- an 80 percent chance that the next five years will bring more of the same: rival factions, and rivals within factions, all continuing to arm and organize; occasional eruptions of serious violence, claiming between 500 and 5,000 civilian lives per year; the Coalition powers generally succeeding in preventing violence from escalating into intense civil war but failing to negotiate a transition from latent civil war to political unity; the distribution of political power and oil revenues, along with many smaller matters, remaining in dispute; and neither rebuilding nor economic development fully pursued because of security concerns.

Scenario C

In this scenario, the United States draws down its military presence to between 5,000 and 10,000 troops, which will pursue special missions, execute rapid responses, and guard key facilities, and simultaneously commits $50 billion to $100 billion annually to the expenses of both occupation and rebuilding. Meanwhile, the government also conducts intense diplomacy among the Iraqi factions and, more crucially, includes all of Iraq's border states in diplomatic efforts to stabilize Iraq. Thus assume the following hypothetical outcome probabilities:

- a 10 percent chance that after five years, a stable, relatively responsive, and rights-respecting Iraqi government that should last twenty-five to fifty years or longer will result;
- a 10 percent chance that Iraq will devolve into violent and intense civil war within five years, as described in scenario B;
- an 80 percent chance of more of the same, as described in scenario B.

While these scenarios are grossly simplified, do not take into account probable American casualties, and are not realistic representations of the kinds of predictions decision makers can confidently make, they do serve to clarify the ethical duties that are at stake. There is a prima facie duty to bear the costs of scenario A based on the ethical responsibility that the United States has acquired. Of course, any practical option akin to scenario A would likely be politically disastrous in a domestic context, where Americans are unwilling to bear such costs. To systematically betray the settled preferences of American citizens would violate exactly the same democratic values that the United States would wish the Iraqi government to observe with respect to its citizens. The difficulty of getting a democratic public to bear the costs associated with providing order and protection to another people is a powerful standing reason against foreign intervention, even (and perhaps especially) those undertaken for humanitarian reasons.[9] Still, it is worth noting that scenarios B and C would look better to political decision makers, not because these options are more ethical but because they are more palatable. Scenarios B and C, if more realistic, are both inferior from an ethical perspective insofar as they expose the Iraqis to increased risks to their lives, their rights, and their common life.

The choice between scenarios B and C is a choice between relative wrongs: both are relatively inferior to scenario A from an ethical perspective, but which is worse? From the perspective of our duties to Iraqis, they are on a par; but from the perspective of duties to Americans, scenario C is obviously superior. (The choice would be vastly more complicated if the probabilities of success associated with scenario B were better than those associated with scenario C; under those circumstances, fulfilling our duties to the Iraqis would again entail significant risks for American soldiers and significant costs for American citizens.) Thus, options resembling scenario C represent the best balance of political palatability and ethical responsibility both to the Iraqis and to Americans.

There is no clear method to weigh the ethical responsibilities to one's own soldiers, to one's own citizens, and to foreigners whose security rests in one's own power. Some preference for one's own people—although ethically controversial from the pure perspective of human equality—is warranted in light of the fact that the United States does not have the same permanent ethical responsibility for the well-being of the Iraqis as it does for its own citizens and soldiers. The United States is not responsible for everything about Iraq, and the Iraqis would not wish it to assume any sort of permanent responsibility. The United States does have temporary duties of a fiduciary or guardianship nature, given that it toppled the Iraqi state (which, if gruesomely tyrannical, nonetheless provided a degree of order).

The duties the United States has acquired toward Iraqis do not fall squarely within the tradition of either *jus ad bellum* or *jus in bello*. They are duties that arise after an invasion (whether its justification was convincing or not) and after the cessation of most combat operations (whether the mode of fighting was just or not). They amount to a kind of "postwar justice," or *jus post bellum*.[10] To the victors go the spoils, or so it used to be said; but when the point of a war is to neutralize an aggressor (as it must be, when wars are fought justly), no such spoils can ever be justified. On the contrary, the sole ethical objective of the postwar period is to establish a state that is sufficiently powerful to defend the basic rights of its inhabitants and is sufficiently legitimate to claim the support of the major social groups in the country such that they prefer to make politics than to make war.

The danger here is that while the United States has acquired some of the duties of a state in Iraq, it has not acquired the procedures of legitimacy: it is not accountable to the Iraqis. Its state-like ethical duties can only be temporary because its power can never be legitimate. To the extent that Iraq has a nominally sovereign government and a procedure for incorporating all major social groups in the establishment of basic law, the United States can be held accountable to the Iraqi government, which in theory invites the U.S. presence and sets the terms for its occupation. By contrast, a coercive power that is unaccountable in every respect to those over whom it exercises force is on a par with a tyrannical power. ("Private" military contractors can come perilously close to this description.) The more the Iraqi government is a fiction rather than a fact and the more it becomes a mere party to civil war, the less legitimate the exercise of U.S. power can be. At the point when the exercise of U.S. power can itself only be described as a party to civil war—because there is no semblance of an Iraqi state—its temporary, quasi-state duty to protect the rights of ordinary Iraqis recedes. At such a point, the United States might, for ethical reasons, choose to back the side that stands poised to most reliably and effectively defend the basic rights of Iraqis were it to win. But in most cases, where it is difficult or impossible to make such calculations about rival parties, the most ethical course is to stand neutral, ready to broker a peace. Whatever the precise course of action, the underlying ethical reason that should govern the occupation and the endgame is to protect innocent life.

Ethics in Counterinsurgency

Civil war is an ever-present possibility when internal enemies, external foes, and terrorists beset the state. It is also a possibility in a fledging state that is striving to attain legitimacy but is harassed by insurgents who prefer war to constitutional politics. Counterinsurgency creates a "much more complex" ethical environment than does conventional warfare, most notably in the elusive distinction between combatants and noncombatants.[11] Fighting a foe that observes no distinctions seems to demand that one's own side be willing to forgo distinctions in order to be effective. Counterinsurgency can seem like warfare without rules.

Indeed, an insistence on moral rules would seem a source of weakness. Some argue that democracies lose small wars against militarily inferior insurgents because they are compelled to abide by ethical standards; indeed, they "find it extremely difficult to escalate the level of violence and brutality to that which can secure victory." As some see it, democracies lose because they cannot be brutal, and when fighting insurgencies, "brutality pays."[12]

However, when the goal of a counterinsurgency is to create a legitimate state, fighting ethically becomes a strategic imperative. As Walzer recently observed, "One might almost say that justice has become a military necessity."[13] The distinctive goal of creating a self-sustaining representative government (rather than the classic goal of capturing resources and territory) puts winning the people's "hearts and minds" at the center of successful counterinsurgency operations.

This strategy has profound consequences. First, as Sarah Sewell points out, Americans must be willing to accept more casualties in order to pursue military strategies that do not systematically offend the resident populations.[14] It is often said that Americans are simply unwilling to tolerate casualties in large numbers. That assertion may be true, but much depends on the extent to which they see the war itself as just and on the likelihood they place on the war's eventual success. Justice in war means, in the end, that American citizens in large numbers must come to see the war itself—the justice of the war—as compelling; only then might they be willing to accept the risk, and the casualties, that fighting in a just manner involves.

Some argue that for the citizenry to debate the justice of the war itself while the country is at war undermines the morale of the troops and emboldens the enemy, for with debate comes dissension and criticism, and some will always oppose the war with passion and eloquence. But the reality is that soldiers themselves cannot easily debate the justice of war. At any rate, they cannot base their willingness to risk their own lives on the outcome of their own debate about the justice of war. They fight in their country's name, when their country, through its civilian leadership, commands them to do so. Citizens, therefore, must do what the soldiers cannot, and debate—freely and openly—the worthiness of the cause. More to the point, only when the citizens themselves are convinced about the justice of the cause and the efficacy of the methods will they be willing to tolerate the length of commitment and numbers of casualties that successful counterinsurgency often involves. Taking the full rationale for war to the public, and debating it in public, does not necessarily diminish but may enhance the probability for success in counterinsurgency operations. Counterinsurgency—especially when the goal is establishing a rights-respecting legitimate state—blurs the distinction between ethical and strategic reasons in war. Moral reasons derive from the duty to respect individuals; in the case of warfare, most of them stem from the duty to respect the right to life of the innocent. Strategic reasons derive from the requirements of victory. Each on its own terms claims priority: moralists claim that where there is a clear moral duty, it should take precedence over other reasons, while strategists claim that where there is a clear strategic necessity, it ought to trump all other reasons. One might say on behalf of strategists that without victory, the moral life itself is imperiled; and on behalf of moralists, without ethics, victory is not worth much. In truth, each is always dependent on the other, and it is a distortion of human judgment and prudence to suppose that either one alone should always be sovereign.

The mutual dependence of strategy and ethics is fully revealed in contemporary counterinsurgency. This dependence creates its own dangers—in particular, the danger of self-righteousness, where whatever we take to be strategically effective, we assume for that reason is also ethical, and where whatever we decide is ethical, we assume will also be effective. Neither politics nor war will ever allow for such an easy marriage of ethics and strategic effectiveness.

The current visible alliance of ethics and strategy in counterinsurgency arises from an insistence on the goal of creating a decent rights-respecting state. This goal is, to be sure, the right one. But exactly what constitutes such a state, and exactly what approximations are acceptable, is not easy to stipulate with precision. Is it enough that a state be "responsive" instead of "democratic"? It is enough that it be "decent" instead of "rights respecting"? Is it enough that a state be "stable" instead of "legitimate"? Given the difficulty of winning a counterinsurgency and the costs involved in trying, we may decide in each of these cases that the lesser goal is enough. If we compromise our goals on multiple standards, we may settle for a state that fails to solicit the affections and convictions (that is, win the hearts and minds) of most citizens most of the time. That concession may be a prudent compromise that serves the national interest, but when it is no longer imperative to win hearts and minds, the visible alliance between ethics and strategic effectiveness will fray. At that point, it will be crucial—for the state of our own hearts and our own minds—to remember that ethical reasons have their own standing that derives from a duty to respect the most elemental and minimal claims of human beings, wherever they are found. To forget this duty—as warfare tempts us to do—ultimately sacrifices something of the pride and self-respect that both our citizens and soldiers deserve.

Notes

1. Augustine, *City of God*, 4.4, Henry Bettenson, trans., (New York: Penguin Books, 1984 [1467]), 139.
2. Michael Walzer, *Just and Unjust Wars: A Moral Argument with Historical Illustrations* (New York: Basic Books, 1977).
3. Ibid., 21.
4. Ibid., 72.
5. One might argue that preemption and intervention constitute exceptions so large as to dilute the principle of nonaggression extremely. See ibid., 74–108.
6. Ibid., 34–47, 179–96.
7. What exactly constitutes a civil war occasioned a great deal of controversy in late 2006, as critics of the Iraq War insisted that it was a civil war while the Bush administration resisted the term. A civil war is simply a condition where two or more organized groups violently contest for political power. Some definitions apply an additional standard of a thousand annual deaths to differentiate civil war from criminal activity, but this standard is arbitrary. See Linda Feldman, "Is Iraq a Civil War?" *Christian Science Monitor*, November 30, 2006; and James D. Fearon, "Iraq's Civil War," *Foreign Affairs* 86, no. 2 (March–April 2007): 2–15.
8. Daniel L. Byman and Kenneth M. Pollack estimate that quelling a full-scale civil war in Iraq would require 450,000 troops; see "What Next?" *Washington Post*, August 20, 2006. James D. Fearon notes that the average duration of civil wars since 1945 has been ten years, and "of the roughly 55 civil wars fought for control of a central government (as opposed to for secession or regional autonomy) since 1955, fully 75 percent ended with a clear victory for one side." Only nine of fifty-five cases ended with power-sharing agreements; see Fearon, "Iraq's Civil War," 8.
9. This view is consistent with John Stuart Mill's skepticism about the ability of one nation to successfully liberate another. See Mill in "A Few Words on Non-Intervention," *The Collected Works of John Stuart Mill*, vol. 21, *Essays on Equality, Law, and Education*, ed. John M. Robson (Toronto: University of Toronto Press, 1984), 109–124, especially 121–24.
10. Michael Walzer, *Arguing About War* (New Haven, CT: Yale University Press, 2004), xiii, 18–22, 92–94, 162–68; and Gary J. Bass, "Jus Post Bellum," *Philosophy and Public Affairs* 32, no. 4 (September 2004): 384–412.
11. *The U.S. Army/Marine Corps Counterinsurgency Field Manual* (Chicago: University of Chicago Press, 2007), 245.
12. Gil Merom, *How Democracies Lose Small Wars: State, Society, and the Failures of France in Algeria, Israel in Lebanon, and the United States in Vietnam* (Cambridge, UK: Cambridge University Press, 2003), 15, 46–47.
13. Walzer, *Arguing About War*, 9.
14. Sarah Sewell, "Introduction," in *Counterinsurgency Field Manual*, 48.

MEASURING WAR AND VICTORY

10
A System Dynamics Modeling Perspective of Iraq's Conflicts

Tarek K. Abdel-Hamid

As in most military-political conflicts, the conflict in Iraq is a conglomerate of interrelated and interdependent factors and processes: military operations, politics, economics, propaganda, and ethnic violence. All these various factors are interconnected, pushing on each other and being pushed on in return. The challenge for us today in addressing the Iraq conflict—and the objective of this research effort—is to "put things back together" again after they have been examined in pieces. Such a holistic perspective does not imply denying the independent roles of the separate factors; rather, it entails integrating the many factors into a broader framework that incorporates the interactions between them, interactions that tend to get lost when the individual mechanisms are examined in isolation.

The objective of this chapter is to build and present a proof-of-concept system dynamics model that integrates the three circles of the Iraq conflict: interstate war (with U.S. military operations), insurgency, and civil war. The purpose is not to determine ultimate solutions for, say, insurgency management—that will require much future work—but rather to demonstrate the potential utility of system dynamics as a tool for the policymaker both to look back and to look forward to understand the past and to assess future options.

System Dynamics Modeling

As with most human systems—indeed, all goal-oriented behavior—military-political conflict belongs to the class of multiloop nonlinear feedback systems. These systems are characterized by a large number of interrelated variables that interact dynamically over time through information-feedback processes.

System dynamics is a technique developed to formally model, analyze, and understand the dynamic behavior of such complex feedback systems. While the words "complex," "dynamic," and "system" have been applied to all sorts of situations, "feedback" is the differentiating descriptor here. Most succinctly, feedback is the transmission of information about the outcome of any process or activity back to its source. For example, a feedback system exists whenever an action taker will later be influenced by the consequences of his or her actions. More generally, feedback refers to the situation of X affecting Y and Y in turn affecting X, perhaps through a chain of causes and effects. One cannot study the link between X and Y and, independently, the link between Y and X and predict how the system will behave. Only the study of the whole system as a feedback system will lead to correct results.

Feedback loops divide naturally into two categories: negative, or deviation-counteracting feedback, loops and positive, or deviation-amplifying feedback, loops. Negative loops counter and oppose change, while positive loops tend to reinforce or amplify whatever is happening in the system. On the one hand, a system dominated by negative feedback is similar to a marble that has been placed at the lowest point of smooth-sided bowl. Pushing the marble off the equilibrium creates a force opposing the displacement.[1] A system dominated by positive feedback, on the other hand, is similar to a ball poised on the peak of a hill, and the slightest disturbance causes the ball to roll off the peak and keep going.

The One-Circle Solution?

For much of the first year after the fall of Saddam Hussein, the United States assumed that it was dealing with a limited number of insurgents that Coalition forces would defeat militarily well before the Iraqi election in 2005.[2]

> As late as July 2004, some senior members of the Bush Administration still seemed to live in a fantasyland in terms of their public announcements, perception of the growing Iraqi hostility to the use of Coalition forces, and the size of the threat. Its spokesmen were still talking about a core insurgent force of only 5,000 . . . [and said they were comprised

of foreigners and hard-line former regime supporters with little popular support]. They also ignored signs of Sunni versus Shi'ite tension, and growing ethnic tension in the north.[3]

The model outlined in figure 10.1 captures the essence of the U.S. mental model of the Iraqi insurgency early in the conflict. The model presents it as a tidy (one-dimensional) military problem.

Fundamentally, it is the archetypical model of goal-seeking behavior in which action is taken to bring the state of a system in line with a goal or desired state. As depicted in the figure, the state of the system—in this case, the intensity of insurgency attacks in Iraq—is compared with the U.S.

Figure 10.1. Model of early U.S. conception of the insurgency of Iraq using stock and flow

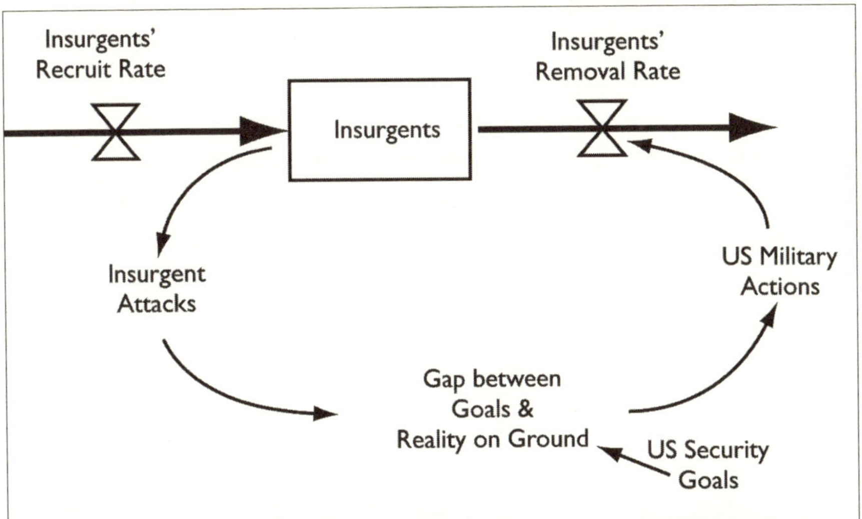

Stock & Flow Diagramming Notation

"Insurgents" is modeled as a stock type variable (represented by a rectangle, suggesting a container).

The "Insurgents' Recruit Rate" is modeled as a rate (represented by a control valve and pipe pointing out, suggesting an outflow from the stock).

In dynamic systems, stocks and flows constitute the two fundamentally different processes that characterize how reality works: accumulation and flow.

desired goals for Iraqi security and stability. A discrepancy between the desired and actual states induces corrective action—in this case, counterinsurgency military intervention to suppress the insurgency—and brings the state of the system in line with the goal. Such a feedback process encompasses many of our conscious and subconscious decisions and underlies all goal-oriented behavior.

How would such a system behave? Not surprisingly, very well. Figure 10.2 shows how such a system drifts slowly but surely toward its goal. It is the kind of behavior that U.S. officials expected (and hoped for) in the Iraqi insurgency early on.

Rather than the expected (and hoped for) exponential decay, however, the number of insurgents and insurgent attacks in Iraq escalated over time. By the end of 2005, insurgent attacks had increased tenfold to more than three thousand per month.[4]

The reason the results from the above (narrow) goal-seeking feedback loop were misleading is precisely that compensating (unanticipated) feedback effects are also active in the system. For example, while the primary target of military intervention is the outflow rate, or the insurgents' removal rate, combat operations and other coercive activities inherent to fighting an insurgency—for example, foreign military patrols, ubiquitous checkpoints, house raids, house searches, and citizen roundups—invariably fan popular

Figure 10.2. Expected decline in number of insurgents based on the early U.S. conception of the insurgency in Iraq

The gradual but nonlinear decline—*exponential decay*—arises because large gaps between desired and actual states tend to generate large responses, while small gaps tend to elicit small responses.

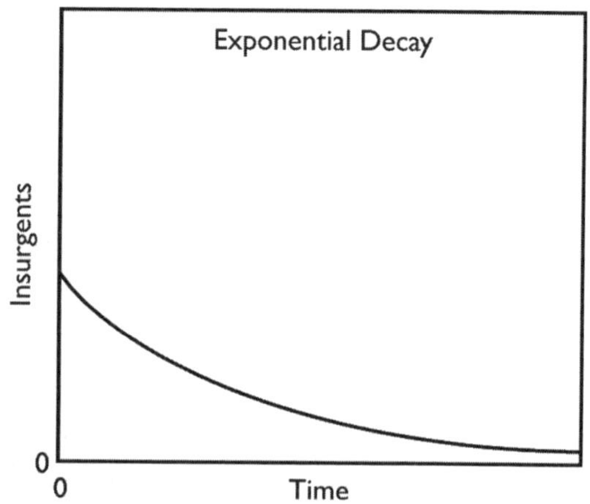

anger and resistance. This simultaneously contributes to the insurgency and increases the inflow rate, or recruitment of insurgents.[5] That is an example of one feedback effect from inside this circle, that is, from the ongoing counterinsurgency military activities. In fact, the insurgents' inflow rate was further fueled by factors from outside this circle, namely, Sunni grievances against the new Iraqi government and ethno-sectarian violence. The cumulative effect of these multiple feedback effects would act to transform the insurgent stock into a "growth stock,"or one that is replenished by an inflow rate that not only compensated for but exceeded the outflow rate.

System Dynamics Model Structure: From One Circle to Three

Figure 10. 3 provides an overview of the system dynamics model structure, depicting the model's three major subsystems—insurgency, U.S. military operations, and civil war/ethno-sectarian violence—together with their key interrelationships.[6] At the heart of the model is the insurgency subsystem, in which the growth of the Iraqi insurgency is modeled as a diffusion process.

The diffusion model—also known as the susceptible-infected (SI) model —was originally conceived to model the spread of infectious diseases. It has been extended to model a wide variety of "social contagion" phenomena, or situations in which people imitate the behavior, beliefs, or purchases of others. As in the spread of a disease, social contagion is driven by a positive feedback mechanism. The key difference is that in social contagion, the pathogen is an idea rather than a biological agent. As those who have already adopted the product or idea come into contact with friends, family, and acquaintances who have not, they expose them to it and infect some of them with the idea or with the desire to adopt the new idea or product. The new believers in turn persuade (infect) others, further increasing the population of adopters.[7]

In the standard SI model, the population of interest is divided into two subpopulations: those susceptible to the disease or idea—referred to as susceptibles (S)—and those who are infectious (I). Connecting the two stocks is an infection rate, or the rate at which people are infected or move from the susceptible stock to the infectious stock.

In applying this model structure to the Iraqi insurgency (see figure 10.4), the S and I subpopulation categories become the potential insurgent popu-

Figure 10.3. System dynamics model of the conflict in Iraq incorporating the three circles of war

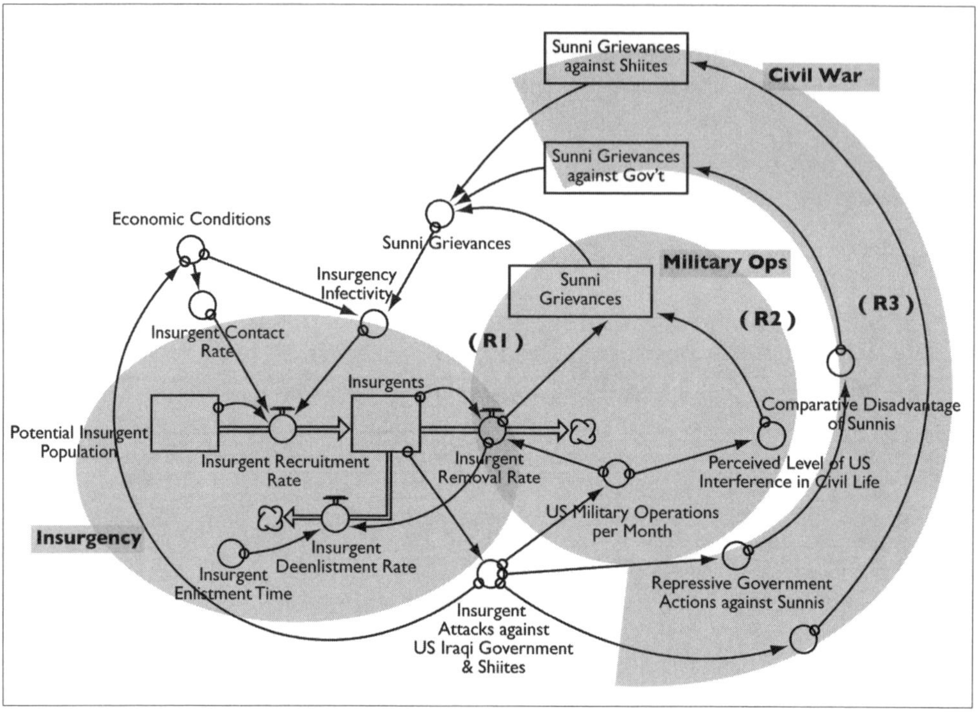

lation and the insurgents, respectively. In the model, the potential insurgent population is primarily a stock of Sunnis, a bloc that dominates the Iraqi insurgency and constitutes the main opposition to the new Iraqi regime and Coalition forces.[8] Not all Iraqi Sunnis are insurgency susceptibles, however. In the model, this stock is disproportionately drawn from young, uneducated or unemployed Sunni males. As in other insurgencies, Paul Collier and others argue, it is the subgroup that is "easily manipulated by propaganda and who find the power that comes from the possession and use of a gun alluring."[9]

Highlighted in figure 10.4 are the SI model's two key loops: the contagion (reinforcing [R], or positive) loop and the depletion (balancing [B], or negative) loop. For any epidemic, it is the interaction of these two types of feedback loops that governs how the epidemic spreads and, if at all, how fast. Typically an infectious disease (or idea) spreads slowly at first, as the

Figure 10.4. Application of the diffusion model, or susceptible-infected (SI) model, to the Iraqi insurgency

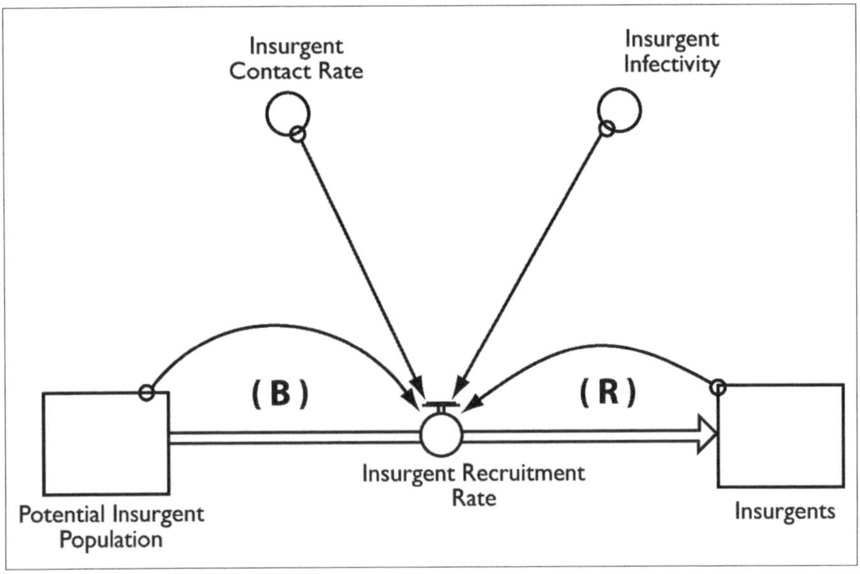

initial few who become infected come into contact with and pass the disease to others who are susceptible. But as more and more people fall ill and become infectious, the number they infect starts to grow more quickly as the process feeds on itself.

As the number of people in the population or community who become infected increases, however, the pool of susceptibles depletes over time. This progression strengthens the depletion loop, slows the rate of new infections, and ultimately ends the epidemic.[10]

The infection rate (IR)—or in this case, the insurgent recruitment rate—is the rate at which susceptible people become infected. In formulating this rate, it is assumed in the SI model that people in the community interact at a certain rate, which is referred to as the contact rate (c) and measured as people contacted per person per time period (1/time period). A susceptible population of size S would thus generate Sc encounters per time period, some of which will be with infectious people. The probability that an encounter with an infectious person will result in infection is a function of the infectivity (potency) of the pathogen (or the appeal of the idea) and is captured in the model by the infectivity parameter i. The infection rate is thus the total number of encounters (Sc) multiplied by the probability that any of those encounters is with an infectious individual $I/(S + I)$ multiplied by the probability (i) that an encounter with an infectious person results in infection: $IR = (Sci)(I/[S + I])$.

For an epidemic to occur, the infection rate must exceed the recovery rate; that is, each infective must, on average, pass the disease to more than one other person prior to recovering. This process, in turn, will depend on the characteristics of the disease (for example, its infectivity and recovery period) and the environment (the contact rate).

This basic SI model—intended to capture the basic process of chronic infection—contains a number of simplifying and restrictive assumptions that needed to be relaxed for a social contagion model. In social contagion phenomena, such as insurgencies, "infected" individuals do not necessarily remain infectious indefinitely. For example, a change in government policy or in economic conditions may alleviate grievances or change the minds of some, transforming them into regime supporters. Alternatively, insurgents can be removed from the system (killed or captured, for example). The two processes by which insurgents "recover" or are removed create two additional negative feedback loops, shown as B2 and B3 in figure 10.5.

Another simplifying assumption in the SI model is that of a homogeneous population. In a social contagion phenomenon, such as an insurgency, different subcultures often behave differently, making it necessary to disaggregate the susceptible population into several distinct subpopulations (for instance, with different contact rates, infectivity, and so on).[11] As shown in both figures 10.3 and 10.5, economic conditions—specifically, the unemployment rate—affect both the contact rate and infectivity in this model.

Some of the young Iraqi Sunnis who join the insurgency are motivated more by financial incentives than ideology.[12] In this model, unemployment increases the population's vulnerability to financial inducements to join the insurgency, bolstering recruitment. Thus, it is assumed in the model that an unemployed young Sunni is twice as likely to become infected as an employed one would. Employment also affects insurgent enlistment time, that is, the average time that a person who joins the insurgency remains active in it. As with most careers, insurgents do not necessarily remain active until either detained or killed. They may also choose to retire or quit, which they are more apt to do when there are more or better employment opportunities available.

Insurgent Reinforcing/Creation Loops

Unlike with biological pathogens, the infectivity of an idea can increase or decrease over time. In the case of the Iraqi insurgency, the rise and fall in infectivity are driven by the ebb and flow in Sunni grievance levels. In this model, three primary sources of Sunni grievances are explicitly captured: those against the U.S. occupation, those against the new Iraqi government, and those against the Shia. The following discussion explains how reinforcing feedback mechanisms acted to feed these Sunni grievances, bolstering the insurgency's contagion loop and driving the tremendous expansion in the insurgency.

The First Mechanism (R1): Grievances Against the U.S. Government

U.S. counterinsurgency military operations have two effects on the insurgency stock. As noted earlier, the primary (intended) target of military in-

Figure 10.5. SI model of Iraq insurgency with initial feedback loops

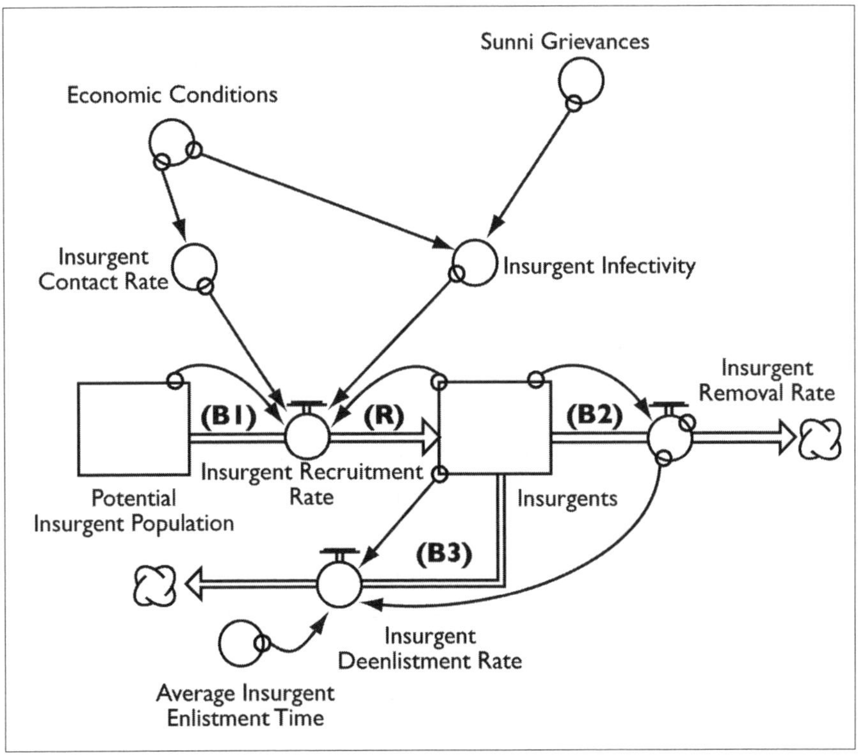

tervention is the outflow, or the insurgents' removal, rate. However, because of limited intelligence, insurgency suppression operations to target, kill, or detain insurgents are rarely surgical affairs. U.S. and Iraqi government forces routinely need to conduct large-scale operations, such as raids on towns and villages, sweeps, and search-and-destroy missions, that often inflict violence on the civilian population. Other coercive activities inherent to fighting an insurgency, such as foreign military patrols, ubiquitous checkpoints, house raids, house searches, and citizen roundups, further rouse popular anger and resistance. The killing and capturing of insurgents thus both weaken them and gain them new adherents—increasing the inflow rate—as those who are harmed or whose family and friends have been victimized harbor hatred and seek retribution.[13]

According to recent polls, 63 percent of Sunni Arabs report unnecessary violence by U.S. or Coalition forces against Iraqi citizens. More worrisome, grievances against the U.S. and Coalition forces translate into an endorsement of violence: 57 percent of all Iraqis called attacks on Coalition forces "acceptable," and Sunnis nearly unanimously hold this view (93 percent).[14] Sunni grievances against the U.S. occupation bolster the insurgency in a second important way, through productivity. Widespread sympathy to the insurgency among the populace allows the insurgents greater mobility and enables them to evade capture more easily. This situation creates a potential for a vicious (positive) cycle because, *ceteris paribus*, an increase in the insurgent stock would lead to more incidents and hence more pressure on U.S. and government forces to suppress the violence. The mounting pressure leads to an increase in the number of military operations and other coercive activities (foreign military patrols, ubiquitous checkpoints, house searches, and so on) against the insurgents. Such interference in Iraqi civil life increases sympathy for the insurgency and ultimately bolsters their ranks, completing the causal loop. Because an increase in the number of insurgents ultimately reinforces itself, this sort of causal loop, depicted as R1 in figure 10.6, is a "reinforcing loop."[15]

Adding further wrinkles to the (unintended) compensatory effect of this reinforcing mechanism is that population grievances and their effects often take some time to percolate through the system.[16] Such time delays create inertia, causing this insurgency-reinforcing process to linger for some time even if U.S. actions subside.

Unfortunately, the insurgency creation process was fueled by more than Sunni grievances against the U.S. occupation. Two additional important drivers are ethno-sectarian rivalry and Sunni grievances against the new Iraqi government. These forces are depicted in figure 10.6 as R2 and R3, respectively.

The Second Mechanism (R2): Grievances Against the Iraqi Government

Iraqi Sunnis who oppose the Coalition forces and the new Iraqi regime have dominated the violent Iraqi insurgency. This development is not surprising. Iraq's Sunni population, which achieved political dominance under Saddam Hussein, feels threatened by the occupation and the new political order that has placed the Shia in the dominant position.

Actions taken by the United States and the Iraqi government—such as de-Baathification—have affected the Sunnis' access to government jobs,

Figure 10.6. SI model of Iraq insurgency with additional feedback loops

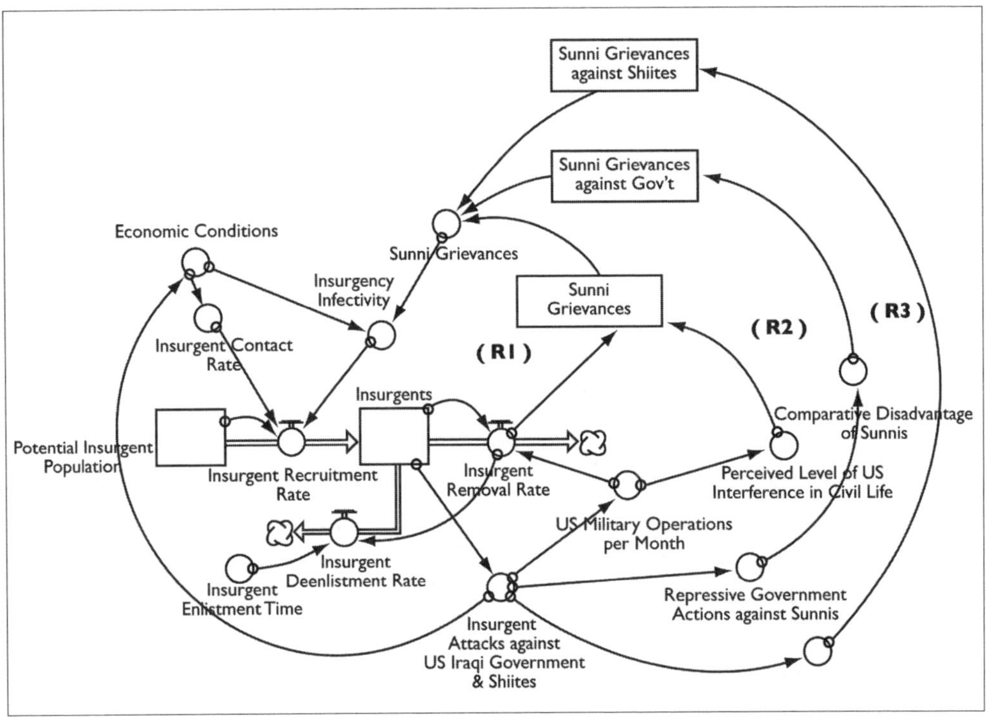

feeding the sense that Sunnis were being held collectively culpable for the crimes of Hussein and his henchmen. Other political actions—such as elections that favored the Shia as the numerical majority—further contributed to a sense that the new order was not for Sunnis.[17] As is often the case, repressive or discriminatory government policies against an ethnic group create comparative disadvantages (real and perceived) for that group, generating opportunities for radicalized ethnic leaders to mobilize the group for rebellion.[18] Over time, hatreds build up, leaving the society polarized.

As with the first mechanism (grievances against the U.S. government), the process is self-reinforcing. Increased insurgency activity in Sunni areas generates a greater intensity of counterinsurgency actions focused on those Sunni areas. This targeting, in turn, creates disproportionately higher numbers of Sunni civilian casualties and a disproportionately higher level of destruction of Sunni districts. Meanwhile, Sunni-dominated violence serves to reinforce the government's mistrust of the Sunni community and its political leaders, leading to further marginalization of Sunnis in the political process. All this turmoil adds up to stress the Sunni perception of having no future in post-Hussein Iraq, completing the feedback loop and driving the cycle forward.

The Third Mechanism (R3): Ethno-Sectarian Grievances

The February 22, 2006, bombing of the Golden Mosque, or al-Askari Shrine, was only the most visible symbol of a pattern of Sunni-Shi'ite clashes that began in 2003, steadily grew in 2004 and 2005, and became a major civil conflict in 2006.[19]

As with many sectarian struggles, the Sunni-Shia conflict is motivated by a struggle for resources and power, including material benefits (land, money, natural resources, and so on), political power (positions in or control of government), and symbolic power (imposition of one's conception of national identity or values on the state). And as in most such conflicts, it invariably leaves a legacy of atrocities. As victims on both sides seek vengeance for killings, a third vicious cycle (R3) of reprisals and counterreprisals is created, often claiming hundreds of lives.[20] Today in Iraq, many observers believe, "the sectarian violence is now propelled as much by revenge for past killings and fear of future ones as it is by instrumental desires to achieve specific political goals."[21]

Exploring Model Behavior Through Computer Simulation

Two simulation experiments based on this model were conducted. The intent of the first—a simulation of the base-case scenario—was to demonstrate that the model replicates, in an approximate qualitative sense, dynamic behavior patterns of key system variables, such as insurgent attacks. In the second experiment, a series of what-if/sensitivity analyses were conducted to demonstrate how the model could be utilized for policy analysis and design and assessments of how different intervention strategies change (or do not change) the behavior of the system.

Experiment 1: Base-Case Simulation

The most salient fact of any insurgency is the violence it generates. Allied with the disruption or destruction of a region's infrastructure and institutions, the significant loss of life often overwhelms whatever political benefits may accrue to either side in the conflict.[22]

Figure 10.7 depicts the model-generated pattern of insurgent attacks between June 1, 2003, and December 31, 2007 (curve 1), together with the pattern based on the actual numbers of insurgent attacks as reported in the literature (curve 2).[23]

A second important metric—and a key determinant of the level of violence—is the size of the Sunni insurgency. As noted earlier, for much of the first year after the fall of Saddam Hussein, the United States assumed that it was dealing with a limited number of insurgents that Coalition forces would defeat militarily well before the Iraqi election. Figure 10.8 compares that initial assumption and the model-generated plot of the insurgent stock size.

The model-generated insurgency follows the typical "epidemic" life cycle: an initial phase of exponential growth (as the reinforcing insurgent creation loops initially dominate the insurgent suppression loops), peak, and decline. The insurgent stock is initialized in the model with ten thousand active insurgents in mid-2003, on the basis of estimates in the literature.[24] The simulation results suggest that the insurgent stock peaks in late 2006 or early 2007 at around seventy thousand people. (Note that in figure 10.8 this simulation is run for a longer period, or ten years, to provide a further projection into the future.)

The good news in figure 10.8 is that the insurgent stock eventually starts to decline after peaking three years into the insurgency. As with the

Figure 10.7. Model-generated and actual patterns of insurgent attacks, June 1, 2003, through December 31, 2007

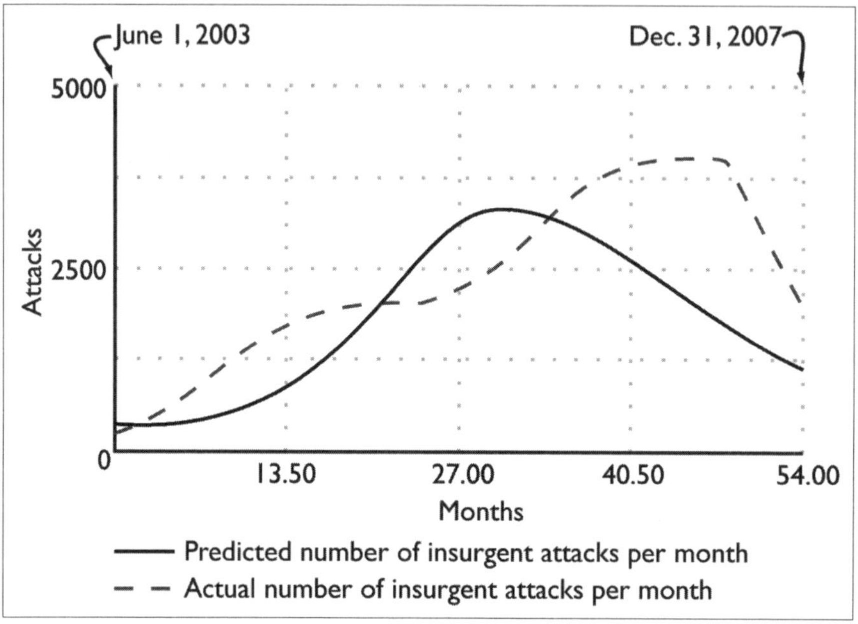

spread of a disease in a population, this decrease eventually happens as the stock of susceptibles is depleted over time (effectively strengthening the balancing depletion loop). The process is akin to a fire that dies out because it runs out of fuel.

The later decline of the insurgent stock means that, at that point, the number of insurgents being removed per unit of time exceeds the number of new recruits added (analogous to a point in an epidemic when the number of infected people recovering exceeds the number of new cases arising). It is important to understand that this "race" between the infection rate and the removal rate is not just part of the final act but is always ongoing. Were the recovery rate to dominate early on, the epidemic would never take off. Unfortunately, in the Iraq conflict, this shift in dominance did not happen early enough to avert the escalation.

Experiment 2: The Search for Leverage

An important utility of simulation-based models is that they allow us to conduct "perfectly" controlled experiments. In the model system, unlike in the

Figure 10.8. Insurgent stock as projected by initial U.S. assumptions and by the system dynamics model

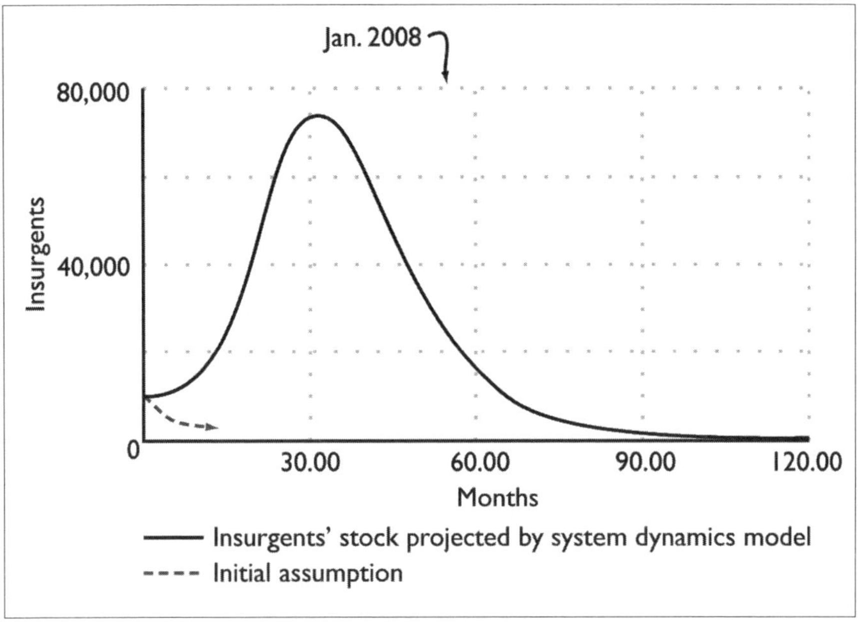

real world, the effect of changing one factor can be observed while all other factors are held unchanged. Experiment 2 was designed to assess the extent to which different intervention strategies could have averted the insurgency epidemic and whether the leverage in the system lies at the outflow side of the equation (insurgent removal) or the inflow side (insurgent creation).

Figure 10.9 compares the base-case scenario (curve 1) to three intervention strategies. In the first strategy (curve 2), the level of counterinsurgency military operations is doubled. Whereas in the base case an insurgent attack induces one counterattack by U.S. and Coalition forces, here it induces two. The model's results indicate that the long-term impact of such a strategy would be positive but modest.

While escalating U.S. counterinsurgency operations would increase the insurgents' removal rate, it would simultaneously bolster the insurgency persuasion pitch and boost the insurgency recruitment rate. Furthermore, such a strategy would not address the other active grievances in the system. The net result is that the insurgency creation loops are able to keep pace with heightened counterinsurgency operations. The results suggest asking the U.S. military alone to carry the full burden of this conflict—the burden of the three reinforcing processes—is asking for too much.

The second intervention tested (curve 3) is economic. Here the effect of decreasing the Iraqi unemployment rate from 30 percent (the assumed average level from 2003 to 2007) to 10 percent is assessed.[25] A comparison of curves 2 and 3 clearly shows that the impact of such an economic intervention would be more significant. Why?

Part of the explanation has to do with the idea of leverage. Not unlike leverage in finance, this economic intervention strategy reaps greater returns because it works on (invests in) a much larger stock, or the potential insurgent population stock. Especially early in the epidemic life cycle, this potential insurgent population stock is significantly larger than the insurgent stock (the target of the first strategy, or military intervention).

An economic intervention can have a significant impact on the Iraqi insurgency because, as argued earlier, just as in most insurgencies, some of the young Iraqi Sunnis who join are motivated more by financial incentives than by ideology. (It is reported, for example, that while Saddam Hussein was in hiding, he paid $250 for the killing of an American.[26]) A lower unemployment rate would thus decrease the potential insurgent population's vulnerability to financial inducements to join the insurgency, dampening recruitment. In addition, a lower unemployment rate would tend to decrease insurgent enlistment time.

In the third intervention (curve 4), the impact of a political intervention to achieve a Sunni-Shia reconciliation is assessed. In terms of model structure, it effectively turns off reinforcing loops R2 and R3—that is, Sunni grievances against the Iraqi government and Sunni grievances against the Shia. Sunni grievances against the U.S. occupation and ongoing military operations (R1) remain active, however.

Note that there is an important distinction between this last intervention and all others. With this political intervention, the number of insurgents never escalates. The distinction is analogous to the one between the stable marble that sits at the lowest point of a smooth-sided bowl (curve 4) and the one rolling off the peak of a hill (curves 1, 2, and 3). The pattern of curve 4 is that of a stable system, an environment in which the insurgency epidemic does not reach its tipping point.

The interesting and important question of whether an epidemic materializes, or reaches its tipping point, is really a question about which feedback

Figure 10.9. Insurgent stock as projected by the systems dynamics model in the base case versus three intervention strategies

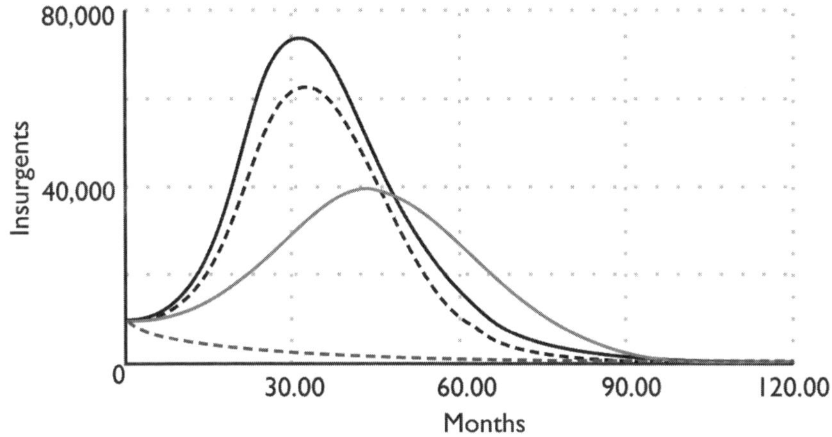

Insurgents' stock in the base case versus three intervention strategies (as projected by the system dynamics model)

loops are dominant when the disease (whether biological or social) arrives in a community. For any contagion phenomenon, some critical combination of contact frequency and infectivity will be just great enough for the positive contagion loop to dominate the negative loops. That threshold is what defines the tipping point. Below the tipping point, the system is stable; thus, the population would be resistant to the epidemic.

This analysis suggests that in the Iraq conflict, the added burden of antigovernment and anti-Shia grievances raises the insurgency infectivity level above that critical threshold. While the military and economic interventions do move the contagion and depletion loops in the right directions—decreasing the former and strengthening the latter—it is only by enough to dampen the spread of this epidemic and not to stop it.

Concluding Remarks

This chapter's objective was not to determine ultimate solutions for the problems of the Iraq conflict but rather to demonstrate that system dynamics is a fruitful avenue for such inquiry. While already commonplace in engineering and in business, advanced methods of dynamic analysis and computer modeling are less widely used in defense analysis. Yet this setting is precisely where complexities are most problematic and where the stakes are highest.

The concern is often expressed that our knowledge is grossly insufficient for building formal mathematical models of a system as complex and messy as the Iraq conflict. But what is the justification for the apparent assumption that we do not know enough to use models of the Iraq conflict but that we *do* know enough to directly intervene in managing the conflict?

It is hoped that this chapter demonstrates that we do know enough to build such models and that doing so is indeed worthwhile.

Notes

1. John D. Sterman, *Business Dynamics: Systems Thinking and Modeling for a Complex World* (Boston: Irwin McGraw-Hill, 2000), 351.
2. Anthony H. Cordesman, "Iraq's Evolving Insurgency: The Nature of Attacks and Patterns and Cycles in the Conflict," working draft (Washington, DC: Center for Strategic and International Studies, February 2, 2006), http://www.csis.org/media/csis/pubs/060202_iraqicombattrends.pdf.
3. Ibid.
4. Michael E. O'Hanlon and Jason H. Campbell, "Iraq Index: Tracking Variables of Reconstruction and Security in Post-Saddam Iraq" (Washington, DC: Brookings Institution, 2007).
5. Kenneth M. Pollack, "After Saddam: Assessing the Reconstruction of Iraq," *Foreign Affairs,* January–February 2004; and Anthony H. Cordesman, "Pandora's Box: Iraqi Federalism, Separatism, 'Hard' Partitioning, and U.S. Policy," working draft (Washington, DC: Center for Strategic and International Studies, October 9, 2007), http://www.csis.org/media/csis/pubs/071009_pandorasbox.pdf.
6. The actual model is more detailed, containing fourteen state variables and close to a hundred causal links.
7. Sterman, *Business Dynamics,* 323.
8. Cordesman, "Iraq's Evolving Insurgency."
9. Paul Collier et al., *Breaking the Conflict Trap: Civil War and Development Policy,* World Bank Policy Research Report (Washington, DC: World Bank and Oxford University Press, 2003), 68.
10. Sterman, *Business Dynamics,* 300.
11. Pollack, "After Saddam."
12. Ibid.
13. Ibid.; John A. Lynn, "Patterns of Insurgency and Counterinsurgency," *Military Review,* July–August 2005, 22–27; and Cordesman, "Pandora's Box."

14. Cordesman, "Pandora's Box."
15. Lynn, "Patterns of Insurgency."
16. Edward G. Anderson, Jr., "A Preliminary System Dynamics Model of Insurgency Management: The Anglo-Irish War of 1916–21 as a Case Study," conference proceedings, 24th International Conference of the System Dynamics Society, Nijmegen, the Netherlands, July 23–27, 2006.
17. Carl Conetta, "Vicious Circle: The Dynamics of Occupation and Resistance in Iraq," Project on Defense Alternatives Monograph 10 (Cambridge, MA: Commonwealth Institute, 2005).
18. Bahadir K. Akcam and Victor Asal, "The Dynamics of Ethnic Terrorism," Rockefeller College of Public Policy and Administration, State University of New York at Albany, 2007.
19. Anthony H. Cordesman with Emma Davies, "Iraq's Sectarian and Ethnic Violence and Its Evolving Insurgency: Developments Through Spring 2007" (Washington, DC: Center for Strategic and International Studies, 2007).
20. Collier, *Breaking the Conflict Trap*, 88.
21. Carlso Pascual and Kenneth M. Pollack, "The Critical Battles: Political Reconciliation and Reconstruction in Iraq," *Washington Quarterly* 30 (Summer 2007): 7–19.
22. Anderson, "A Preliminary System Dynamics Model."
23. O'Hanlon and Campbell, "Iraq Index."
24. Cordesman, "Iraq's Evolving Insurgency."
25. O'Hanlon and Campbell, "Iraq Index."
26. Pollack, "After Saddam."

11
Metrics in Iraq's Complex Conflict Environment

Karen Guttieri

> "This difficulty of seeing things correctly, which is one of the greatest frictions in war, makes things appear quite different to what was expected."
>
> —*Carl von Clausewitz*[1]

Reporting to Congress on progress in Iraq in April 2008, Gen. David Petraeus and Ambassador Ryan Crocker asserted that facts on the ground would determine future U.S. troop levels.[2] Measures from the field, as Petraeus and Crocker imply, are vital to the assessment of strategies in war. Is the strategy appropriate? Is its implementation on track? Are resources efficiently employed? What is the adversary up to? Analysis of data collected can shape strategy to great advantage, but a false reading of the environment is potentially disastrous.

This chapter discusses the utility and limitations of metrics in assessments of the conflict in Iraq. The U.S. General Accountability Office (GAO) has repeatedly stated that U.S. efforts in Iraq lack strategies "with clear purpose, scope, roles and performance measures."[3] There is no dearth of data; numbers abound. Rather, assessments fail to address the multilayered challenges in Iraq, to articulate concepts, and to reconcile the criteria of diverse stakeholders across bureaucratic divides. This chapter describes the environmental and organizational measurement challenges in Iraq's complex conflict ecology, focusing particularly on the need for a theory of the problem in order to develop program outcome metrics. New and broader indicators of conflict transformation are required to complement the combat-centric metrics of the existing literature, and new approaches to data collection are needed to provide operational relevance in the dispersed decision environment.

Goals

U.S. aims in Iraq are stated in reports the Department of Defense (DOD) submits to Congress on performance indicators and measures of progress: "The strategic goal of the United States in Iraq remains a unified, democratic and federal Iraq that can govern, defend and sustain itself and is an ally in the war on terror."[4] These reports, first issued in July 2005, depict the political, economic, and security environment of Iraq in narratives and graphics on oil production, electricity supply and demand, attacks, casualties, training of Iraqi security forces, and surveys of Iraqi perceptions.

Even with this level of detail, assessment in war is often murky. In April 2008, some congressional leaders openly disputed claims Petraeus and Crocker made of progress in Iraq. Moreover, one study declared a surge in U.S. troops was a tremendous success, with "dramatically improved security in Baghdad and throughout Iraq,"[5] while another rated only three of eighteen benchmarks accomplished and the stated goal—to create space for political reconciliation among Iraqis—as unfulfilled.[6] Army chief of staff Gen. George W. Casey, Jr., cited a side effect of the American troop increase—exhaustion. "The surge has sucked all of the flexibility out of the system," he warned.[7]

The noise of multiple competing goals, statistics, and interpretations makes it difficult to judge progress. The multilayered conflict ecology in Iraq amplifies that noise. Numerous incoherent and hostile factions vie against one another and against a weak new government. Internal alliances shift while regional powers attempt to manipulate the outcome. In this regard, the layered complexities depicted by General Petraeus in September 2007 (see figure 11.1) must be considered when setting goals and developing programs to achieve them.

Problem Assessment

Analysts supporting the U.S. effort seem to have collected data while blind to entire layers of the conflict. Iraqi resistance to occupation was ignored for

Figure 11.1. Major threats to Iraq

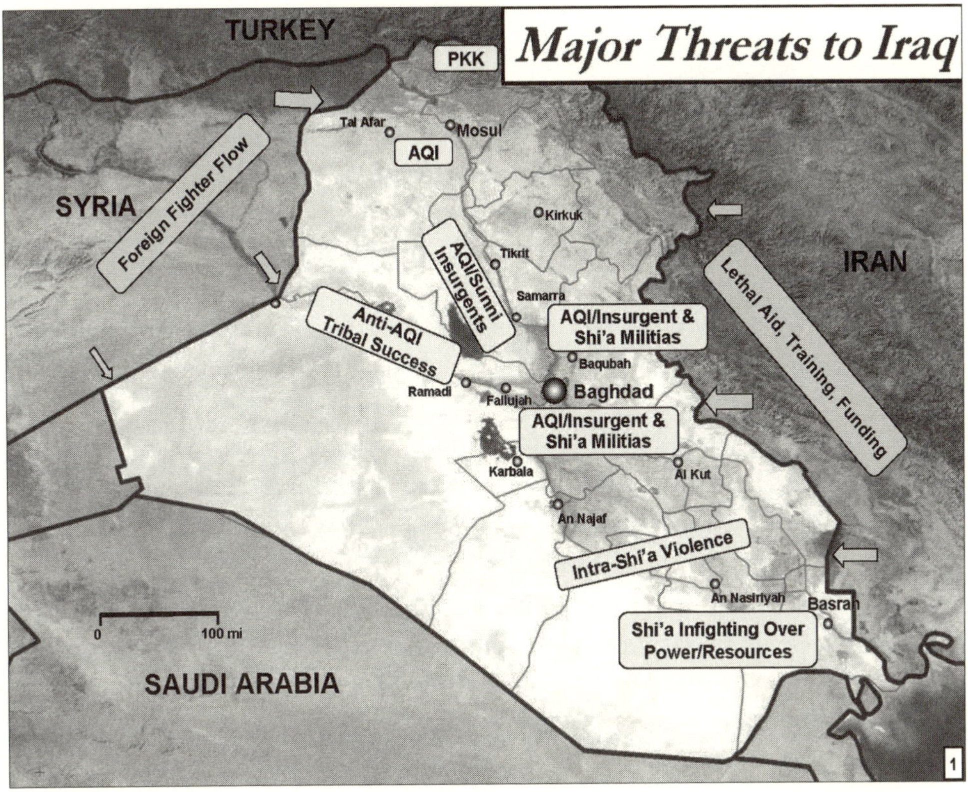

Source: Gen. David M. Petraeus, "Report to Congress on the Situation in Iraq," September 10–11, 2007, 11, at http://foreignaffairs.house.gov/110/pet091007.pdf, accessed December 12, 2009.

months; intrastate and interstate dimensions of the conflict were ignored far longer. The "National Strategy for Victory in Iraq," presented by President Bush on November 30, 2005, addressed three kinds of enemies—Sunni rejectionists, Saddamists, and terrorists—with no mention of the Shia elements that had been troublesome in 2004 and were again in 2006.[8] Civilian casualties create antibodies to any foreign presence, but they were purposefully neglected at first because, as Gen. Tommy Franks, who led the invasion of Iraq, put it, "We don't do body counts."[9]

Effective programs require a viable theory of the problem. Until May 2006, DOD reports on Iraq focused solely on the political, economic, and security developments that were key to establishing the legitimacy of the government against the insurgency. The reports did not address the geostrategic conflict dimensions—the influence of Iran and Syria—until then. U.S. military statistics did not measure sectarian violence until January 2006.[10] The report of February 2006 was naively reassuring: "Terrorist attacks have failed to create and spread sectarian conflict, and polls of Iraqi perceptions continue to show the isolation of terrorists and foreign fighters from the Iraqi people."[11] Although the bombing of the al-Askari Shrine (Golden Mosque) in Samarra on February 22, 2006, clearly marked an intense phase of internecine violence, the May 2006 report cited the bombing only to portray Iraq's new leadership as resilient: "Iraqi leaders stood together in a united front against further violence and continued with the political process."[12]

Attacks as indicators of violence were in the range of a thousand a month before April 2004. In January 2006 the average *weekly* number of attacks was around seven hundred and by January 2007 around fourteen hundred. By the end of 2006, members of competing Shia factions—the Badr and Mahdi militias—had heavily infiltrated the Iraqi Interior Ministry and many police units. Many Iraqi Army units were also unreliable because of sectarian divisions.[13] By every account, civilian casualties rose, as illustrated in figure 11.2 from a June 2008 GAO report.[14]

Relief came when Shia cleric Moqtada al-Sadr ordered his Mahdi Army to cease fire in August 2007. Despite wide variance in the reports on Iraq Significant Activities (SIGACTS), depicted in figure 11.3, consensus formed around a downward trend in overall violence.

Indicators

The complexity of stability operations exhausts the capacity of analytic tools developed for conventional war, including the combat-centric metrics dominating the literature on military effectiveness.[15] In November 2005, DOD defined stability operations as civilian and military activities to restore or ensure order, with priority on a par with major combat operations.[16] Stability operations require a "whole of government" approach, as it is currently called in U.S. government policy circles, because it requires many government agencies to work together. Stability operations require a "whole of community" effort, including coordination with governmental and non-governmental agencies from the host nation and the international

Figure 11.2. Enemy-initiated attacks

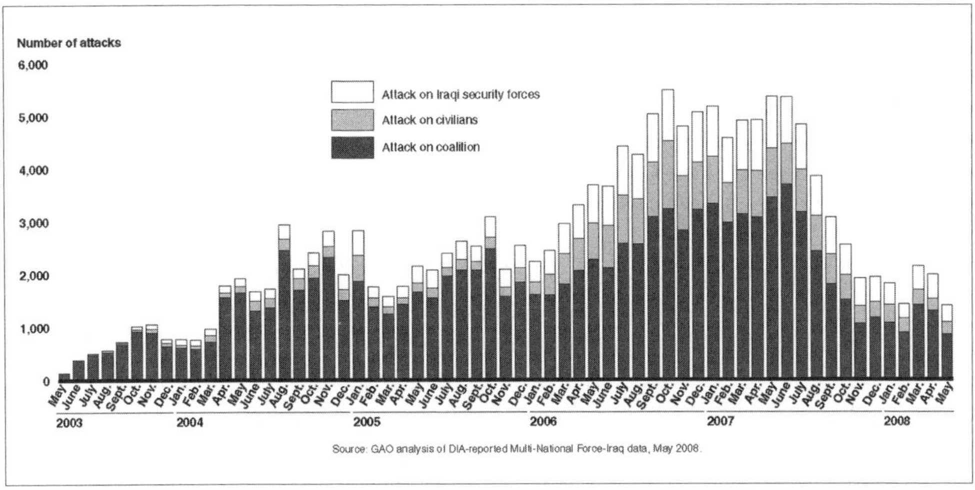

Source: U.S. Government Accountability Office, "Securing, Stabilizing, and Rebuilding Iraq: Progress Report: Some Gains Made, Updated Strategy Needed," Report to Congressional Committees (GAO-08-837), June 2008, http://www.gao.gov/new.items/d08837.pdf; compiled from GAO analysis of Defense Intelligence Agency–reported Multi-National Force–Iraq data, May 2008.

community. This type of engagement characterized the economic assistance and other non-kinetic U.S. efforts in Vietnam that became known as "the other war." The result was diffuse responsibility with poor results.[17] Parties to that diffuse responsibility collect and interpret information differently. Although they may be participants in a larger strategy, it is understandable that particular agencies and people within them focus on the aspects of their own programs that are working.[18] An evaluator might broaden the lens to take in a more attractive tableau or narrow it to obscure surrounding ugliness.

How information is displayed affects how it is interpreted. In the monthly "Iraq Index," the Brookings Institution compares data for any given month in a series of years, although different indicators are reported in each issue, which undermines the data's continuity and comparability.[19] General Petraeus, in his September 2007 briefing to Congress, illustrated trends in Iraqi ethno-sectarian violence beginning in May 2006 (see figure 11.4). With a high level of ethnic violence in the spring of 2006 as the baseline, rather than the comparatively low levels of attack in previous years, his graph portrays a rosier picture of progress.

Figure 11.3. Civilian deaths, January 2006–February 2008

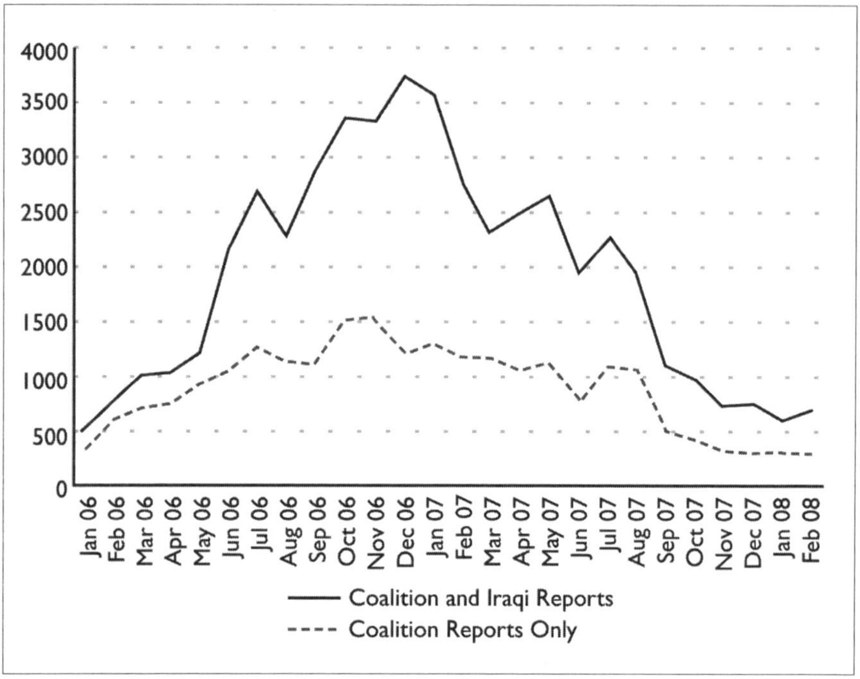

Source: General Petraeus, "Report to Congress on the Situation in Iraq," 13.

The last six months of 2006 marked the worst period of violence in the history of the war: "Only in comparison to that could the first half of 2007 be regarded as an improvement. Despite any efforts put into the surge, the first six months of 2007 was [*sic*] still the most deadly first six months for civilians of any year since the invasion."[20]

A rational decision model suggests that organizations track indicators in order to measure policy or strategy effectiveness and consider changing strategies at determined thresholds of satisfaction or dissatisfaction.[21] However, Scott Gartner observes that decision makers do not have fixed preferences but fixed criteria; they assess strategies on the basis of rates of change in dominant indicators. Curvilinear changes in key indicators capture attention. For example, the World War I British leader David Lloyd George noted that the "alarming rate at which our ships were being sunk was rapidly increasing."[22] Similarly, in December 2006, the bipartisan Iraq Study Group's assessment argued that the situation was "deteriorating" and

Figure 11.4. Ethno-sectarian violence

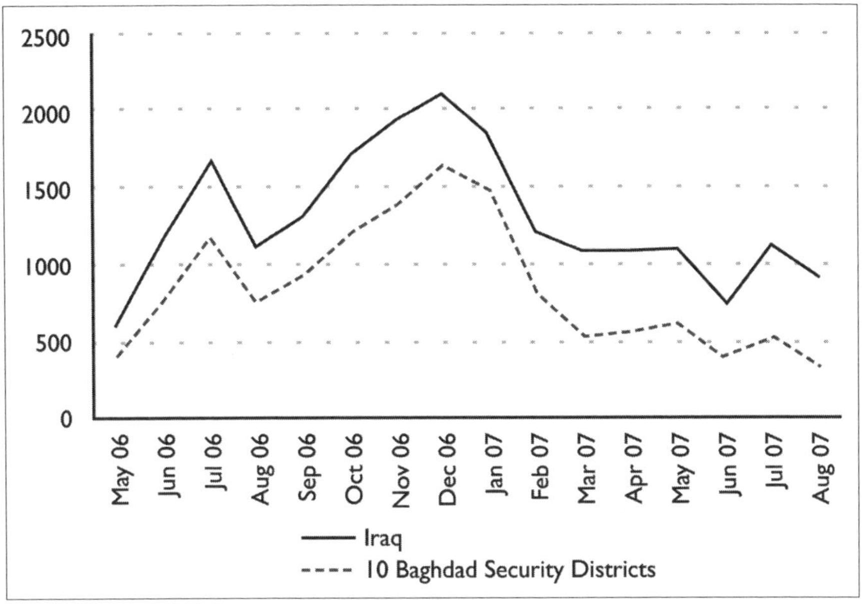

Source: General Petraeus, "Report to Congress on the Situation in Iraq," 14.

that "the ability of the United States to shape outcomes is diminishing."[23] In January 2007, President Bush conceded in his State of the Union address, "It's clear we need to change our strategy in Iraq." He proposed a "surge" of 21,500 new troops in a plan called "The New Way Forward in Iraq."[24]

When many problems compete for attention, some more loudly than others, program resources tend to chase moving targets. The improvised explosive device (IED) problem offers an example. IED attacks have been responsible for two-thirds of American combat deaths to date, so intense scrutiny of the problem is understandable.[25] However, within this narrow topic, the Pentagon's focus on data was selective—an IED was considered effective only if it caused a Coalition casualty—and was based on the assumption that the purpose of an IED attack is to erode American political will.[26] Figure 11.5 provides an example of how DOD presented IED data according to the attacks' "effectiveness." Note that there are no values on the y-axis. A 2008 Rand study reported that the United States lacked a formal system for measuring Iraqi civilian casualties, although the think tank had begun work with the Joint IED Defeat Organization (JIEDDO) to address the shortcoming.[27] The total number of attacks grew at a much more rapid rate than Coalition casualty rates did in part because of countermeasures.[28]

In what may be the first official declaration of the strategy, in mid-2007 Lt. Gen. Ray Odierno, commander of the Multi-National Corps–Iraq, issued a ten-point "Counterinsurgency Guidance" that included instructions to "look beyond the IED—get the network that placed it."[29] JIEDDO analysts began to widen their framework to estimate the number of ineffective attacks as well as the number of IEDs found and cleared. As it became obvious that the adversary was adapting more quickly than the Americans were innovating, the counter-IED effort shifted from a technical approach to a broader focus on networks. As illustrated in table 11.1, the IED problem exists at several levels of analysis.

What metrics are useful in such a complex operational environment? A project called Measuring Progress in Conflict Environments (MPICE), conducted by the U.S. Institute of Peace, the U.S. Army Peacekeeping and

Figure 11.5. IED incident trends

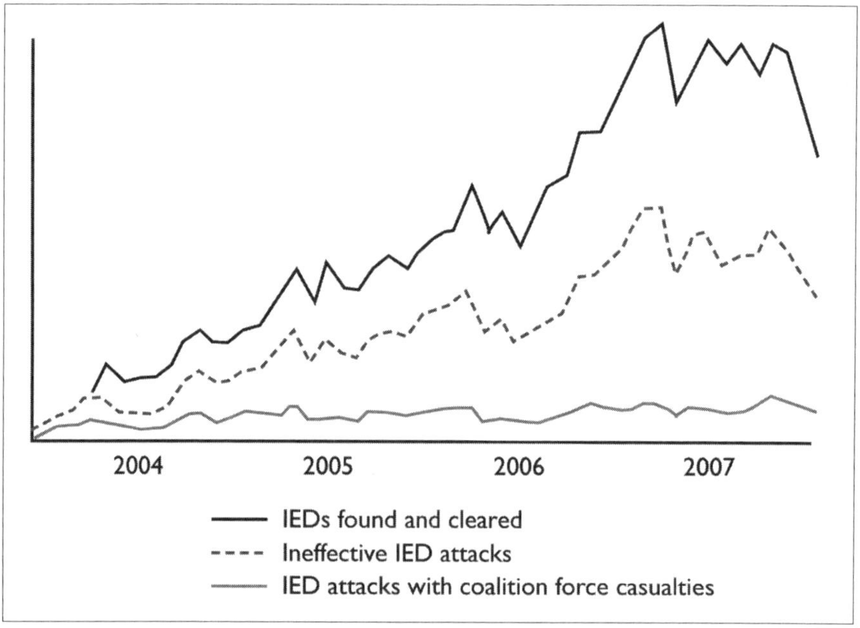

Source: Joint Improvised Explosive Device Defeat Organization Annual Report, 2007, 4, https://www.jieddo.dod.mil/content/docs/2007_JIEDDO%20Annual%20Report_(U).pdf, accessed December 12, 2009.

Table 11.1. The Improvised Explosive Device (IED) Problem

Level of focus	Illustrative metrics
IED device	▪ Emplaced devices found and neutralized by appropriate technical means ▪ Device avoided with joint/Coalition tactics, techniques, and procedures (TTP) ▪ Protective measures mitigate damage effects of the detonated device
IED network or system	▪ IED suppliers and bomb makers arrested ▪ Confiscation of key IED stockpiles (weapons and matériel) ▪ Numbers of surveillance/patrols in key target areas to deter/prevent IED emplacement ▪ Numbers of active and passive measures to neutralize emplaced IEDs
Defeat the insurgency	▪ Increase in capture/kill rate of insurgents and their leaders ▪ Reduction in recruitment for insurgency ▪ Reduction in matériel and funding available to insurgency ▪ Increase in ability of government, commercial sector, or others to provide services to population ▪ Increase in active support of population to government and counterinsurgency
Defeat the movement	▪ Increase in capture/kill rate of terrorists and their leaders ▪ Reduction in recruitment rate for particular terrorist movement ▪ Reduction in matériel and funding available to terrorist movement ▪ Reduction in support/sympathy for terrorist movement objectives and methods by larger Muslim community (both the general populace and key religious leaders)

Source: John Benedict and L. Dean Simmons, briefing slides presented to Military Operations Research Irregular Warfare Analysis Workshop, Naval Postgraduate School, Monterey, California, December 2007 (adapted with permission from the authors). Benedict and Simmons depict insurgency within a broader context of transnational terrorism, rather than interstate competition.

Stability Operations Institute, and the U.S. Army Corps of Engineers, offers interagency metrics in key sectors of conflict stabilization and transformation.[30] MPICE assesses conflict transformation in five sectors: political moderation and stable democracy, safe and secure environment, rule of law, sustainable economy, and social well-being. In each sector, the accounting focuses on the drivers of conflict—for example, injustice when the legal system is used as an instrument of repression, as measured by the percentage of citizens who fear law enforcement or by measures of torture or inhumane treatment. Measures of institutional performance—for example, accountability of law enforcement agencies as measured by enforcement of codes and percentages of investigated complaints—offset those negative factors.

The choice of indicators influences strategy. In Vietnam, the U.S. Marine Corps advocated, futilely, for the inclusion of crop production as a measure of success. The U.S. military focused on body counts rather than crop production, creating incentives to emphasize the kinetic fight rather than the "other war."[31] As in the Marine Corps' desire to track crop production as a measurement in Vietnam, MPICE metrics may facilitate a cognitive shift away from overreliance on kinetic war fighting, which can be counterproductive to conflict transformation. MPICE includes metrics relevant to each of Iraq's conflict genres. This tool may provide measures of progress toward reduction of conflict drivers and increased indigenous capacity, but it does not provide immediate recommendations as to how to prevent terrorist networks from forming or guidelines on how to apply the instruments of national power to mitigate or disrupt them once formed.

Treatment Evaluation

In a complex environment like Iraq's, many agencies of government and many actors outside its sphere of control define problems and apply treatments to goals that may differ or that they may weight differently than do other partners in conflict transformation. The U.S. strategy, according to the GAO, lacks coherence and continues to fail at strategic planning. When agency leaders were interviewed by GAO auditors, they "generally agreed on the importance of having clear strategies but provided various comments on how to best implement those strategies."[32] DOD presented strategies that only partially identify agencies responsible for implementation, do not address how to integrate goals with those of the Iraqis and the international community, and only partially specify costs.

Measuring implementation is a different task from measuring outcomes. Counting the number of patrols, for example, is worthwhile if patrols are part of a treatment program and the evaluator wants to determine whether the program is being implemented as designed. The numbers of viable Iraqi security forces have been a common metric to help determine the feasibility and timing of a transition from U.S. to Iraqi control. These numbers have been volatile and perhaps even deceptive. In 2006, even as Iraq met political milestones and its increased numbers of security forces took on more responsibility for security, conditions continued to deteriorate. Iraqi-led missions, such as Operation Together Forward, cleared Baghdad neighborhoods of insurgents only temporarily.[33] Without adequate numbers, the "clear, hold, build" approach was not fully implemented.

According to the GAO, the inability to implement programs is a weakness of both the U.S. and the Iraqi governments. Congress has obligated nearly $400 billion for Iraq since 2003; of that, "$40 billion has supported reconstruction and stabilization efforts." Meanwhile, the Iraqi government's capacity to spend reconstruction funds is severely limited, with only about 24 percent of its 2007 capital budgets allocated by mid-July 2007.[34]

Collection

Metrics are subject to distortion in the collection process. In his memoir of his days with a military advisory team in Vietnam, David Donovan reflected on the role of data in the Hamlet Evaluation System and Territorial Forces Evaluation System. These programs involved standardized lists of questions about troop strength, morale, numbers of houses with tin roofs, numbers of televisions, and the like. "Meeting the deadline for submission of the report was the important thing," he recalled, "not accuracy."[35] The Vietnamese authorities and the U.S. district chiefs both understood that an A rating in the Hamlet Evaluation System put them in good light. Donovan wrote, "If I recall correctly, the month the infamous Tet offensive broke out, the country was reported to be over ninety-percent pacified."[36]

Data collection too often imposes an additional burden on implementers without any utility to the collector. Reports go up the chain of command and undergo classification, but do not return to the collectors in the form of analysis that they need. As various kinds of reports streaming through different channels produce variance in the format of data, the interoperability of data becomes limited, which in turn also reduces the data's utility for evaluation.

Next Steps

Program theory for complex conflict environments must emphasize the development of a multilayered theory of effects. Analysis must examine the causal mechanisms that link the treatments, processes, and outcomes.[37] What is the causal chain that connects a given treatment (for example, increased patrols) with a particular effect (for example, a safe and secure environment)? What unintended consequences does the treatment produce? If the desired effect is achieved, does the treatment account for that success? If the desired effect is absent, is it because the treatment failed? Empirically testable propositions about treatment effects in conflict environments can be studied in controlled case comparisons or, if the effects are quantifiable, through statistical studies.

Next, the effects in relation to the multiple layers of the conflict environment must be considered. To the extent that factors can be identified and weighted, it may be possible to develop algorithms to inform decisions about treatment compositions. Situating analysis in time introduces the potential for temporal markers that can help decision makers anticipate cycles in conflict transformation. Strategy involves moves and countermoves of competitive players; thinking in time must anticipate a range of responses from the various competitors in the complex environment.

Finally, data feedback is a vital element of the evaluation system. Without it, the incentives for clean and reliable information collection diminish, and the entire enterprise of evaluation fails in its mission to serve the frontline agents of conflict transformation.

Notes

1. Carl von Clausewitz, *On War*, trans. J. J. Graham (New York: Barnes and Noble, 2004).
2. "Petraeus, Crocker Criticize Iran, Call for Halt to Troop Pullout," *CNNPolitics.com*, April 8, 2008, http://www.cnn.com/2008/POLITICS/04/08/iraq.hearing/.
3. A GAO report to Congress indicated: "Three GAO reports illustrate a recurring problem with U.S. efforts in Iraq—the lack of strategies with clear purpose, scope, roles

and responsibilities, and performance measures. Our reports assessing (1) the National Strategy for Victory in Iraq (NSVI), (2) U.S. efforts to develop planning and budget capacity in Iraq's ministries, and (3) U.S. and Iraqi efforts to rebuild Iraq's energy sector show that clear strategies are needed to guide U.S. efforts, manage risk, and identify needed resources." See U.S. Government Accountability Office (GAO), "Securing, Stabilizing, and Rebuilding Iraq: GAO Audits and Key Oversight Issues," statement of Joseph A. Christoff, director, International Affairs and Trade, testimony before the Committee on Appropriations, Subcommittee on State, Foreign Operations, and Related Programs, U.S. House of Representatives (GAO-08-231T) (Washington, DC: GAO, October 30, 2007).

4. U.S. Department of Defense, "Measuring Stability and Security in Iraq," June 2008 Report to Congress in Accordance with the Department of Defense Appropriations Act 2008 (Section 9010, Public Law 109-289), June 13, 2008, iii, http://www.defenselink.mil/pubs/pdfs/Master_16_June_08_%20FINAL_SIGNED%20.pdf.
5. Kimberly Kagan, "How They Did It: Executing the Winning Strategy in Iraq," *Weekly Standard* 13, no. 10 (November 19, 2007).
6. Center for American Progress, "Iraq Benchmark Report Card: One Year After the Surge," January 24, 2008, http://www.americanprogress.org/issues/2008/01/benchmark.html.
7. Quoted in Ann Scott Tyson, "Army Chief May Shorten Tours In Iraq, Afghanistan by Summer," *Washington Post*, January 17, 2008.
8. Office of the Press Secretary, the White House, "Fact Sheet: Strategy for Victory: Defeating the Terrorists and Training Iraqi Security Forces," http://georgewbush-whitehouse.archives.gov/news/releases/2006/03/20060313-6.html; and National Security Council, "National Strategy for Victory in Iraq," November 2005, http://georgewbush-whitehouse.archives.gov/infocus/iraq/iraq_national_strategy_20051130.pdf.
9. Quoted in Edward Epstein, "How Many Iraqis Died? We May Never Know," *San Francisco Chronicle*, May 3, 2003.
10. Michael R. Gordon, "A Fuller Picture: U.S. Looks to Iraqi Data," *New York Times*, December 1, 2007.
11. U.S. Department of Defense, "Measuring Stability and Security in Iraq," February 2006 Report to Congress in Accordance with the Department of Defense Appropriations Act 2006 (Section 9010), February 17, 2006, 3.
12. U.S. Department of Defense, "Measuring Stability and Security in Iraq," May 2006 Report to Congress in Accordance with the Department of Defense Appropriations Act 2006 (Section 9010), May 26, 2006, 3.
13. Office of the Director of National Intelligence, *National Intelligence Estimate: Prospects for Iraq's Stability: A Challenging Road Ahead*, Washington, D.C., January 2007.
14. GAO-08-837, "Securing, Stabilizing, and Rebuilding Iraq," http://www.gao.gov/new.items/d08837.pdf.
15. Allan R. Millett, Williamson Murray, and Kenneth H. Watman, "The Effectiveness of Military Organizations," in *Military Effectiveness*, ed. Allan R. Millett and Williamson Murray (London: Allen & Unwin, 1988); and Risa Brooks and Elizabeth A. Stan-

ley, eds., *Creating Military Power: The Sources of Military Effectiveness* (Stanford, CA: Stanford University Press, 2007).

16. U.S. Department of Defense, "Military Support for Stability, Security, Transition, and Reconstruction (S.S.T.R.)," Directive no. 3000.05, November 28, 2005.
17. Robert W. Komer, *Bureaucracy Does Its Thing: Institutional Constraints on U.S.-GVN Performance in Vietnam* (Santa Monica, CA: Rand, 1972).
18. Richard Armitage, a former Bush administration official who played a key role in the early occupation of Iraq, described this as "a common . . . Washington dilemma." See *No End in Sight*, directed and produced by Charles Ferguson (New York: Magnolia Pictures, 2007).
19. Michael E. O'Hanlon and Ian Livingston, "Iraq Index: Tracking Reconstruction and Security in Post-Saddam Iraq" (Washington, DC: Brookings Institution, Saban Center for Middle East Policy, ongoing),http://www.brookings.edu/iraqindex.
20. "The Baghdad 'Surge' and Civilian Casualties," *Iraq Body Count*, http://www.iraqbodycount.org/analysis/numbers/baghdad-surge/.
21. Richard Cyert and James March, *Behavioral Theory of the Firm* (Englewood Cliffs, NJ: Prentice Hall, 1963); Herbert Simon, *Administrative Behavior* (New York: Free Press, 1957); and John D. Steinbruner, *The Cybernetic Theory of Decision: New Dimensions of Political Analysis* (Princeton, NJ: Princeton University Press, 1974). For an example of a work assuming fixed preferences, see Barry Posen, *The Sources of Military Doctrine: France, Britain, and Germany Between the World Wars* (Ithaca, NY: Cornell University Press, 1984).
22. Scott Sigmund Gartner, *Strategic Assessment in War* (New Haven, CT: Yale University Press, 1997); and David Lloyd George, *War Memoirs of David Lloyd George* (Boston: Little, Brown and Company, 1933).
23. James A. Baker III et al., *The Iraq Study Group Report: The Way Forward––a New Approach* (New York: Vintage Books, 2006), 32.
24. Although the plan's name reflected the title of the Iraq Study Group's report, on the contrary, the report's authors advocated a reduction of troops.
25. Rick Atkinson, "'The Single Most Effective Weapon Against Our Deployed Forces,'" *Washington Post*, September 30, 2007.
26. Ibid.
27. Katharine Hall and Dale Stahl, *An Argument for Documenting Casualties: Violence Against Iraqi Civilians, 2006* (Santa Monica, CA: Rand, 2008).
28. Rick Atkinson, "'The IED Problem Is Getting out of Control. We've Got to Stop the Bleeding,'" *Washington Post*, September 30, 2007. The ratio of casualties per blast was reduced by a combination of technology and new procedures for troop movement. Some, such as a "porcupine approach," in which patrols assume an aggressive posture, may have other effects on Iraqi perceptions and relations with Coalition forces.
29. Editors, "HQ M-NC-I Counterinsurgency Guidance by Lt. Gen. Ray Odierno," *Small Wars Journal*, June 15, 2007, http://smallwarsjournal.com/blog/2007/06/hq-mnci-counterinsurgency-guid/.
30. This effort builds on the work in Jock Covey, Michael J. Dziedzic, and Len Haw-

ley, eds., *The Quest for a Viable Peace: International Intervention and Strategies for Conflict Transformation* (Washington, DC: United States Institute of Peace Press, 2005); the Conflict Assessment System Tool (CAST) by the Fund for Peace; the Pre-Conflict Anticipation and Shaping (PCAS) tool developed by the Defense Advanced Research Projects Agency; Country Analytic Studies (CAS) indicators developed by U.S. Agency for International Development; and various metrics developed by the American Bar Association, the Geneva Centre for Democratic Control of the Armed Forces (DCAF), the World Bank, the International Monetary Fund, the United Nations Development Program, and the Center for Public Integrity.

31. Gartner, *Strategic Assessment in War*.
32. GAO, "Securing, Stabilizing, and Rebuilding Iraq."
33. John F. Burns, "U.S. And Iraqis Are Wrangling over War Plans," *New York Times*, January 15, 2007.
34. GAO, "Securing, Stabilizing, and Rebuilding Iraq: Iraqi Government Has Not Met Most Legislative, Security, and Economic Benchmarks," Report to Congressional Committees (GAO-07-1195) (Washington, DC: GAO, September 2007), http://www.gao.gov/new.items/d071195.pdf.
35. David Donovan, *Once a Warrior King: Memories of an Officer in Vietnam* (New York: McGraw-Hill, 1985), 149.
36. Ibid., 150.
37. Huey-Tsyh Chen, *Theory-Driven Evaluations* (Newbury Park, CA: Sage, 1990).

12

System Modeling of U.S. Efforts as Applied to the War on Terrorism in Iraq and Iraq's Infrastructure Resiliency: The Indicators of Force Multipliers (INFORM) Model

William P. Fox

> "The attack took place on American soil, but it was an attack on the heart and soul of the civilized world. And the world has come together to fight a new and different war, the first, and we hope the only one, of the 21st century. A war against all those who seek to export terror, and a war against those governments that support or shelter them."
>
> —*President George W. Bush, October 11, 2001*

The strategic goal of the United States in Iraq is the creation of a unified, democratic, and federal Iraq that can govern, defend, and sustain itself and is an ally in the war on terrorism. The purpose of the modeling effort presented in this chapter is to provide a tool for leaders and decision makers to measure the effects of proposed actions, or treatments, on all facets of the total mission in Iraq as well as to measure unforeseen events and their potential impact on Iraq's stability. Mathematical models can not only provide insights into real-world behavior but also serve as tools that decision makers can use to determine possible effects of what-if scenarios. Our Indicators of Force Multipliers (INFORM) model is a layered model, initially going to a depth of one or two layers. If our efforts provide fruitful results, the model can be expanded to more layers as needed.

The INFORM model uses the circles-of-war approach described in chapter 1.[1] All three types of war—interstate war, insurgency, and civil war—have occurred during the conflict in Iraq, at times simultaneously. The conflict began as an interstate war when the United States and allied forces invaded Iraq in 2003. After deposing the Saddam Hussein regime, U.S.-led forces soon faced an insurgency led by Sunni factions—and including some al Qaeda elements—fighting the presence of Coalition troops and the Shia-dominated Iraqi government and security forces. In 2006, the conflict began increasingly to take on the characteristics of a civil war, causing the government to split along Sunni and Shia lines, replete with reprisal attacks between Sunni and Shia militias. While the conflict in Iraq might currently be characterized as a civil war, it still contains elements of an insurgency and an interstate war, with threats of additional interstate involvement from Iran and Turkey.

The three types of war overlap, and incidents may involve elements of more than one dimension. For example, some insurgency is "pure" terrorist activity executed by al Qaeda in Iraq (AQI), other acts are insurgent motivated, and yet others exhibit a prominent sectarian dimension. Most incidents, in fact, include elements of two dynamics or of all three. The three types of war may be thought of in terms of a Venn diagram of overlapping circles (see figure 12.1), each constantly changing in size. Any incident can be plotted somewhere within the interaction of the three dynamics.

Figure 12.1. View of the strategic problem in Iraq

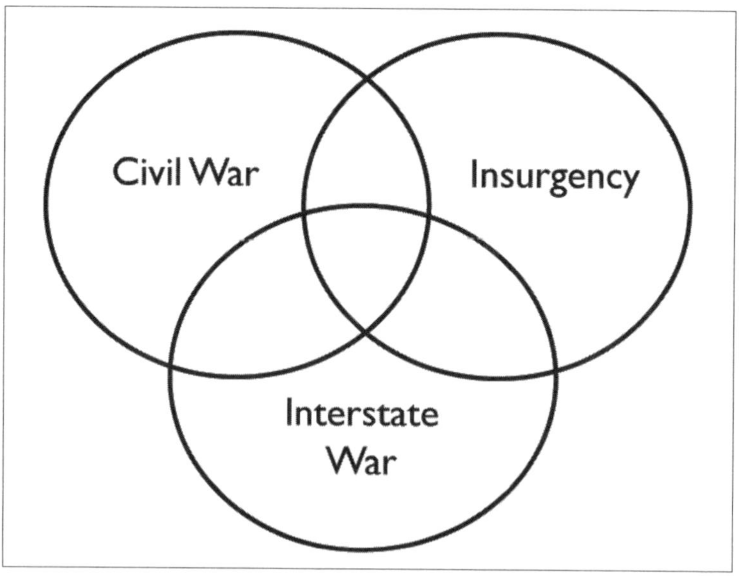

An underlying assumption of the model as applied to this conflict is the need for nation building in Iraq. Pervasive security problems prevent us from getting at many of the underlying problems—crime, weak infrastructure, economic and social alienation, weak governance, and so on—that need to be addressed in order to deal with the nation-building requirement. The inability to get at these underlying problems perpetuates and exacerbates the security problems in Iraq as well as the three types of war.

The three types of war can be mutually reinforcing—that is, each can make the others worse. Terrorism provokes communal conflict, which in turn makes the insurgency more intractable, which in turn gives rise to terrorism, and so on.

The solution sets to each problem also tend to be countervailing—that is, the solution to one tends to make the others worse. For example, defeating the insurgency requires building indigenous security forces. But in a society that has weak national institutions and is divided along sectarian lines, a buildup of indigenous security forces can make the communal conflict worse. Resolving the communal conflict requires working with all community groups, including those groups that currently support terrorists. This effort may create animosity and increase the support of terrorist factions. Countering terrorist cells implies disrupting terrorist support, but that interference can make the insurgency worse—and so it goes, in an endless loop.

In this chapter, the first five steps of the following eight-step model-building process[2] are applied to examine the problem of the three dynamically interacting types of war as well as the construct in figure 12.2.

Step 1. Understand the problem or the question asked.
Step 2. Make simplifying assumptions.
Step 3. Define all variables.
Step 4. Construct a model.
Step 5. Solve and interpret the model.
Step 6. Verify the model.
Step 7. Identify the strengths and weaknesses of the model.
Step 8. Implement and maintain the model for future use.

We begin with the real-world system and apply many simplifying assumptions so that we can employ mathematical models to measure the effects, as illustrated in figure 12.3.

Figure 12.2. Modeling process to be used

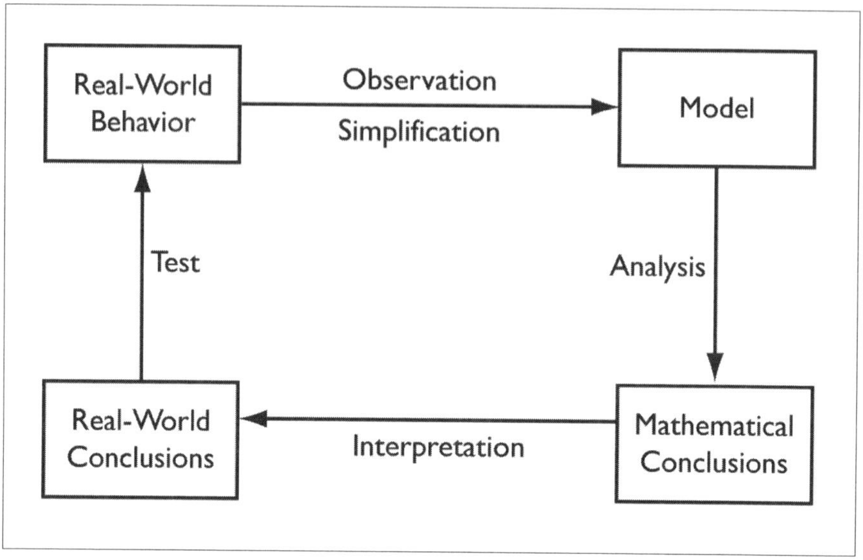

Model I: A Model Using Game Theory

We initially used game theory to model the U.S. decision to invade Iraq. Military officers in our defense analysis courses on models of conflict did the classwork and yielded the game theory model and its results. Given the assumptions that the United States will meet the imperatives of the war on terrorism and that the Iraqi regime under Saddam Hussein provided support to terrorists, military action emerges as the ultimate result. Classical game theory determines the optimal strategy via the minimax criterion. The equilibrium strategy in this case is a pure strategy for each of the two players and is referred to as the Nash equilibrium. For this game, the equilibrium strategies are as follows: the Iraqi strategy is to support the terrorists, and the U.S. strategy is to use military action. The model is explained in more detail in section 1 of this volume's appendix.

Model II: A Dynamical System's Model

We created the INFORM model of the war in Iraq as a dynamic systems model of both military and nonmilitary effects as applied to the war on terrorism in Iraq and the resiliency of Iraq's own infrastructure. The basic form of this model stems from a Department of Homeland Security model.[3] This

Figure 12.3. Mathematical models and the real world

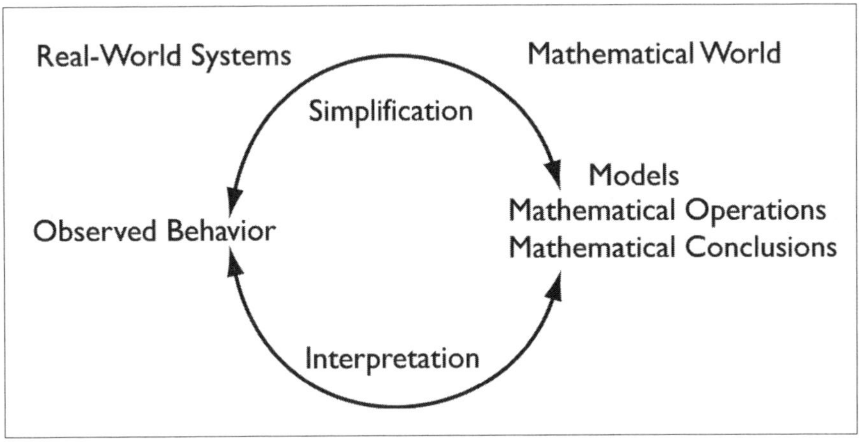

model and the modified algorithm used in providing examples are further explained in the appendix. The current effort is only the skeleton of a larger proposed stochastic model.

Dynamic Modeling

We used a discrete dynamic modeling structure to capture the effects over time as well as the results of interactions. We used the paradigm

Future = Present + Change

in order to build our dynamic model structure. The basic model without shocks is provided in the following equation:

$$\begin{bmatrix} p_i(t+1) \\ s_k(t+1) \end{bmatrix} = \begin{bmatrix} Q_{pp} & Q_{ps} \\ Q_{sp} & Q_{ss} \end{bmatrix}^T \begin{bmatrix} p_i(t) \\ s_k(t) \end{bmatrix}$$

Notatio:

$i = 1, 2, \ldots, I$	major elements
$J = 1, 2, \ldots, J$	critical services related to elements
$k = 1, 2, \ldots, K$	set of *i*, *j* physical element-service pairs
pi(t)	physical condition state of infrastructure element *i* at time *t*
sk(t)	service process condition state for pair k at time *t*
Q = [Qik(t)]	state interactivity level matrix at time *t*

Two additional vectors for degradation over time and maintenance over time can serve as multipliers in this model. We note the following:

$di(t^*)$	degradation of the physical system by natural causes
$dk(t^*)$	degradation of the service system by natural causes (between physical systems, services, and physical-service pairs)
$mi(t^*)$	maintenance for physical layer for infrastructure i at time t
$mk(t^*)$	maintenance for critical infrastructure service j for infrastructure i at time t

- Q is assumed to be partially time invariant, asymmetric, and state independent in the basic model.
- The block structure of Q represents the pairwise influence effects between state components as a result of linked interdependencies.
- The scale chosen for Q components represents a complete effects cycle.
- The state vector at time $t = 0$ represents a conservative estimate of current state condition levels.
- The degradation and maintenance vectors represent planned periodic resource investments for state conditions according to (possibly unique) periodic time sequence t^*.

Examples of some Homeland Security layers that were used include physical layers such as energy, transportation, public health, finance, and so on. Their respective service layers could be used to supply residential electricity, provide rail and bus service, control disease, facilitate business transactions, and so forth.

Modifying these layers to fit our dynamic model for Iraq, we begin with six variables, move to eight variables in our examples, and suggest a thirty-variable model to be constructed. Our variables and their definitions, along with some brief discussion of data, are detailed in section 2 of the appendix.

We iterate the dynamic model and its interaction over time. We can affect the model with both degradation (natural degradation) and maintenance (upgrades) as necessary. We can "hit" the system with a "shock," or subject it to various stimuli; analyze which elements go out of control; and measure the net percentage change in these elements.

In our group discussions, we discovered our model needed to react to various stimuli, or shocks to the system. These shocks can be passive or aggressive stimuli. We built several scenarios based on shocks for preliminary analysis. Based on the results of our model and our analysis of these results, we believe this model is worthy of further development.

Modeling with Shocks

Let $c(\tau)$ be a shock due to an outside force (insurgency attack, bombing, reduction of U.S. troops, and so on). We can measure its effect throughout the elements (infrastructures) to determine courses of action to improve the situation. The model allows experts to create a vector of scalars for the shock effect (or a distribution of the effect if not accurately known). The shock is applied after the period indicated for the shock. The new vector is then used for subsequent calculations within that scenario.

$$\begin{bmatrix} p_i(t+1) \\ s_k(t+1) \end{bmatrix} = \begin{bmatrix} Q_{pp} & Q_{ps} \\ Q_{sp} & Q_{ss} \end{bmatrix}^T \begin{bmatrix} p_i(t) \\ s_k(t) \end{bmatrix} \begin{bmatrix} c_i(\tau) \\ c_k(\tau) \end{bmatrix}$$

where

$$\begin{bmatrix} \tilde{Q}_{pp} & \tilde{Q}_{ps} \\ \tilde{Q}_{sp} & \tilde{Q}_{ss} \end{bmatrix}^T = \left(\begin{bmatrix} Q_{pp} & Q_{ps} \\ Q_{sp} & Q_{ss} \end{bmatrix}^T + \begin{bmatrix} c_{pp} & c_{ps} \\ c_{sp} & c_{ss} \end{bmatrix}^T \right)$$

This modeling format can allow for the user (decision maker) to consider responsive actions and policies.

Model with Responsive Actions and/or Policies

$$\begin{bmatrix} p_i(t+1) \\ s_k(t+1) \end{bmatrix} = \left(\begin{bmatrix} \tilde{Q}_{pp} & \tilde{Q}_{ps} \\ \tilde{Q}_{sp} & \tilde{Q}_{ss} \end{bmatrix} + \begin{bmatrix} P_{pp}(\delta) & P_{ps}(\delta) \\ P_{sp}(\delta) & P_{ss}(\delta) \end{bmatrix} \right) \begin{bmatrix} p_i(t) \\ s_k(t) \end{bmatrix} * \begin{bmatrix} m_i(t^*) \\ m_k(t^*) \end{bmatrix} * \begin{bmatrix} c_i(\tau) \\ c_k(\tau) \end{bmatrix} + \begin{bmatrix} p_i(\delta) \\ p_k(\delta) \end{bmatrix}$$

$$\begin{bmatrix} p_i(t+1) \\ s_k(t+1) \end{bmatrix} = \left(\begin{bmatrix} \tilde{Q}_{pp} & \tilde{Q}_{ps} \\ \tilde{Q}_{sp} & \tilde{Q}_{ss} \end{bmatrix} + \begin{bmatrix} R_{pp}(\delta) & R_{ps}(\delta) \\ R_{sp}(\delta) & R_{ss}(\delta) \end{bmatrix} \right) \begin{bmatrix} p_i(t) \\ s_k(t) \end{bmatrix} * \begin{bmatrix} m_i(t^*) \\ m_k(t^*) \end{bmatrix} * \begin{bmatrix} c_i(\tau) \\ c_k(\tau) \end{bmatrix} + \begin{bmatrix} r_i(\delta) \\ r_k(\delta) \end{bmatrix}$$

Dynamic pairwise effects imposed on the composite system by Q are proportional to the "health" of the "transmitting" system component. Specifically:

$$p_i(t+1) = ((p_i(t) + \sum_{j \neq i} q_{ji} p_j(t) p_i(t)) m_i(t)) env(t)$$

Since many of these variables stem from distributions, it is envisioned that a future simulation can be overlaid on the model and run thousands of times to capture the output statistics, which can then be analyzed. We illustrate these results below in scenario 5.

Model's Algorithm

The algorithm for the model in its current state is provided in step-by-step detail in section 3 of the appendix.

Model's Variables and *Q* Matrix

Although our goal for this model is to include fifteen physical variables and fifteen service variables that capture most of the key aspects of Iraq's infrastructure and the forces for security and combat (see the master list in section 4 of the appendix), in this report we limit our model to six physical and eight service variables selected and modified from our master list.

The values of the variables are derived from reports to Congress from 2003 to 2008, which we downloaded from the Internet and analyzed to extract the data. Many of the data elements were probability distributions, and we calculated the statistics to include means and standard deviations. In this version of the model, we used the means and then normalized them to values between 0 and 1.

The *Q* matrix is a key element of the model. Experts must provide the values of the interactive effects of layers of the data. These interactions are essential to the model, as they show the net effects of the shocks they propagate throughout the other layers of the model.

Illustrative Examples

We built and ran five scenarios in which we allowed a shock or multiple shocks to affect the dynamic system. The descriptions below provide only a summary. A more detailed description, with both inputs to and outputs from the model (including graphical output), is provided in section 5 of the appendix.

Scenario 1

In this example, we consider only three physical and three service layers: "electrical power" and "provide hours of power," "Iraqi police" and "provide local security," and "terrorist activity" and "weekly attacks." We watch the system dynamics operate until a shock hits the system directly at time period 6. In this case, car bombs are directed at police targets. This shock effect lowers the percentage levels of the physical condition of the police and their ability to provide local security directly, as we would expect. This outcome is reflected in the tables (see section 5 of the appendix) showing a reduction over time of the police physical condition to less than 20 percent and provision of local security to less than 5 percent. The model shows the other effects as well: it predicts that the electrical power physical condition and the provision of power are diminished by more than 10 percentage points and that the number of terrorist attacks increases by more than 20 percentage points. Analysis of these factors suggests that we need to monitor the electrical power system in Iraq and concentrate additional efforts to deter terrorist activities. If we consider options, we can measure their impact on the system to try to restore the system as quickly as possible and even improve it.

Scenario 2

In this example, we consider only three physical and three service layers: "economy" and "unemployment rate," "Iraqi police" and "provide local security," and "terrorist activity" and "destabilize government through weekly attacks." We watch the system dynamics operate until a shock hits the system directly at time period 6, and here again, car bombs are directed at police targets. This shock effect lowers the percentage levels of the police physical condition and their ability to provide local security directly, as we would expect. This outcome is reflected in the tables (see section 5 of the appendix), which show a reduction of the police physical condition to less than 20 percent and provision of local security to less than 5 percent. The model shows the other effects as well: it predicts that the economy is decreased by about 10 percent and provision of jobs by more than 15 percent and that the number of terrorist attacks increases more than 18 percent. Analysis of these factors suggests that we need to monitor the economic system in Iraq and concentrate additional efforts to deter terrorist activities. If we consider options, we can measure their impact on the system to try to restore the system as quickly as possible and even improve it.

Scenario 3

In this example, we consider only four physical and four service layers: "U.S. military" and "casualty rate," "Iraqi police" and "provide local security," "insurgents" and "destabilize the government," and "civil war" and "discontent." We watch the system dynamics operate until a shock hits the system directly at time period 6. Here again, car bombs are directed at police targets. This shock effect lowers the percentage levels of the police physical condition and their ability to provide local security directly, as we would expect. This outcome is reflected in the illustrations of values (see section 5 of the appendix) showing a reduction of police effectiveness to less than 45 percent and provision of local security to less than 52.5 percent. The model shows the other effects as well: it predicts that U.S. military effectiveness decreases by about 17 percent and casualties increase by 150 percent. The insurgency, which becomes the object of all Coalition efforts, is temporarily decreased 72 percent and destabilization by only 10 percent. The civil war increases by 4 percent while discontent increases by 30 percent. Analysis of these factors suggests that we need to increase our efforts against the insurgents in order to stop insurgent activities and maintain our level of effectiveness in Iraq. We should also concentrate additional efforts in other areas to curb the increase in the population's discontent. If we consider options, we can measure their impact on the system to try to restore the system as quickly as possible and even improve it.

Scenario 4

In this example, we consider only four physical and four service layers: "U.S. military" and "casualty rate," "Iraqi military" and "provide security," "insurgents" and "destabilize the government," and "civil war" and "discontent." We watch the system dynamics operate until a shock hits the system directly at time period 6. In this case, the U.S. military withdraws substantial troops, and the Iraqi military gains minor improvement in overall effectiveness. This shock effect lowers the percentage levels of the effectiveness of the U.S. military and increases the casualty rate. The Iraqi military remains

93 percent effective, and its provision of security is at 85 percent. Both variables show slight decreases. Insurgents and their ability to create instability are both decreased by these shocks, and the civil war and discontent levels both increase. We should recommend not having any rapid withdrawal of U.S. troops until we can do so without causing any increase in casualties.

Scenario 5: Stochastic Simulation

Inputs and Outputs:

In this model, we allowed the state conditions of the variables to be uniform distributions with the means as the values in scenario 4. We also allowed the shock multipliers to be uniform distributions with the means as the values in scenario 4. We captured the end state as distributions using a thousand runs of the simulated model from scenario 4.

The simulated outputs are provided in section 5 of the appendix. In each case, the expected value or mean is established, but a probability distribution is shown for all possible other output values.

Analysis:

The model results show the possible range of values and the probabilities of obtaining those values. Sensitivity analysis shows some typical and atypical results. The variability in the lowering of U.S. military effectiveness is a function of the force and its drawdown; the effect is typical. The same is true for the variable for the Iraqi military. The variability in the insurgency is atypical and is a function of the insurgency, but it is also 27.4 percent owing to the Iraqi military and 16.6 percent to civil war activities. The variability in the U.S. casualty rate is affected by the civil war and the effectiveness of the Iraqi military.

Conclusions and Recommendation

The INFORM Iraq modeling effort should continue to be developed as a planning tool to help decision makers make informed decisions about actions taken relative to Iraq. The model, in its infant stages, has been shown to be capable of capturing and explaining the dynamics of events occurring in Iraq and their effects on other components in Iraq. The larger model will incorporate more infrastructure variables, since rebuilding is critical to the achievement of peace and stability in Iraq.

Notes

1. A three-ring view of the Iraq situation was initially proposed by David Kilcullen, who saw terrorism, insurgency, and sectarian conflict as overlapping security problems in the conflict. See David Kilcullen, "A Framework for Thinking About Iraq Strategy," *Small Wars Journal*, January 12, 2007, http://smallwarsjournal.com/blog/2007/01/a-framework-for-thinking-about.
2. Frank R. Giordano, Maurice D. Weir, and William P. Fox, *A First Course in Mathematical Modeling*, 3rd ed. (Pacific Grove, CA: Brooks-Cole Publishers, 2003).
3. Patrick J. Driscoll and Niki Goerger, "Stochastic Systems Modeling of Infrastructure Resiliency," presented at the 48th Annual Conference of Operational Research Society, Bath, England, September 2006.

SHAPING PERCEPTIONS AND MILITARY STRATEGY

13
Strategic Communications

Robert Reilly

In 2003, President Bush announced Operation Iraqi Freedom as the centerpiece of an effort to transform the Middle East from authoritarian to democratic rule. This attempted transformation was part of a larger strategy to win the "war of ideas" against a malignant Islamist ideology that animated the September 2001 terrorist attacks on the United States and threatened to overtake the entire Muslim world. As the White House's "National Strategy for Combating Terrorism" stated, "In the long run, winning the War on Terror means winning the battle of ideas."[1] If ever an ambitious objective needed a communications strategy to help implement it, this was it.

Iraq was considered the key in the strategy insofar as its development into a decent, democratic, rule-of-law constitutional order would, over time, transform the entire Middle East, the locus of terrorist ideology, by showing that there is a way other than the typical Arab tyranny. The problem with this scenario was that not everyone in the Middle East wished to be transformed. In fact, in terms of the states in the region, not one did. In other words, it was in no one's interest in the Middle East that the United States should succeed in the terms in which it was describing success.

How could the United States prevail in such an environment, and what kind of communications strategy would it need to do so? As far as the war against Iraq was concerned, it clearly needed a regional communications strategy aimed at Iraq's neighbors and the broader Middle East, as well as a strategy to communicate with the Iraqis before, during, and after the invasion.

What follows is an analysis of the regional and local communications strategies of the United States, or the lack thereof, in the Iraq conflict from the months immediately prior to the 2003 invasion to the present. It attempts to draw some general lessons concerning the interaction of the interstate, insurgency, and civil war components of the Iraq conflict that may be pertinent for future strategic communications efforts.

Of course, it should be noted that a communications strategy can only be as good as the larger strategy it supports. It cannot make up for policy errors. For example, it was certainly effective to inform Iraqi military conscripts before the invasion that they were just as much victims of Saddam's regime as the Iraqi people and that if they stayed in garrison and did not fight, the United States would take care of them. However, no amount of communications could remedy the damage done when the United States then failed to do so and disbanded the Iraqi Army without making any provisions for its soldiers.[2] Likewise, when an announced purpose of Operation Iraqi Freedom was the liberation of Iraq, strategic communications could not by itself solve the problems created when U.S. forces later occupied the country.

Regional Communications Strategy

The United States needed to communicate its policy to the Middle East at a time when 24/7 Arab satellite television stations, whose broadcasts had become the favorite means for obtaining information in the region, had revolutionized the communications environment. The influence of Al Jazeera and certain other Arabic-language satellite television stations throughout the Middle East can hardly be overstated. Al Jazeera in particular had established itself as the default channel for strategic communication pronouncements by al Qaeda's top leadership.

The United States lacked any similar facility in the region to counter this influence. The U.S. Broadcasting Board of Governors (BBG) launched an Arabic TV channel, Alhurra, in 2004 with a $62 million budget, but it began far too late to influence events in the immediate aftermath of Operation Iraqi Freedom. Moreover, in the still-influential radio broadcast arena, the BBG had eviscerated its capabilities by shutting down the twelve-hour, content-rich Arabic service of the Voice of America (VOA) in 2002 in favor of a youth pop-music station, Radio Sawa. The VOA had an explicit charter-driven obligation to present and explain U.S. policy; Radio Sawa did not. In the same spirit, in 2003, the State Department launched an Arabic-language youth lifestyle magazine, *Hi International*, which offered Arab males advice on such burning issues as exfoliation (publication was suspended in 2005).[3] In short, the United States had not yet developed adequate means to communicate with the region's people, and the means it did employ lacked serious content.

One could argue that even with better content, efforts at winning the Arabs' hearts and minds for the United States would not necessarily translate into success for Arab democratic allies because there was too much to overcome historically in terms of regional prejudices and misconceptions vis-à-vis the United States. In other words, many Arabs were only too willing to dismiss peremptorily any message from the United States as an expression of American self-interest rather than accept it as an appeal to moral principles. While the United States should have sought to explain itself—it had to do so, particularly in a time of war—the ultimate vindication of American policy in the region would come only with the success of Arab democrats. For the time being, it may have been more effective for Arabs to speak to Arabs about the merits of democracy and against terrorism. Their success must come first in the sense that a favorable disposition toward democracy within Arab countries is more important in achieving the strategic goal than is developing their good opinion of the United States.

Also, Arab-to-Arab communication was particularly important in delegitimizing radical Islamist ideology. Muslim moral and theological authorities are far more effective in performing this task, for obvious reasons. Also, this effort did not need to be undertaken in an overtly polemical way; it could instead be dramatized, for example, through effective TV programs.

Indeed, if the United States wished to be successful in "translating" its message to the cultural landscape of the Arab-Muslim world, perhaps it should have looked to some successful regional examples of such programming for guidance, such as the Saudi television program *Experiences in the Name of Jihad: Deception*. In this prime-time television program airing on the main state TV channel in Saudi Arabia after the evening news, real-life former jihadists and Islamic extremists repent and recount their personal narratives of their seduction into Islamic extremism by radical sheikhs, their training camp experiences, and the targeting of Saudi Arabia by the extremist movement.

Also from Saudi Arabia came the long-running and popular Ramadan show *Tash ma Tash* ("Whatever Comes, Comes"). Taking on polemical modern issues facing Saudi society, one episode dealt with Islamic extremism and went so far as to ridicule Islamic extremists, portraying them as incompetent morons. The Egyptian series *The Beautiful Virgins* ran during Ramadan and was written by a confessed former member of al Qaeda. It detailed a young Saudi male's struggle over whose version of Islam he should follow—that of a militant sheikh or that of a moderate one.

Unfortunately, before 2003 or afterward, there was no concerted U.S. effort to develop and support indigenous media efforts in the Middle East that would generally have helped shape attitudes toward democracy and against terrorism. Although there were knowledgeable people in the U.S. government who recognized the need to do this work, they had no institution from which to do it. Another egregious omission was the lack of anticipation by the U.S. government of how Iraq's neighbors would attempt to influence events within Iraq after liberation. Because its announced goals in Iraq were inimical to the long-term interests of Syria and Iran, the United States should have expected attempts by these countries to undermine the project in Iraq and been prepared to counter them. What would a democratic, constitutional order in Iraq mean for these neighbors? For Baathist Syria, it would probably mean the regime's ultimate demise. The proximity of a successful Iraq would, if only by force of its example, undermine the only remaining Baathist regime and its national socialist ideology. A similar fate is possible in Iran but at a more theological level. Once the Shia in Iraq were free to practice their faith, the Iranians would face a shift of the theological center of gravity from Qum back to Najaf and Karbala, where Grand Ayatollah Ali al-Sistani and his quietist version of Shiism might hold sway. The heterodox theocratic doctrine of Ayatollah Ruhollah Khomeini embodied in the current Iranian regime would then be undermined.

There seems to have been no strategy to counter Syria's and Iran's gross interference in Iraq beyond whatever ephemeral effects the "shock and awe" campaign might have had on these state sponsors of terrorism. When asked to explain the reason for this vacuum, Lt. Gen. Ricardo Sanchez, U.S. Army (Ret.), responded with the phrase "significant neglect."[4] As a consequence, the interference was cost free for Syria and Iran. It encouraged them to continue.

While Syria allowed the pro–al Qaeda Al-Zawra television station to operate from its territory, its interference came primarily from serving as a safe haven for senior Baathists and as a pipeline for jihadi terrorists. To further its political ambitions, Iran, meanwhile, had prepared to play a major media role in Iraq. Saddam Hussein had built huge transmitters to jam Iranian terrestrial TV stations that were powerful enough to reach Baghdad from inside the Iranian border. With Hussein's removal, Iranian TV was no longer blocked. Two 24/7 TV stations blanketed Iraq before the United States had any TV transmissions in place and well before the Iraqi government was able to communicate with its own people. Iran even had the temerity to move radio transmitters inside Iraq's borders to improve its broadcast capabilities.[5]

It can be argued that the U.S. failure to take a more vocal stance against Iranian interference in Iraq from the outset, as well as its failure to take effective measures to control the Iran-Iraq border, was a major contributing factor both to the developing insurgency and to the Sunni sense of beleaguerment at the hands of increasingly well-armed Shia in the Iraqi Army and police forces as well as the private militias. The United States did not seem to recognize the intensive Iranian propaganda and political warfare activities in Iraq for the threat they were, nor did they effectively counter them.

Local Communications Strategy

The media environment in Iraq was radically changed by the overthrow of Saddam Hussein. Under the Baathist regime, satellite TV dishes were forbidden, and possessing a satellite telephone was a capital crime. Within weeks of the invasion, Iraq was flooded with cheap Chinese satellite dishes; they sprouted on the rooftops of Baghdad like mushrooms. An information-starved society was now inundated with scores of Arabic, Farsi, and other channels, most of which, if not all, were hostile to the United States.

In this atmosphere, one would have expected U.S. and Coalition forces to make a major communications effort to educate the people of Iraq concerning the goals of Coalition forces and the transition to democratic rule. However, the United States seemed to have had no real outreach plan. The Department of Defense (DOD) attempted to set up an Iraqi Media Network (IMN) that would have been able to reach the Iraqi public with such programming, but it ran into insurmountable problems.

One of them was indecision within DOD itself as to whether there should even be such an effort. When the IMN leadership presented its plan to the special assistant to the secretary of defense, Larry Di Rita, he explained that no such endeavor would be undertaken. Rather, the Iraqis could start whatever media they wished. The IMN leader argued, unsuccessfully, that the "let a hundred flowers bloom" approach would only produce a sectarian and highly partisan media that would have a fissiparous effect on the Iraqi population.[6] Other than expatriates, Iraqis had zero experience with free media and journalistic standards. The Coalition needed to offer a standard, on some kind of public broadcasting basis, that would show the way. Relatively early in the occupation, a decision was made (to quote a DOD official at the time) not to "try to structure the information environment" in the country.[7] The results were predictable.

However, Lt. Gen. Jay Garner, U.S. Army (Ret.), the head of the Office for Reconstruction and Humanitarian Assistance, embraced the ambitious vision of IMN. Garner approached the National Security Council and the Office of Management and Budget to obtain funds for it. The modest start-up money he received allowed for a contract with Science Applications International Corporation (SAIC) to begin recruiting Iraqi expatriate journalists. However, in less than two months, the small IMN team was deployed to Kuwait to wait for the invasion.

IMN's concept of success was proffered by way of analogy to North Korea. What if the people of North Korea, who live in a totally controlled information environment, turned on their TVs and radios one morning and saw and heard South Korean media? The effect would be revolutionary. (This kind of thing had been seen in slow motion from the effect of the terrestrial leakage of West German TV broadcasts into East Germany.) If IMN could be ready to do something like that in Iraq, also a state with totalitarian media control, it could galvanize the population and influence it in the right direction.

The problem, of course, was that there was no equivalent of the South Korean media in the Arab world to draw upon; rather, IMN faced the opposite, as exemplified by Al Jazeera. Therefore, IMN would have to start from scratch to create programming not otherwise available in the Arab world that would also specifically address Iraqi concerns. Such a project would take several years of planning and a large budget. It would require recruiting the best expatriate Iraqi artistic and journalistic talent. Recruitment would require multiyear contracts. However, IMN was reduced to offering three- to six-month contracts to established figures who did not consider such offers serious.

The IMN project began too late (January 2003) and lacked adequate resources. Without even considering the costs of infrastructure and security, IMN would have required at least $150 million per annum for several years to have a reasonable chance of success on TV and radio and in print. It started with several million dollars and failed. When the media vacuum in Iraq became too obvious to ignore, a large contract for $96 million to run and expand IMN was given to the Harris Corporation/Lebanese Broadcasting Corporation (LBC)/Al Fawares group. It too failed.

Al-Iraqiya, the TV station begun by IMN, turned into another Arab state media organ, except this time it was a strongly Shia one that did not hesitate to broadcast insults about the first three caliphs, material sure to inflame the Sunni population. Meanwhile, the "let a hundred flowers bloom" strategy had performed as predicted, as other start-up Iraqi media tore away at the remaining fabric of Iraqi society for the sake of tribe, party, ethnicity, or religion.

If this squandered opportunity had been successfully pursued, it could have had a significant impact on the Iraqi population and, by satellite, the peoples of the Middle East. It might also have helped counter the pressures that led Iraq to the brink of civil war after the bombing of the al-Askari Shrine (Golden Mosque) in February 2006. IMN fell short of its initial goals for various reasons, the most striking of which was that it was not part of a consistently held communications strategy.

It is more than ironic that the one part of IMN that came closest to fulfilling initial expectations was the part that was abandoned. The newspaper *Sumer*, named to appeal to pride in Iraq's pre-Islamic past as the cradle of civilization, was a first-class journalistic enterprise designed to attract the intelligentsia of Iraq to the democratic transition. *Sumer* represented the face of a new Iraq, with Arab, Kurdish, Chaldean, Assyrian, Turkoman, Christian, and Jewish contributors. (It is the only Arab paper ever to have had regular Israeli contributors—namely, Samir Naqqash and Sasson Somekh, both Jews of Iraqi origin.) Nevertheless, the Coalition Provisional Authority (CPA) shut it down. Another paper, *al-Sabah*, had been started mostly with indigenous Iraqi talent, and, despite its amateurish cast, it was favored by the CPA. While the superior quality of *Sumer* was beyond dispute, the CPA communications chief told the IMN head that Iraq did not need its equivalent of the *Wall Street Journal* at the time; it only needed a broadsheet to announce weapons turn-in checkpoints.[8]

The gradual emergence of a dangerous insurgency in Iraq after 2004 reflected a convergence of interests among former regime elements, the Sunnis (particularly the powerful tribes in the Sunni Triangle), and the largely foreign fighters who made up what came to be called al Qaeda in Iraq (AQI). The United States was slow to recognize this development and failed to devise an effective strategy to counter it, including a strategic communications effort designed to drive wedges in between these groups.

However, al-Iraqiya did develop some effective programming to delegitimize the al Qaeda terrorists on the one hand and the intransigent Baathist elements on the other, the two of which together constituted the core of the insurgency. *Terrorism in the Hands of Justice* became the most popular TV program on al-Iraqiya. In it, captured terrorists are interviewed and exposed as venal. It showed that the government could act against the terrorists and win. The second most watched program was "Light" (or "Legacy of Evil"), produced by the Iraq Memory Foundation (with support from DOD and the State Department), which concentrates on filming and archiving people's stories about the atrocities of the Hussein era and the structures of the government and the party that committed them. Many Iraqis only know their own stories and not the pervasive nature of Hussein's crimes against all Iraqis.[9] This program helped support the ideas behind constitutional structures that would prevent the recurrence of such crimes, further discredited the Baathist revanchists, fostered reconciliation, and put the trials of Hussein and others into a larger context. As an indication of its importance, Prime Minister Nouri al-Maliki ordered al-Iraqiya to play "Light" every day during Ramadan.

It should also be noted that while the U.S. satellite TV station, Alhurra, failed to develop much of an audience in the broader Middle East, its specially fashioned Iraqi programming stream has succeeded in winning a significant Iraqi audience. It has come to be considered, despite recent controversy, the only source of TV information in Iraq that is not partisan or sectarian. It has belatedly achieved what IMN failed to accomplish with al-Iraqiya in this respect.

The estrangement between Anbari Sunnis and al Qaeda operatives over the course of 2007 seems to have been owed most to the mistakes of al Qaeda—notably, its brutality toward Iraqis who got in its way—rather than to positive U.S. actions or communications. AQI's grotesque torture and execution videos not only terrify; they repel. Nevertheless, a growing awareness of what needed to be done was clearly reflected in the U.S. Army's new field manual, *Counterinsurgency* (December 2006), which encouraged U.S. forces to "exploit inconsistencies in the insurgents' message as well as their excessive use of force or intimidation."[10] In any case, the United States has been increasingly successful in taking advantage of this situation to solidify a de facto alliance with the Sunni tribes against al Qaeda and to hinder and discredit al Qaeda–inspired terrorist activity generally. Al Qaeda also seems to have realized (as reflected in Ayman al-Zawahiri's widely publicized correspondence with Abu Musab al-Zarqawi) that its strategy of fomenting civil war in Iraq was leading to its losing Iraq. Iraqis were increasingly repelled by al Qaeda's Muslim-on-Muslim violence and its extreme *takfiri* ideology that demonizes anyone who does not agree with it.

The counterinsurgency strategy pursued by Gen. David Petraeus from early 2007 had a significant local communications component. Recognizing the political and symbolic importance of Baghdad, it focused on visibly restoring order and security to the capital. It started by increasing the visible presence of American troops and their Iraqi counterparts in small operating bases close to the local population. Regular interactions with this population not only significantly facilitated allied intelligence on insurgent activities but also provided important psychological reassurance and a new spirit of cooperation with American forces in restoring order and basic services throughout Baghdad and beyond.

Despite its lack of a strategic communications strategy, the United States might still succeed in Iraq through what may be called the diplomacy of the deed. What U.S. forces have done in Iraq has been far more persuasive than what the United States has said. Of course, deeds always matter, but these two elements—words and deeds—should have been supporting and reinforcing each other from the beginning. The question remains: how much higher has the price been because they were not? It also remains to be seen whether the United States can win the larger war of ideas that almost every national strategy document states is the sine qua non of victory in the war against terrorism. The United States continues to pay the price for the 1999 dismantlement of the U.S. Information Agency (USIA), from which it used to be able to fight wars of ideas.

When this mission belonged to USIA at the height of the Cold War, the agency had some ten thousand employees (including foreign nationals) and a $1 billion budget. After the end of the Cold War, USIA's functions were dispersed to the State Department and the Broadcasting Board of Governors. Within the State Department, public diplomacy functions were further dispersed to regional and other bureaus, making coordination and control by the new Under Secretary for Public Diplomacy problematic. As a consequence, no single government institution has sole responsibility for the war of ideas. Thus, without a central U.S. government organization responsible for it, policy, personnel, and budget cannot be deployed coherently and over an extended period of time to implement a multifaceted communications strategy.

It may be time to consider the re-creation of an institution whose primary responsibility is to win the war of ideas, that is, to articulate and promulgate American ideals and institutions to the world and to undermine the enemy's ideology by attacking its moral legitimacy. A new communications agency could maintain a strategic focus on aiding Muslim allies and moderates and not get lost in daily "spin" control. It should facilitate the creation and reinforcement of an antitotalitarian social and intellectual network throughout the Islamic world.

Such an organization should be independent of the State Department, which may be inclined to downplay differences for the sake of overall relations with a particular state or group of states. It should have the funds to promote the free exchange of ideas in the Islamic world and elsewhere and to support those who also find the radical Islamist ideology repugnant.

There could be grant mechanisms within this new agency, similar to the National Endowment for Democracy but far better endowed, that would provide concrete support to Islamic liberals and moderates and to others in vital regions of the world. The new agency should have the authority and funds to provide equipment and operating funds to responsible broadcast and print journalists in Muslim societies to initiate news and features broadcasts via, for example, FM transmitters and to start up newspapers or journals with the necessary print equipment.

The organization needs to be staffed by people who know substantively what the war of ideas is about and have the regional expertise to operate across the Muslim world and in other vital regions. They should have at their disposal all non-military U.S. government radio and TV broadcasting, as well as Internet access and print presses for books, magazines, and newspapers, to tell the U.S. side of the story.

When the United States took the war of ideas seriously in past conflicts, it was able to prevail. As late as it may be in this new war, it is not too late to take it seriously and begin the work to win it.

Notes

1. White House, "The National Strategy for Combating Terrorism," 2006, http://georgewbush-whitehouse.archives.gov/nsc/nsct/2006/.
2. Remarks by Gen. Anthony Zinni (Ret.), National Defense University, Washington, DC, May 8, 2008.
3. "Sharp-Dressed Men," *Hi International*, April 2005.
4. Response to the author's question at the Military Reporters and Editors' Conference, Crystal City, Virginia, October 12, 2007.
5. Constantine C. Menges, "Iran's Covert Actions in Iraq," Hudson Institute, April 14, 2004, http://www.hudson.org/index.cfm?fuseaction=publication_details&id=3280: "Iran has spent heavily seeking to dominate radio and television broadcasting in Iraq. A survey by Radio Free Europe/Radio Liberty found that Iran is the source of 33 of 59 AM broadcasts and of 41 of 63 AM/FM/TV broadcasts heard in Iraq. In comparison, the U.S.-supported Iraq Media Network has a total of one television station, two radio stations, and one newspaper." See also Menges's "Iranian Direct and Indirect Efforts to Infiltrate Iraq," Hudson Institute, April, 29, 2004, http://www.hudson.org/index.cfm?fuseaction=publication_details&id=3295.
6. Author's conversation with Lawrence Di Rita, Kuwait, April 2003, http://www.defense.gov/releases/release.aspx?releaseid=8956.
7. Carnes Lord, unpublished paper.
8. Remarks by Dan Senor and John Buck, acting CPA head of communications, to the author, Republican Palace, Baghdad, Iraq, June 11, 2003.
9. Letter from Iraqi Media Network, al-Iraqiya TV, October 5, 2005, to Iraq Memory Foundation: "According to the surveys and statistics conducted by the Study and Research Center in Iraqi Media Network every two months, during August and September 2005 your program Iraqi Testimonies prized [sic] as the second most popular show as selected by the viewers after the program 'Terror in the Grip of Justice'."
10. Department of the Army, *Field Manual 3-24: Counterinsurgency* (Washington, DC: Department of the Army, December 2006), 1–18, http://www.usgcoin.org/library/doctrine/COIN-FM3-24.pdf.

14
Strategic Dimensions of the Iraq Conflict

John Arquilla and Douglas A. Borer

The subtle interplay of traditional interstate conflict, insurgency, and civil war in Iraq has been perhaps most evident in the realm of military strategy, a cross-cutting category of thought that has suffused and affected virtually every area of U.S. endeavor in that country. At this late stage of the U.S. intervention in Iraq—more than seven years on from the invasion—there is probably no more urgent task than to craft a well-hedged endgame strategy capable of performing effectively at each of the three levels of war. This chapter analyzes the military strategies employed over the past years, reviews the results achieved, and considers the various courses of action (COAs) that might guide U.S. forces in the next—hopefully last—phase of the war.

The basic pattern to date has been for the U.S. military to respond slowly to strategic shifts in the conflict. The character of the war has varied, with conventional operations predominating at the outset, then giving rise to an insurgency, and then, when the focus finally shifted to counterinsurgency, developing into an incipient civil war. The challenge now is to anticipate what might come next and act early to shape the situation rather than simply react in the wake of unfolding events. Attentiveness to and understanding of the three levels of conflict should help this analysis. At the same time, this exercise may also improve our understanding of what has already transpired, providing both assistance now and a helpful framework to rely upon when contemplating or coping with the consequences of future interventions.

Phase 1: The March up Mesopotamia

The initial phase of operations in Iraq, which ran roughly from March through July 2003, was dominated by a conventional mechanized offensive and its immediate aftermath. Coalition forces on the ground, benefiting from air and naval mastery, dealt swiftly with light Iraqi resistance. Indeed, military historian John Keegan sees the absence of fighting during this phase as "a mystery."[1] The Iraqis appear to have been poised to "melt away," and they moved swiftly to an insurgent strategy, avoiding the severe punishment they would have suffered in conventional engagements while at the same time being able to land some irregular counterblows. There is some evidence that beyond his prewar formation of the irregular forces—whose initial efforts to slow the invasion foreshadowed unconventional things to come—Saddam Hussein himself developed a defensive strategy aimed at sparking an insurgency.[2]

But there were other, non-regime-related actors among the Sunni in Iraq who had interests in shifting to such an approach, and some in the Shia community as well were eager to begin flexing their muscles when events presented a great opportunity for asserting themselves and shaping their country's future. Then there were some groups outside Iraq, including al Qaeda and its network of affiliates, that intended to seize the opportunity to strike at the U.S.-led occupation of a Muslim land.[3]

Added to all this opposition and hostility was the Coalition's confused and slow-moving response to the rioting and civil unrest that soon followed Saddam Hussein's fall from power.[4] This period saw enough suffering in the country both to antagonize Iraqis and to energize foreign fighters. In short, the explosive materials for launching an insurgency were largely in place, but the fuse was lit by the inability of Coalition forces to impose and sustain order and return life in Iraq to some semblance of normalcy. It was under such circumstances that insurgent violence soon flared up. In retrospect, it is clear that initial U.S. responses that sought to diminish the gravity of the situation—as in Secretary of Defense Donald Rumsfeld's comment about the unrest that "freedom is messy"—or to downplay American responsibility only fanned the flames of insurgency.

Phase 2: From Conventional War to Insurgency

Given the various sources of recruitment and support for fighters who would resist the occupation—along with al Qaeda's opportunism and Sunni discontent—it is unsurprising that a vigorous insurgency erupted in the late summer of 2003. This phase of the conflict commenced with a series of near-simultaneous strikes against power and water infrastructure, coupled with attacks against nongovernmental organizations. These "stuns of August" culminated in the bombing of the United Nations (UN) headquarters in Baghdad and the death of the UN representative in Iraq, Sergio Vieira de Mello, a clear blow designed to drive humanitarian civil society actors out of Iraq. Thus the fundamental character of the conflict in Iraq had shifted from one of conventional war to insurgency, with Coalition forces responding only slowly to this profound change.[5]

By 2004, the overall strategic initiative in Iraq had passed to the insurgents,[6] despite two American tactical offensives—one in the spring and another in the fall—in the city of Fallujah. These attacks, looking almost as conventional as the city fighting in Hue during the Vietnam War, did little to stop the overall insurgency, which only grew in intensity. This upsurge happened despite the claim of a Marine general that the fighting in Fallujah would "break the back" of the insurgency.[7] Throughout the rest of Iraq, U.S. forces were also slow to grasp the nuances of counterinsurgency-style operations. Areas were subjected to "sweeps"—so redolent of Vietnam-era notions—both in urban areas and rural border zones. American troops, laagered in for the most part on about three dozen large forward operating bases (FOBs), were necessarily slow to reach sites that had been attacked, predictable in their patrolling movements and of little deterrent value.[8]

For al Qaeda in Iraq (AQI), meanwhile, this theater of operations had become a fruitful "economy of force" campaign. While its own fighters made up a small fraction (perhaps just 5 percent) of the resistance forces, it had still caused great disruption and imposed huge operating costs on the Coalition.[9] Despite the inherent edge the insurgents enjoyed in this sort of strategic interaction, there was some dissent and a growing desire to expand the scale of operations. At this point Abu Musab al-Zarqawi came to the fore, in particular with his direct challenge to the authority of al Qaeda's leadership. He believed that insurgency alone would not suffice to defeat the Coalition, so he lobbied hard for adding the element of civil war to the strategic mix.

Zarqawi made his case in a letter purportedly sent to al Qaeda's senior leadership in April 2004, arguing that the Shia of Iraq, by negotiating a relatively peaceful modus vivendi with the government and the occupiers, had betrayed their faith.[10] Initially, Osama bin Laden and his second-in-command, Ayman al-Zawahiri, were reluctant to embrace the notion of a shift from insurgency to civil war, in part because of bin Laden's reluctance to antagonize Shia communities in general and Iran in particular.

But Zarqawi proved impossible to control from a distance, and he soon began freelancing acts of sectarian violence anyway, which, it turned out, *did* create the kind of chaos that al Qaeda sought. In December 2004, bin Laden formally—perhaps grudgingly—embraced Zarqawi's leadership in Iraq and associated al Qaeda with a strategic shift in the campaign, aimed at moving from insurgency to a Sunni-Shia civil war.[11] In February 2006, AQI bombed the al-Askari Shrine (Golden Mosque) in Samarra, one of Shia Islam's most holy sites, a signature act of violence that would spark the large-scale sectarian strife that followed.

Phase 3: Toward Full-blown Civil War

For the next two years—roughly from March 2005 until March 2007—irregular resistance to foreign military occupation continued, but after the February 2006 bombing of the al-Askari Shrine in Samarra, the principal focus of Sunni insurgent and al Qaeda terrorist energy was on striking at the Shia, who, for their part, staged retaliatory raids and terrorist attacks against the Sunni. For the most part, the Shia kept to an uneasy truce with the Americans that had been arranged in 2004 after some hard fighting around the city of Najaf. Thus, in the wake of the Samarra bombing, a civil war began to manifest itself. At its height in 2006 and the first months of 2007, about a hundred Iraqis were dying from the violence each day.[12] By this point, Zarqawi had been killed, but the networked, hydra-headed structure of the Sunni-led insurgency was relatively undamaged by this "counter-leadership" targeting coup—much as the capture of Saddam Hussein in December 2004 had done little to stem the tide of violence. As for the Shia, their own "death squads" began acting in reprisal for Sunni attacks, and the escalatory spiral of revenge attacks became the dominant dynamic.[13]

A further complication arose during this period, raising the specter of interstate involvement in the war. Iran increased its support for the Shia, most likely providing them with training and arms, including such sophisticated items as explosively formed projectiles. This assistance both allowed the Shia to hold their own in the civil war against the Sunnis and to improve their capacity for sustaining an insurgency against American forces and their allies. Against this rising tide of trouble, the Coalition's response was twofold: stepped-up efforts to field more friendly Iraqi troops—a kind of latter-day version of Vietnamization—and military threats against Iran in an effort to tamp down Tehran's support for the Shia.

Both initiatives were effective, but only at the margins. Indigenous forces, while not as professional as other Coalition units, were indeed able to function well with even small amounts of leavening from allies. And threats against Iran, although they ran some risk of igniting the interstate aspect of the conflict again, did appear to encourage more circumspection on Tehran's part. Still, the strategic situation was a stalemate.

Phase 4: The Surge and the Swarm

At this point, in the first half of 2007, a new Coalition strategy emerged, one that can best be summarized by the phrase "outpost and outreach," consisting of both quantitative and qualitative elements. At scores of locations—almost all initially in Baghdad—small, platoon-size allied units were co-located in "hot spots" with similar-size, friendly Iraqi forces. U.S. military leadership felt comfortable in doing so because a surge of reinforcements—roughly thirty thousand combat and support troops in five brigade combat teams—had arrived.[14]

This new quantitative presence in so many places created a coverage network within which response time to violent incidents was sharply reduced compared with that of units still located on large FOBs. Now the insurgents and terrorists had to worry about quick response from any of a number of directions—for example, in such fast-moving operations as Phantom Strike and Iron Harvest—and not the usual slow, predictable movements that they were used to facing.[15] In short, al Qaeda and its affiliates were facing a "defensive swarm." And wherever there were outposts, levels of violence soon dropped sharply.[16]

The shift to an outpost network strategy came at the same time that al Qaeda had made itself vulnerable to Coalition influence operations because it had overreached in Anbar Province. Al Qaeda began consolidating a kind of harsh governance over the Iraqis, claiming it had come to "liberate [them] from American oppression." Al Qaeda thus had sharia Islamic courts up and running under its control, trying and sometimes executing Iraqi defendants.[17] The terrorists also began to demand local brides for foreign fighters and to assert control in ways that soon alienated the Anbaris. In late summer 2006, Al Qaeda's overreaching extended even to the assassination of some sheikhs and other dissenters, including a tribal leader, Sheikh Abdul Sattar Abu Risha,[18] whose murder led to the Anbaris' profound disaffection.[19]

At this moment, the more qualitative outreach aspect of U.S. strategy came to the fore, as numerous small negotiations were undertaken with tribal leaders, encouraging them to switch sides and take up the fight against al Qaeda. In just a few months, the membership of Awakening Councils and Concerned Local Citizens groups willing to take up arms against AQI grew to more than fifty thousand people.[20] But the key point is that the qualitative elements in the outreach were as important as the increased numbers of troops in the surge's success with the Sunni tribes. Instead of simply chasing insurgents and returning to large bases, many of these new forces helped secure the local population and thus broke their connection with the AQI insurgents. This enhanced security situation, combined with al Qaeda's excesses, resulted in growing trust—a critical element in any successful intelligence-gathering process—between the Americans and the Sunnis. Then, as Americans acted on the new intelligence in more precise, discreet, and culturally attuned operational practices, the legitimacy of their presence slowly increased while the collateral damage among civilians decreased.

Indeed, while the increased numbers and a wider distribution of nodes are certainly part of the Anbar success story, the U.S. ground forces' eventual adaptation of a "best practices" approach[21] to counterinsurgency was the key element in the surge. Coupled with the emerging network of local outposts and the swarm-like raids by increasingly well-informed strike forces, this qualitatively superior outreach effort soon succeeded wildly in Anbar, where all twenty-three tribes signed up to fight the terrorists. Soon it was piloted in other parts of the country as well.

Al Qaeda cells, attacked from seemingly every direction, were put on the run by this strategic swarm, and the initiative moved decisively back to the Coalition. Levels of violence dropped by more than half from mid-2007 to mid-2008. In short, things had improved a great deal.[22] The question now is, what strategy should guide the next, and perhaps final, phase of the war? There are at least three principal ways to answer this query.

Endgame Considerations

The main strategic courses of action break down as follows: (1) reduce U.S. forces slowly until most leave at the end of 2010; (2) keep the drawdowns but reinsert "residual" troops into the small outposts that they left in the summer of 2009;[23] and (3) instead of thinking about the future primarily in terms of the quantity of U.S. forces in Iraq, focus intently on the qualitative element of U.S. troops in Iraq. The rationale behind this third approach is that if the right type of U.S. forces, with distinctive skills and capabilities, can be made available in sufficient numbers, then they can be distributed widely as advisers in an expanded outpost network in support of Iraq's rapidly expanding security forces.

We dismiss the notion of simply exiting from Iraq completely at any foreseeable near-term future point, as such a course of action would almost certainly fan the flames of civil war, encourage interstate military intervention—most likely by Turkey in the north and Iran in central and southern Iraq—and spark an insurgency against any effort to provide central governance from Baghdad. In short, a residual force – even if a small one – should remain in Iraq indefinitely.

Each of the three viable courses of action has its merits and its concerns. For example, COA 1 would best deter any sort of return to interstate war. Given an American garrison that stayed in the 50-100,000-troop range, as will likely be the case until late in 2010, neither Turkey nor Iran would be likely to contemplate any sort of serious intervention. Such a continuing presence would no doubt also serve as an effective deterrent to an all-out civil war, as U.S. forces would be able to tamp down such violence quickly. However, as part of COA 1, the ongoing outreach to the Sunni tribes would entail further arming them, thus improving their now-growing capability to wage civil war while at the same time providing a disincentive for bridging the sectarian divide. In addition, without any further efforts to expand the outpost distribution, COA 1 would result in less efficiency in countering a renewed insurgency. With the vast majority of remaining American forces still on large FOBs, it would be possible for al Qaeda and its affiliates over time to reestablish their hold. The present outpost network—already bereft of U.S. forces—would simply lack sufficient response nodes to extirpate them.

COA 2 addresses this distribution deficiency by using more of the remaining U.S. forces in "outpost mode." This approach would ramp up the pressure on the insurgents, ever reducing the range of places in which they might go to ground and regroup. Furthermore, expanding the number of nodes in the outpost network would probably also mitigate the risk of a return to civil strife. Given a great increase—the Coalition could easily double or triple its number of outposts—in the presence of order-keeping forces throughout the country, they could both deter internecine conflict and provide added security to rebuilding projects.

Where COA 2 might be less effective would be at the interstate conflict level. If most of the residual forces were deployed to outposts, then, as drawdowns continued, with U.S. forces being replaced as new Iraqi units stood up, other countries might feel less inhibited when it came to launching short, sharp military actions in Iraq. The Turks would probably feel less at risk in engaging in "hot pursuit" of Kurdish fighters, for example, or striking at Kurdistan Workers' Party (PKK) bases inside Iraq.

COA 3 has in common with COA 2 the idea of expanding the outpost network but differs from both COAs 1 and 2 in its focus on the qualitative aspect of the remaining U.S. forces, using the unique quality and capabilities of specific units to maximize the overall economy of force. COA 3 would require small units that are highly skilled in foreign internal defense, which includes training foreign forces in the best practices of counterinsurgency; have experience in operating in hostile environments with minimal security and the skills and training to rapidly form bonds of trust with their Iraqi counterparts; and are trained to make rapid and accurate assessments of local economic and security needs and are empowered with sufficient resources to meet those needs in a timely fashion.

The benefit of COA 3's "less is more" approach is that, as in COA 2, there would be a sustained training and advising presence locally throughout Iraq, while at the same time there would be a clear signal of the American desire to depart, with the withdrawal of most American troops in 2010. Such a signal might in itself help reduce insurgent recruitment among some

Iraqis whose nationalist sentiments inspire them to fight foreign forces. The downsides of COA 3 would include a greater risk of brief military incursions by Turkey or Iran—a risk shared with COA 2—and, at the margin, a reduced ability to deter or cope with a return to civil war. But just as air power could be used to deal with invading foreign armies, it could also help in heading off or coping with the more massive violence that would accompany a raging civil war.

Concluding Analysis

Each of the first two strategic COAs deals with two of the three levels of conflict very well, but each leaves a strategic "coverage gap." COA 1—as close to staying the course as possible—would not intensify the pressure on insurgents. COA 2 would pursue this strategy but might be less a deterrent of interstate military incursions. Still, this latter concern can be mitigated by good diplomacy, and American air power would remain in position to dissuade others from violating Iraq's territorial sovereignty. With these considerations in mind, COA 2 has the edge on COA 1, as the risk of a return to "insurgent Iraq" is one that should remain a priority concern, given that neither diplomacy nor air power are optimized to confront small, dispersed cells of violent non-state actors.

With regard to the latent threat of interstate military conflict, COAs 2 and 3 stand equal. U.S. air power would still be present to deter or deal with Turkey, Iran, or any others. As to civil war, both COAs would rely on networks of outposts and would thus have the same deterrent effect, although COA 3 would accomplish this objective with fewer residual American troops in country. In terms of counterinsurgency, COA 3's requirement that Special Forces be placed in the lead gives this COA the edge. In light of the patterns of strategic interaction that have emerged over the past seven-plus years in Iraq; the interplay of traditional conflict, insurgency, and civil war; and the options available, our conclusion is that COA 1 is clearly the least acceptable path to pursue. COAs 2 and 3 each have their merits, with COA 2 being more appealing to the risk-averse mind and COA 3 being attractive to those open to the possibility that recent improvements in Iraq were not simply the result of having sent more forces into the country. The intriguing possibilities suggested by these courses of action are analyzed in detail in the chapter 15.

Notes

1. See John Keegan, *The Iraq War* (New York: Alfred A. Knopf, 2004), chapter 1, "A Mysterious War."
2. Loretta Napoleoni, in *Insurgent Iraq: Al Zarqawi and the New Generation* (New York: Seven Stories Press, 2005), 145, describes the network of financiers and arms suppliers that Saddam Hussein developed to support resistance fighters.
3. On the many parties interested in fomenting insurgent activity in Iraq, see Ahmed S. Hashim, *Insurgency and Counter-Insurgency in Iraq* (Ithaca, NY: Cornell University Press, 2006), especially chapter 2, "Origins and Motives of the Insurgency."
4. The key studies critiquing U.S. planning at this stage are Donald P. Wright and Timothy R. Reese, *On Point II: Transition to the New Campaign* (Carlisle, PA: Army War College, 2008); and Nora Bensahel et al., *After Saddam: Prewar Planning and the Occupation of Iraq* (Santa Monica, CA: Rand, 2008).
5. On this point, see Thomas E. Ricks, *Fiasco: The American Military Adventure in Iraq* (New York: Penguin, 2006). In fairness, there were those, Gen. David Petraeus among them, who saw the insurgency clearly early on. But many did not, particularly in the Pentagon, where there was much reluctance even to use the term "insurgency." See George Packer, "The Lesson of Tal Afar," *New Yorker,* April 10, 2006.
6. This position is taken in Hashim, *Insurgency and Counter-Insurgency,* 35–47, where he analyzes the evolution of the insurgency during 2004.
7. The officer in this case was Lt. Gen. John F. Sattler, USMC. See Richard A. Oppel, Jr., and Robert F. Worth, "G.I.'s Open Attack to Take Falluja from Iraq Rebels," *New York Times,* November 8, 2004.
8. This point is also made in Packer, "The Lesson of Tal Afar."
9. See Anthony H. Cordesman's report, "Iraq's Evolving Insurgency and the Risk of Civil War," working draft (Washington, DC: Center for Strategic and International Studies, February 2, 2006), http://www.csis.org/media/csis/pubs/060424_iraq insurgrpt.pdf.
10. This correspondence is described in Fouad Hussein, " The Caravan is Moving: The Second Generation of al Qaeda," *Al Quds al Arabi,* June 2005.
11. Napoleoni, *Insurgent Iraq,* 167.
12. The United Nations Assistance Mission in Iraq conducted the most widely accepted survey of this human carnage. Its *Human Rights Report, 2006* (New York: United Nations, 2007), concluded that more than thirty-five thousand Iraqi civilians had been killed in 2006.
13. On this point, see Ken Silverstein, "Minister of Civil War: Bayan Jabr, Paul Bremer, and the Rise of the Iraqi Death Squads," *Harper's,* August 2006.
14. A good overview of this phase of the war can be found in Jon Lee Anderson, "Letter from Iraq: Inside the Surge," *New Yorker,* November 19, 2007.
15. The Institute for the Study of War provides descriptions of these operations at http://www.understandingwar.org/iraq-project/operations.
16. Andrew Marshall, in "In Badlands South of Baghdad, U.S. Says Surge Working," *Reuters,* November 16, 2006, recounts the sharp drop in violence in the vicinity of the outposts.

17. Al Qaeda's excesses in Anbar are examined in Frederick W. Kagan, "Al Qaeda in Iraq: How to Understand It, How to Defeat It," *Weekly Standard,"* September 10, 2007.
18. "Obituary: Abdul Sattar Abu Risha," *BBC News,* September 13, 2007, http://news.bbc.co.uk/2/hi/6993370.stm.
19. See Joshua Partlow, Ann Scott Tyson, and Robin Wright, "Bomb Kills a Key Ally of U.S.; Sheikh Had Organized Rival Tribes in Anbar to Oppose Extremists," *Washington Post,* September 14, 2007, http://www.washingtonpost.com/wp-dyn/content/article/2007/09/13/AR2007091300490.html.
20. According to Alissa J. Rubin and Stephen Farrell, in "Awakening Councils by Region," *New York Times,* December 22, 2007, the number of friendly Sunni fighters in the Awakening movement had risen to more than seventy thousand near the end of 2007.
21. See Kalev I. Sepp, "Best Practices in Counterinsurgency," *Military Review,* May–June 2005.
22. On this point, see Kimberly Kagan, "How They Did It: Executing the Winning Strategy in Iraq," *Weekly Standard* 13, no. 10 (November 19, 2007).
23. As of the summer of 2008, there were more than a hundred platoon-size outposts in Iraq, most in Baghdad. But well upward of 80 percent of U.S. troops remained on large FOBs. A good unclassified summary of the numbers, disposition, and impact of the outposts can be found in Tim Cocks, "Outposts Help U.S. Troops Quell Violence in Iraq," *Reuters,* February 19, 2008.

CONCLUSIONS

15
Considerations for Leaving Iraq

Heather S. Gregg, Hy S. Rothstein, and John Arquilla

Unfortunately, discussions about the future of U.S. involvement in Iraq have rarely gone beyond how quickly forces can be redeployed home and how deep force reductions can go. In chapter 14, John Arquilla and Douglas A. Borer offer a retrospective view of what the U.S. strategy in Iraq seemed to be from the invasion that started in March 2003 through the relative calm today, which is attributed in large part to the "surge" that began in early 2007. The chapter delves more deeply into the complexities of achieving U.S. political objectives in Iraq and concludes by outlining three alternative military courses of action. Since a fast and deep drawdown has become the center of attention, this concluding chapter begins with this reality and backs into an even more meaningful discussion about how to achieve a positive outcome in Iraq.

We begin by outlining some of the assumptions that should inform the discussion on leaving Iraq, stressing that military action—specifically troop drawdowns—does not constitute a complete strategy for Iraq. The section then builds on discussions from the previous chapters to outline the political, security, economic, and regional conditions that should be in place to achieve stability in Iraq. Second, we balance the three military courses of action described in chapter 14 against a range of conditions necessary for reducing the military footprint without jeopardizing the achievement of U.S. objectives for Iraq. This discussion considers the benefits and risks associated with drawing down U.S. forces without these conditions present, including the implications for the three circles of war: insurgency, civil war, and regional interstate conflict. Finally, we identify potential "shocks" that could significantly alter the course of events in the Middle East and require alternative courses of action.

Assumptions for a Stable Iraq

The first and most important assumption is that a military course of action in and of itself does not constitute a complete strategy. Achieving a positive outcome in Iraq will require the United States to wield and integrate multiple instruments of statecraft. While most Americans and Iraqis support a quick and deep drawdown of U.S. forces, they also want these past years of depleted blood and treasure to produce something good and lasting. Therefore, discussions about a military drawdown require a sober assessment of what must precede such action to avoid a potential calamity. Continued investments are needed to mitigate the risks associated with the departure of U.S. forces; it is too easy to assume that the current relative calm in Iraq is not reversible.

The previous chapters offer important insights about the necessary conditions for creating a stable Iraq. William P. Fox in chapter 12 on indicators of force multipliers (INFORM) modeling and Tarek K. Abdel-Hamid in chapter 10 on system dynamics modeling argue that multiple variables—such as the government, infrastructure, economic development, insurgents, U.S. forces, Iraqi forces, and regional actors—act and react to one another in a nonlinear, multiloop feedback system. Such systems are characterized by a large number of interrelated variables that interact dynamically over time to produce an outcome. The chapter on INFORM modeling proposes conducting an analysis of a total of thirty variables that affect Iraq's stability. While certain variables may have a greater effect than others do, no one variable is solely responsible for success or failure in Iraq. Therefore, it is necessary to consider these variables holistically. Moreover, in chapter 11 on measures of effectiveness Karen Guttieri contends that an overemphasis on U.S. troop fatalities, improvised explosive device (IED) attacks, and troop size has meant the omission of other important variables necessary for measuring stability in Iraq. These other, less measurable variables, which are equally important for lasting success, are detailed here.

Governance

Improved security in Iraq has revealed that Iraqi governance, particularly at the federal level, has not developed at a sufficient pace. In chapter 2 on political development Heather S. Gregg argues that U.S. efforts to democratize Iraq have suffered as a result of Sunni alienation, produced by the Coalition Provisional Authority's policies, and of an unreasonable timetable for political transformation. A stable Iraq in the near term will most likely require reduced expectations for a fully functioning democracy and emphasize a political system that will maintain order and cohesion for the country. This interim political stability should allow for the growth of social capital, civic society, and national identity, all of which are necessary ingredients for a healthy democracy.

Society

Currently, Iraqi society is fractured along tribal, ethnic, and religious lines. As described by Glenn E. Robinson in chapter 1 on Iraqi identity and by Arquilla and Borer in chapter 14 on military strategy, U.S. policy has used these divisions to stabilize certain areas in Iraq, such as drawing on tribal leaders in Anbar Province to drive out al Qaeda in Iraq (AQI) or undermining support for Moqtada al-Sadr within the Shia community. These near-term fixes, however, could be setting the stage for societal disintegration and civil war. For Iraq to remain intact as a state, Iraqi society needs a sense of national identity and purpose (see chapter 2 on political development). Political, economic, security, and informational tools of statecraft need to be better coordinated for this purpose in order for Iraqis to find common ground as Iraqis.

Ethical and Legal Issues

Russell Muirhead, Jr., in chapter 9 on ethics and Christopher M. Ford in chapter 8 on legal issues argue that the United States has an obligation—although not an unconditionally open-ended one—as an occupier to establish a degree of stability in Iraq before ending the occupation. While the international laws that govern war do not have rigorous enforcement mechanisms, allowing the country to return to a state of chaos, including perhaps through a premature withdrawal, would likely further tarnish the

U.S. image in the region and throughout the world (see also Robert Reilly's discussion on strategic communications in chapter 13). Equally important, it would undermine the achievement of one of the war's objectives, namely, establishing an Iraqi government that represents its people.

Security

Iraq faces several challenges to its security. Michael E. Freeman in chapter 5 on the financing of insurgency and terrorism, Dorothy E. Denning in chapter 6 on use of the Internet in the Iraq conflict, and Arquilla and Borer in chapter 14 on military strategy all discuss the myriad threats to Iraq's security: notably transnational terrorist movements, crime and trafficking, and Iran's and Turkey's meddling in Iraqi affairs. Iraq also faces domestic security challenges, including the persistence of extra-governmental militias, that are outside the control of the federal government, unrelenting but somewhat muted domestic insurgents, crime, and ethno-sectarian violence. The need for unpoliticized, accurate intelligence on the various international and external security threats that Iraq faces, as described by Joshua Rovner, actually grows as American military presence diminishes.

A stable Iraq requires security forces that can defend Iraq's borders, root out terrorist and criminal threats, and maintain a reasonable level of law and order within its borders. In chapter 4, Hy S. Rothstein argues that the country needs better-trained army and police forces and local security to fight a spectrum of conventional and irregular threats. The Iraqi Army shows signs of engaging these enemies successfully, but the police have not yet attained the level of training or professionalism necessary to successfully maintain law and order.

Economy

Iraq has the resources for economic prosperity, including substantial oil reserves, rich agricultural land, a port, and potentially even tourism to Iraq's historic cities. However, efforts at economic development in Iraq have been uneven and hindered by poor planning and weak security. Moreover, Iraq continues to struggle with corruption and crime, including crime to pay for the insurgency and terrorism (see chapter 5). In chapter 3 on economic development, Raymond E. Franck, Jr., argues that development efforts need to be focused on projects and localities where they are likely to succeed and gain momentum before the country's economy can stabilize and move toward its promising potential.

Regional Security

Iraq faces several challenges to its stability and sovereignty from regional threats, from both state and non-state actors. Turkey has made several incursions into northern Iraq with the aim of cracking down on the Kurdistan Workers' Party (PKK). Iran continues to meddle in Iraq's affairs by aiding Iraqi Shia militias, and Iranian Special Forces, such as the Quds Brigade, have reportedly operated within Iraqi borders. Iraq also faces challenges to its sovereignty through the presence of foreign fighters affiliated with AQI and other insurgent groups. Other states, especially Saudi Arabia, Syria, and Jordan, will continue to play an important role in Iraq's affairs, particularly relating to border security, refugees, and transnational terrorist organizations. To effectively combat these challenges to its sovereignty, Iraq needs to develop its diplomatic capabilities and normalize relations with its neighbors, in addition to establishing improved border security and defense capabilities. These efforts will not be possible without a functioning government that can engage in international relations and employ and control its security forces.

Military Courses of Action, Necessary Conditions, and Risks for War

Arquilla and Borer in chapter 14 on military strategy recognize that some minimal level of U.S. strike and deterrent capability must remain in Iraq for a few years but concludes with the popular discussion of troop drawdowns in Iraq. It outlines three courses of action (COAs): stay the present course by drawing down U.S. forces slowly until all "combat forces" leave late in 2010, maintaining forward operating bases (FOBs) and outposts as long as possible; keep the element of slow drawdowns but put more of the troops that do remain into small outposts, in contravention to the current status of forces agreement (SOFA); and last, draw down with the focus on a qualitative shift in the composition of U.S. forces, including better-qualified advisers to aid Iraqi forces. Next, each of these courses of action is assessed for its benefits to stability and its risk of insurgency, civil war, and transnational conflict, building on the previous section's discussion of necessary conditions for ensuring a stable Iraq.

COA 1

With the first course of action, the military would draw down U.S. combat forces, but a small residual force would remain for a period of several years while maintaining FOBs and outposts. It would also require renegotiating the SOFA in order to allow residual American forces to be stationed in the small outposts. This course of action provides several benefits for the continuing stabilization of Iraq:

- In the absence of a strong government, even a small continuing U.S. military presence could provide a security guarantee to the government and prevent Iraqi disintegration, creating the security space needed for social capital, civil society, the economy, and Iraqi identity to develop.
- Even a small military force in the country could intervene if one group were to secede or if full-scale civil war were to erupt.
- It would constitute a forward presence that would most likely deter large-scale intervention from Iran or Turkey.
- This presence could also support regional stability.
- It would give U.S. forces the ability to deal with a variety of shocks (see "Feedback Loops and Shocks" later in this chapter).

This COA also comes with risks:

- Residual forces might be less likely to successfully tamp down an insurgency if the majority of the troops remained concentrated in FOBs and not in outposts sprinkled among the population.
- The visible presence of even small numbers of U.S. forces in Iraq could spark continued violence from Islamic and nationalist terrorists who want the United States out of the Middle East.
- The presence of U.S. forces as a security backup could weaken Iraqis' motivation to rely on their own capabilities and thus retard the development of capable Iraqi security forces.
- A long-term presence, if more than just of minimal size, would continue to stress an already worn-down U.S. military force structure.

COA 2

In the second course of action, the military would also conform to President Obama's call to draw down U.S. combat forces quickly in 2010 but would place more troops in outposts than on FOBs. Doing so would also require renegotiation of the SOFA. This COA offers several benefits for the continued stabilization of Iraq:

- The presence of outposts would ramp up the pressure on the remaining insurgents, who seemed to be getting back on their feet early in 2010, by reducing the range of places where they might hide and regroup.
- Outposts could mitigate the risk of a return to civil strife, if the rules of engagement called for intervention in response to such violence.
- The outposts could provide added security to reconstruction efforts.
- The smaller U.S. military footprint might reduce Islamic and nationalist insurgent activities aiming to oust U.S. forces from the region.
- Outposts would provide continuing support for and monitoring of Iraqi security forces.

This COA also comes with risks:

- Outposts would be unlikely to prevent the secession of one group from the country or a large-scale societal disintegration.
- If most of the remaining forces were deployed to outposts, the ability to deter other countries from invading may be reduced.
- Dispersed troops would have a reduced ability to deal with shocks (again, see "Feedback Loops and Shocks" later in this chapter).

COA 3

This course of action calls for the drawdown in 2010 to result in a qualitative change in the residual forces. COA 3 offers benefits for the continued stabilization of Iraq:

- Specially qualified forces could train Iraqi troops while maintaining a small footprint, which would help in building rapport and trust.
- Units trained in foreign internal defense and stabilization operations, such as Special Forces and civil affairs teams, could work on improving microeconomic and security needs.

This COA has associated risks that are similar to those listed for COA 2. However, COA 3's level of risk is deemed to be lower as a result of the qualitative improvement of the individual advisers and the manner in which they are employed.

Feedback Loops and Shocks

Finally, it is important to think about two additional factors that could affect Iraq's stability—feedback loops and shocks. In chapter 10 on system dynamics modeling, Abdel-Hamid argues that changes in policy or military courses of action have a delayed reaction and produce a nonlinear feedback loop with both counteracting and amplifying variables. It is important to anticipate the delayed response and effects of these feedback loops.

In chapter 12, Fox uses INFORM modeling to consider shocks to the system, or those events that would greatly alter the trajectory of progress in Iraq and require a change in policy. Such events could be aggressive, such as the outbreak of civil war, or passive, such as are occurring with the drawdown of U.S. troops. The chapter considers five scenarios that combine service variables, such as security forces, and physical variables, such as the country's infrastructure. The scenarios demonstrate that attacks that affect more than one variable simultaneously have an impact on Iraq's stability and that certain variables, particularly security, affect stability more than others do.

Several specific shocks are worth considering in light of the necessary conditions for stabilizing Iraq and the U.S. military's courses of action outlined above. We will address three in particular.

Shock 1: The Collapse of Iraq's Government

This shock could be caused by a number of scenarios, including the inability of the government to build consensus and pass legislation, the fracturing of the government along ethnic or religious lines, or the assassination of a high-level Iraqi politician or official. The collapse of Iraq's government would present significant domestic and regional problems, including the possibility of one group or area seceding from the state (see shock 2), civil war, refugee flows, and possibly invasion from a neighboring country. The lack of a functioning central government in Iraq could also open the door for transnational terrorist groups seeking ungoverned territory for sanctuary.

Given this range of possible outcomes for the collapse of Iraq's government, the United States would have good reason to intervene again militarily to maintain Iraq's cohesion and prevent regional instability. Intervention, however, would require a sizable force that either had remained in Iraq—which will not be the case under current U.S. policy—or could be rapidly deployed there.

Shock 2: Secession

Another shock that would be domestically and regionally destabilizing is one ethnic group's secession from Iraq. Secession by the Kurds in particular would present several challenges to regional stability. Domestically, the Kurds could not secede without causing disputes over certain cities—especially Mosul, Tal Afar, and the oil-rich city of Kirkuk—that are ethnically mixed or have historical significance to the Kurds, regardless of the numbers still living there.[1] Kurdish secession would include these cities because the Kurds see them as part of their historical patrimony. This historical basis for their inclusion would run head-on into resistance both from the large Sunni populations in these areas and from Shia and Sunni factions that would deem the areas' valuable resources as essential to post-occupation Iraq's national health and wealth. Kurdish secession would therefore undoubtedly cause domestic turmoil.

Perhaps more important, Kurdish secession would be regionally destabilizing. Iraq's bordering countries—particularly Turkey, Iran, and Syria—have a vested interest in preventing Kurdish secessionism in Iraq because a run for independence could spark separatist movements within these countries' Kurdish communities as well as transnational efforts to create an independent Kurdistan carved out of territories from several countries. It is reasonable to assume that Turkey would take some form of military action if the Kurds were to secede, making the conflict regional.

As with the collapse of Iraq's central government, secession could also require U.S. military intervention to prevent the conflict from rapidly escalating and drawing in multiple states. But it might also be possible to head off an interstate war sparked by Kurdish secession with timely deterrent signals to Turkey and others, coupled with energetic crisis bargaining.

Shock 3: Escalating Conflict with Turkey or Iran

Both Turkey and Iran have involved themselves in Iraq's domestic affairs since the U.S.-led invasion in 2003. Iran has reportedly funded and armed Shia militias, political parties, and insurgents, in addition to dispatching special forces inside Iraq's borders. Turkey has staged several cross-border incursions into northern Iraq via ground forces and air raids to crack down on Kurdish insurgents. While less dramatic than a government collapse or secession, these continued low-level violations of Iraq's sovereignty could escalate, especially if one side miscalculates as a result of significant U.S. force reductions. Turkey and Iran are both larger than Iraq and most likely have better prepared conventional and irregular forces, making Iraq's sovereignty vulnerable. An escalated conflict with Turkey could be resolved through diplomatic means and diplomatic efforts from other North Atlantic Treaty Organization (NATO) countries. However, in the case of an escalation between Iran and Iraq, fewer diplomatic options would be available, making a military response the likely course of action, especially if Iran were unresponsive to deterrent signals from the United States.

Finally, in addition to shocks, another consideration could necessitate further U.S. and presumably international intervention: what happens if the Iraqis are eager to go it alone but are incapable of doing so successfully? Negotiations between the United States and Iraq led to Iraqi authorities demanding a relatively short time line for the withdrawal of U.S. combat forces. As this scenario unfolds, it creates a tricky dilemma: the United States would not like to see its efforts put at risk, but the legalities of staying after a sovereign government asked U.S. forces to leave would be complicated. Still, ethical and perhaps legal considerations could call for the United States to keep at least a minimal residual force in place if leaving entirely meant the likelihood of bloody chaos after its departure.

Conclusion

On balance, the endgame in Iraq is likely to be characterized by sustained tension animated by the reduction of U.S. forces on the ground and persistent governance problems. Force drawdowns are unfolding in a "swift and deep" pattern in 2010. Governance problems may range from gridlock to outright collapse and secession. These possibilities suggest four broad scenarios—that is, the three shocks and Iraq's decision to go it alone. Each of these scenarios offers different levels of risk for rekindling the insurgency or civil war or sparking a fresh round of interstate warfare. Our study has tried to identify the fault lines as well as the interconnectedness among these three faces of conflict, the implication for policymakers being that a hedged strategy will have to be formulated that finds a risk equilibrium among the three.

Of the four scenarios outlined above, the two that suggest little change in Iraqi governance in the near term—one perhaps featuring a slightly larger U.S. presence and the other a smaller one—may not differ too greatly from each other in their levels of risk. In other words, with a standing Iraqi government, however fractious, that draws representation from all major groups in the country, it may be that deterring internal or interstate conflict would be a lesser challenge for the United States. Meanwhile, the "collapse of governance" scenarios clearly seem to entail greater risks of all three types of conflict. These possibilities would put substantial demands on both American deterrent and counterinsurgent capacities. Yet, even under these difficult conditions, it is possible to see external intervention thwarted by clear signaling of American resolve and internal strife tamped down by a smaller residual force specifically attuned to the problems posed by internal conflict.

Beyond these four worst-case scenarios, however, the study holds out the hope that our various findings regarding the way ahead for Iraq's economy, the prospects for social reintegration and political conciliation, and the broader involvement of the international community suggest the path to yet another future for Iraq—one in which the government is stable and functional, the need for military action is much diminished, and the three faces of conflict no longer look out quite as grimly upon a people who have suffered so much.

Notes

1. See International Crisis Group (ICG), "Iraq and the Kurds: Resolving the Kirkuk Crisis," Middle East Report No. 64 (Kirkuk/Ammand/Brussels: ICG, April 19, 2007).

Postscript

The chapters of this book were drafted in the first half of 2008, and since their completion, several events have affected Iraq. Some were expected while others have come as a total surprise. These changes show that unforeseen and seemingly disconnected events can have an impact on Iraq's road to stabilization.

The global economic crisis, which took nearly everyone by surprise, has forced the United States to refocus its priorities. While we drafted these chapters, Iraq was the top concern on the U.S. public's mind. Now Iraq has been replaced by the more immediate concerns of unemployment rates, housing foreclosures, the national deficit, and the stability of U.S and global financial institutions. The economic crisis raises serious questions about the U.S. public's willingness to fund wars and other operations overseas, including stabilizing Iraq and the continuing war in Afghanistan.

Along the lines of the economy, fluctuating oil prices could affect Iraq's road to recovery. Not only is Iraq's economic health dependent on developing its petroleum exports, but the oil industry is also supposed to finance Iraq's continued reconstruction. Iraq has the potential for other economic markets; however, the path for developing these markets runs through the viability of its oil market. Fluctuating oil prices may impede getting Iraq up on its economic feet, which, in turn, could affect the country's ability to provide meaningful work for its population and establish domestic stability. Indeed, an oil-driven economic crisis should be seen as the one shock most likely to spark renewed civil strife in Iraq, as ethnic factions vie for their shares of a diminished pool of national revenues.

The U.S. presidential elections in 2008 brought a new administration to power with a different approach to foreign policy. President Barack Obama has stated his willingness to talk with both Iran and Syria as a necessary first step to work toward reducing tensions between the United States and these key Middle Eastern countries and as a possible means of reducing tensions throughout the region more broadly. Talks with Iran could pave the way for reducing its interference in Iraq's domestic affairs. Likewise, talks with Syria could lead to a reduction of illicit goods and people traveling over its border with Iraq. In contrast, failed talks could push Iran and Syria further away from normalization and regional integration and perhaps toward greater efforts in destabilizing Iraq.

In January 2009, Iraq held another round of provincial elections. Election day was relatively peaceful (although candidates were killed leading up to the polls), suggesting that Iraqis are becoming more familiar with the process of elections. But the results still show Iraqis voting primarily along ethnic and religious lines, signifying deep divisions in society and suggesting that the voters do not see themselves first as Iraqis. These results demonstrate that democracy is much more than just elections, and the necessary institutions that support a healthy democracy, especially a strong civil society, have yet to take hold in Iraq. These institutions do not happen by accident; they require time and conscious construction.

President Obama announced at the end of January 2009 that the U.S. combat mission in Iraq will end by August 31, 2010; that the troop size will be reduced from 142,000 to between 35,000 and 50,000; and that all troops will be out in 2011, in accord with the status of forces agreement between Iraq and the United States. Prior to the 2011 complete withdrawal, the remaining forces will be tasked with training and advising Iraqi forces (provided they remain nonsectarian), protecting civilian and military efforts in Iraq, and conducting targeted counterterrorism missions, a plan that looks similar to course of action 3 in this volume.

Simultaneous to the troop reduction in Iraq, Afghanistan is undergoing an increase in troop strength, possibly similar to the surge strategy undertaken in Iraq in 2007. Greater numbers of U.S. troops in Afghanistan may mean that these forces will not be at the ready to aid Iraq in any significant numbers should there be a shock to that country's stability. Additionally, it is not clear that the Obama administration or the American people have the stomach for renewed combat operations in Iraq, especially while the investment in Afghanistan grows.

Increased attention to Afghanistan could cause the United States to take its eye off of Iraq. The contributors to this volume have argued that a stable, functioning Iraq requires more than just the absence of violence. Ethnic and religious tensions need to be reduced and civil society strengthened. The economy needs to be developed so that it can provide meaningful work to the population. The government needs to be responsive to its population and protect its minorities. The military needs to defend its borders and prevent foreign intrusions. The judicial and police systems need to provide law and order. And the government needs to have rotation of leadership. Iraq is not there yet. It still needs mentoring and support from the United States and the wider international community as the country continues on its path to recovery. The global economic crisis and the reduction of U.S. capabilities and attention to Iraq place greater burdens on the Iraqis just as domestic and external pressures are likely to increase in Iraq.

Until this process of restoration is complete, one or all of the three faces of conflict whose interplay forms the core concern of this book—civil war, insurgency, and interstate warfare—may flare up once again. Our hope is to have provided early warning of the ways to head off such crises or, in the face of renewed conflict, to have outlined the most expeditious means for restoring Iraq's stability. Ultimately, one can only conceive of winning in Iraq in the context of an absence of conflict, one that allows for the growing security, freedom, and prosperity of the Iraqi people.

Appendix:
Formal Modeling of Iraq Using Game Theory and Dynamic Systems

©*William P. Fox*

Section 1: Modeling and Problem Identifications

In our descriptions, we refer to non-state actors. These non-state actors are the terrorists operating within the state. In Iraq, they operate with the regime's knowledge and support. Thus, the terms "non-state actors" and "Iraq" are considered interchangeable in this description.

Two problem identifications were considered in this initial modeling effort:

Problem identification 1: determine the proper strategies that the United States and non-state actors should employ to accomplish each side's goals or objectives. The resulting model should establish the courses of action to be taken to accomplish the objectives in the war on terrorism.

Problem identification 2: determine the relationships between and among the three circles of war and their effects on each other.

Modeling the War on Terrorism Using Game Theory

Problem Identification

Determine the proper strategies that the United States and non-state actors should employ in order to accomplish each player's goals or objectives.

Assumptions Bearing on the Model

- Non-state actors are reasonable and rational.

- The United States can actually try to use diplomatic measures to work with non-state actors.
- Non-state actors have goals that they want to accomplish that are not zero sum.

U.S. strategies

- unilateral military action
- unilateral diplomatic or political strategies

Non-state actor strategies

- support terrorism and national violence
- do not support terrorism

Criteria

- *timeliness*: ability to react
- *sustainability:* ability to sustain effort
- *suitability:* likelihood of success
- *feasibility:* right tool for the right job
- *acceptability:* willingness to accept solution

Payoff Matrix Using Utility Theory

On a scale of 1 to 4, with 4 being the best option and 1 the worst, we assume the rankings depicted in table A.1 for a United States objective of coercing a given state to stop sponsoring terrorism.

Table A.1. U.S. options: Utilities for payoff

4. Best choice: State stops sponsoring terrorism; military force not required
3. Next best choice: State stops sponsoring terrorism; military force used
2. Next choice: State continues sponsoring terrorism; military force used
a. United States able to punish enemy for terrorist acts committed; use of cruise missiles and air strikes limit United States casualties
b. United States does not look weak by taking no action at all
c. Helps with public support
1. Option: State continues sponsoring terrorism; United States takes no military action

On a scale of 1 to 4, with 4 being the best option and 1 the worst, we assume the rankings depicted in table A.2 for a non-state actor's objective of continuing to use terrorism to further its objectives.

Table A.2. Non-state actor's options: Utilities for payoff

4. Best choice: United States does nothing; continues sponsoring terrorism
3. Next best choice: United States strikes militarily; continues sponsoring terrorism because although some damage and loss of life are sustained, know strikes are limited and will not be sustained
2. Next choice: United States does not strike militarily; stops sponsoring terrorism
a. No collateral damage or loss of life
b. Regime stays in power
1. Worst choice: United States strikes militarily; stops sponsoring terrorism
a. Reason for stopping most likely owing to severe damage to infrastructure and loss of life
b. United States has denied state the ability to continue sponsoring terrorism
c. May result in loss of regime's hold on power

Results from Game Theory Analysis

A Nash equilibrium in a game exists when no player can obtain a better payoff by switching to some other available strategy while all other players adhere to their specified strategies. Figure A.1 represents the analysis of tables A.1 and A.2 and shows that a pure Nash equilibrium emerges at the U.S. strategy of striking militarily and the non-state actor strategy of supporting terrorism (2, 3). The values used in this game theory model are not as important as their relative ordering. Provided the ordering is the same, the result will still be a pure Nash equilibrium at the strategies shown above. The U.S.-Iraq conflict followed this result.

The position the United States favors is "do not strike militarily," perhaps in favor of a diplomatic or political strategy. However, this strategy appears to be unattainable under normal conditions. The United States might consider strategic moves (such as threats, promises, combinations of threats and promises, negotiations, and so on) in order to get the key players—the

Figure A.1. Payoff matrix and movement diagram

		Non-state Actor: Sponsor terrorism		Non-state Actor: Stop sponsoring terrorism
U.S.	Strike militarily	(2,3)	←	(3,1)
		↑		↑
	Do not strike militarily	(1,4)	←	(4,2)

United States and the non-state actor—to move toward nonviolent strategies. There are no stable strategies in this game. Since we are involved in this military (United States) and violent (non-state actor) strategy, we need to build a more fluid model to determine how we are doing and how we can react to terrorist activities. However, this part of the modeling shows how we initially got into the conflict with Iraq.

Even as we add more strategies, the military/violence strategy is the pure Nash equilibrium. This option may not be the strategy of choice, but it may be the strategy of necessity. The United States would like to find viable methods to allow for alternative strategies to prevail.

Conclusions from the Game Theory Model

We have outlined an approach using game theory to evaluate the strategies of the two opponents considered for this analysis. We believe this approach offers a useful way to structure generic problems of this nature. We also believe this analysis is incomplete. We focused only on the United States versus Iraq in the early stages. We have not fully explored all the options of Iraq, from Iraq's perspective, and we have not considered any resource constraints on the problem. This analysis is not adequate to support public policy, but it does provide some limited insights into the original problem.

Given that our model suggests military intervention, let us turn our attention to that model and its effects within the three circles of war.

Section 2: Model II for Stochastic Dynamic Systems Modeling of U.S. Efforts in Iraq and Iraq's Infrastructure Resiliency Within the Three Circles of War Using the Inform Model

It is our hypothesis that the conditions in Iraq (measured by the lack of rebuilding, which resulted in the infrastructure failure in the power system, politics, the economy, health care, transportation, security, and so on) led to the growth of the insurgency and the outbreak of civil war. Furthermore, we assume that efforts in one arena of the three circles of war might hinder efforts in the other arenas. The proposed model should help to identify these effects.

Problem Identification

Build a mathematical model that relates infrastructure dynamics to shock effects of "war" activities. We will consider war activities to be terrorist acts, insurgency operations, and civil war activity. We must address three issues:

1. How can the infrastructure of a metropolitan area or country be modeled so that we can better understand "resilience" with respect to major system shocks from war activities?
2. What is an appropriate balance between preparedness and responsiveness for strategic planning?
3. How can the loss in productivity imposed by response plan implementation be captured in the model?

Modeling Assumptions and Variables

We want to consider the following in our modeling:

- *hearts and minds:* infrastructure and political resiliency in Iraq
- *terrorists/insurgents:* mission to destroy U.S. resolve and presence in other countries
- *U.S. strategy:* mission to secure the United States from direct attack, to secure strategic access and retain global freedom of action, to strengthen alliances and partnerships, and to establish favorable security conditions
- *U.S. military strategy in Iraq:* protect, prevent, prevail

We will use the seventeen critical infrastructures as defined by the Department of Homeland Security: energy, transportation, water, public health, emergency services, telecommunications, dams, commercial assets, agriculture and food, banking and finance, defense industrial base, nuclear power, postal and shipping, government facilities, information technology, national monuments and icons, and chemical and hazardous materials. Within each major area, the dynamics can be measured in a manner similar to that used in control charts, with upper and lower bounds for normal functions. We assume that experts can define these boundaries.

Dynamic Modeling

We will use discrete dynamic modeling structure to capture the interactions. The basic model without shocks is as follows:

$$\begin{bmatrix} p_i(t+1) \\ s_k(t+1) \end{bmatrix} = \begin{bmatrix} Q_{pp} & Q_{ps} \\ Q_{sp} & Q_{ss} \end{bmatrix}^T \begin{bmatrix} p_i(t) \\ s_k(t) \end{bmatrix}$$

Notation:

$i = 1, 2, \ldots, 17$	major infrastructure elements
$j = 1, 2, \ldots, J$	critical infrastructure services
$k = 1, 2, \ldots, K$	set of *i*, *j* physical element-service pairs
xi(t)	physical condition state of infrastructure element *i* at time *t*
sk(t)	service process condition state for pair *k* at time *t*
Q = [Qik(t)]	state interactivity level matrix at time *t* (between physical systems, services, and physical-service pairs)
mi(t)*	maintenance for physical layer for infrastructure *i* at time *t*
mk(t)*	maintenance for critical infrastructure service *j* for infrastructure *i* at time *t*

Notation:

- *Q* is assumed to be partially time invariant, asymmetric, and state independent in the basic model.
- The block structure of *Q* represents the pairwise influence effects between state components as a result of linked interdependencies.
- The scale chosen for *Q* components represents a complete effects cycle.

- The state vector at time t = 0 represents a conservative estimate of current state condition levels.
- The maintenance vector represents planned periodic resource investments for state conditions according to (possibly unique) periodic time sequence t^*.

Modeling with Shocks

Let $c(\tau)$ be a shock due to an outside force (insurgency attack, bombing, and so on). We can measure its effect throughout the infrastructures to determine courses of action to improve the situation.

$$\begin{bmatrix} p_i(t+1) \\ s_k(t+1) \end{bmatrix} = \begin{bmatrix} Q_{pp} & Q_{ps} \\ Q_{sp} & Q_{ss} \end{bmatrix}^T \begin{bmatrix} p_i(t) \\ s_k(t) \end{bmatrix} \begin{bmatrix} m_i(t^*) \\ m_k(t^*) \end{bmatrix} \begin{bmatrix} c_i(\tau) \\ c_k(\tau) \end{bmatrix}$$

where

$$\begin{bmatrix} \tilde{Q}_{pp} & \tilde{Q}_{ps} \\ \tilde{Q}_{sp} & \tilde{Q}_{ss} \end{bmatrix}^T = \left(\begin{bmatrix} Q_{pp} & Q_{ps} \\ Q_{sp} & Q_{ss} \end{bmatrix}^T + \begin{bmatrix} c_{pp} & c_{ps} \\ c_{sp} & c_{ss} \end{bmatrix}^T \right)$$

Model with Responsive Actions and/or Policies

$$\begin{bmatrix} p_i(t+1) \\ s_k(t+1) \end{bmatrix} = \left(\begin{bmatrix} \tilde{Q}_{pp} & \tilde{Q}_{ps} \\ \tilde{Q}_{sp} & \tilde{Q}_{ss} \end{bmatrix} + \begin{bmatrix} P_{pp}(\delta) & P_{ps}(\delta) \\ P_{sp}(\delta) & P_{ss}(\delta) \end{bmatrix} \right) \begin{bmatrix} p_i(t) \\ s_k(t) \end{bmatrix} * \begin{bmatrix} m_i(t^*) \\ m_k(t^*) \end{bmatrix} * \begin{bmatrix} c_i(\tau) \\ c_k(\tau) \end{bmatrix} + \begin{bmatrix} p_i(\delta) \\ p_k(\delta) \end{bmatrix}$$

$$\begin{bmatrix} p_i(t+1) \\ s_k(t+1) \end{bmatrix} = \left(\begin{bmatrix} \tilde{Q}_{pp} & \tilde{Q}_{ps} \\ \tilde{Q}_{sp} & \tilde{Q}_{ss} \end{bmatrix} + \begin{bmatrix} R_{pp}(\delta) & R_{ps}(\delta) \\ R_{sp}(\delta) & R_{ss}(\delta) \end{bmatrix} \right) \begin{bmatrix} p_i(t) \\ s_k(t) \end{bmatrix} * \begin{bmatrix} m_i(t^*) \\ m_k(t^*) \end{bmatrix} * \begin{bmatrix} c_i(\tau) \\ c_k(\tau) \end{bmatrix} + \begin{bmatrix} r_i(\delta) \\ r_k(\delta) \end{bmatrix}$$

Dynamic pairwise effects imposed on the composite system by Q are proportional to the "health" of the "transmitting" system component. Specifically:

$$p_i(t+1) = ((p_i(t) + \sum_{j \neq i} q_{ji} p_j(t) p_i(t)) m_i(t)) env(t)$$

It is envisioned that a simulation can be overlaid on the model and run thousands of times to capture the output statistics, which can then be analyzed. Following is a a small example from our proposal.

Scenario

Consider an attack on a Baghdad police station, its personnel, and its police cruisers. Let us measure the effects of this attack over discrete time intervals. Our goal is to show that the attack on the police station affects not only the police and their mission but also other dynamics within the infrastructure whose subeffects can be missed by response and policy operations in the arena. Knowing this information, we can use this analysis to better plan a response and our actions to improve the overall infrastructure in an effort to maintain hearts and minds in Iraq and perhaps in the world. We use the Excel spreadsheet to facilitate the model.

The model (see the illustrations in section 5) shows that the attack on the police stations not only disrupts the police functions and their ability to enforce laws but also has subsequent effects on roads and bridges, affecting safe movement. These effects would not have been examined in normal operations to improve the condition of or to do repairs on the police station. Thus, this model helps provide decision makers with other layers of information that are useful in keeping the state's infrastructure sound, which is critical in maintaining a stronger balance against the other dynamics in the country (terrorist activity, civil war, and so on).

We allow the model to operate for some length of time before hitting the system with a terrorist attack on the police station. We hit the system with the shock effect (see table A.3).

Table A.3. System shock effects

Variable	Shock multiplier
Garbage trucks	1.0
Police cruisers	0.7
Roads and bridges	1.0
Trash removal	1.0
Enforcing laws	0.4
Safe, effective movement	1.0

We ran a before and after analysis that shows garbage trucks' effectiveness decreased by 26 percent, police cruisers by 66 percent, roads and bridges by 15 percent, trash removal by 33 percent, enforcing laws by 87.5 percent, and safe, effective movement by 3.33 percent. We might expect that these other areas would be ignored unless we knew they were affected indirectly.

One result is illustrated in figure A.2.

Figure A.2. Service Condition (Enforcing Laws)

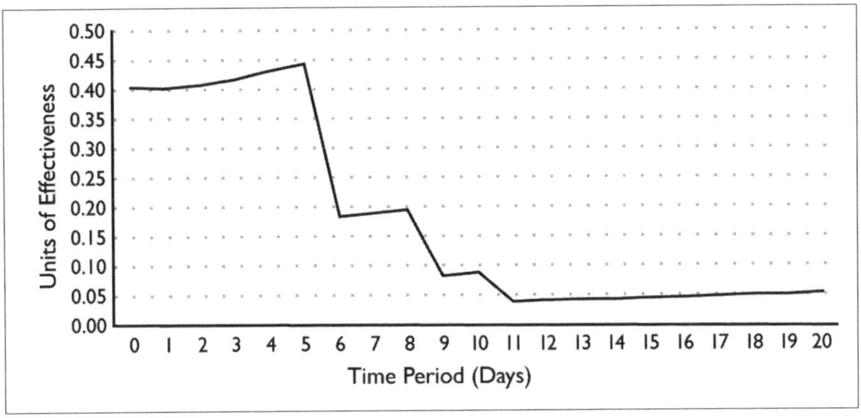

Section 3: INFORM Iraq Model Algorithm

Inputs: physical and service variables and values, Q matrix of interdependencies and its transpose, shock state, and shock values

Output: physical and service values over time

Step 1

Set $t = 0$, and read in all input values. The column vector of physical and service variables should be scaled to accommodate a value between 0 and 1. The Q matrix is a matrix of interdependencies among the variables. It is suggested that these be established by a group of experts. Enter the transpose of the matrix as it is used in the calculations.

$$Q^T\,matrix = \begin{bmatrix} Q_{11} & Q_{21} & \cdot & \cdot & \cdot & Q_{61} \\ Q_{12} & Q_{22} & \cdot & \cdot & \cdot & Q_{62} \\ Q_{13} & Q_{23} & \cdot & \cdot & \cdot & Q_{63} \\ Q_{14} & Q_{24} & \cdot & \cdot & \cdot & Q_{64} \\ Q_{15} & Q_{25} & \cdot & \cdot & \cdot & Q_{65} \\ Q_{16} & Q_{26} & Q_{36} & Q_{46} & Q_{56} & Q_{66} \end{bmatrix}$$

Step 2

Create a scaled effects matrix from the starting state conditions of the physical and service input variables. The main diagonals are all set at 0, and the matrix is symmetric, with the upper triangular being the product of the variables with all other variables one at a time.

Example: Given the initial physical and service values, then the scaled matrix is:

$$\begin{bmatrix} 0 & p_1 * p_2 & p_1 * p_3 & p_1 * s_1 & p_1 * s_2 & p_1 * s_3 \\ p_1 * p_2 & 0 & p_2 * p_3 & p_2 * s_1 & p_2 * s_2 & p_2 * s_3 \\ p_1 * p_3 & p_2 * p_3 & 0 & p_3 * s_1 & p_3 * s_2 & p_3 * s_3 \\ p_1 * s_1 & p_2 * s_1 & p_3 * s_1 & 0 & s_1 * s_2 & s_1 * s_3 \\ p_1 * s_2 & p_2 * s_2 & p_3 * s_2 & s_1 * s_2 & 0 & s_2 * s_3 \\ p_1 * s_3 & p_2 * s_3 & p_3 * s_3 & s_1 * s_3 & s_2 * s_3 & 0 \end{bmatrix}$$

Step 3

Take the sum product (dot product) of the scaled effects matrix in step 2 with the $Q^T(_{ik})$ transpose matrix. This yields an *n by 1* matrix of scalars. Take row 1 of each and dot their entries. For example, position 1,1 would be:

$$O*Q11+P1*P2*Q21+P1*P3*Q31+P1*S1+Q41+P1*S2*Q51+P1*S3*Q61$$

The column matrix is as follows:

Dynamic effect vector =[

$$\begin{bmatrix} 0*Q_{11} + p_1 * p_2 * Q_{21} + p_1 * p_3 * Q_{31} + p_1 * s_1 * Q_{41} + p_1 * s_2 * Q_{51} + p_1 * s_3 * Q_{61} \\ p_1 * p_2 * Q_{12} + 0 * Q_{22} + p_2 * p_3 * Q_{32} + p_2 * s_1 * Q_{42} + p_2 * s_2 * Q_{52} + p_2 * s_3 * Q_{62} \\ . \\ . \\ . \\ p_1 * s_3 * Q_{16} + p_2 * s_3 * Q_{26} + p_3 * s_3 * Q_{36} + s_1 * s_3 * Q_{46} + s_2 * s_3 * Q_{56} + 0 * Q_{66} \end{bmatrix}$$

Step 4

Add these dynamic effects to the end-state physical and service values to obtain their values at the end of the next state to obtain the new state vector.

However, for example, if a road network is used as a variable, the degradation could be 0.95, meaning that the road is worn by a small percentage each time period. If road maintenance is performed in a time period, then a maintenance factor, such as 1.05, could be used. These factors, which should be provided by experts, can be applied to any variable used in the model.

Step 5

If degradation factors and/or maintenance recovery factors are to be used, those scalars can be multiplied to the new state vector to obtain its final state value. In these examples, we started by using no degradation or recovery factors. In later example runs, we included the degradation factor.

Step 6

Repeat steps 2 through 5. This process continues from period 1 until one time period beyond the shock effect. We assume that it takes one period for the shock to take effect.

Step 7

Induce a shock effect on the system. It is done by taking a set of scalars with most values as 1 (noting no change) and a multiplicative value for the physical and/or service values receiving the shock.

For example, consider a bomb on *P2* that also affects *S2*, where *S2* is the service provided by *P2*. Let's assume the bomb removes 10 percent of the *P2* capability and 30 percent of the *S2* capability. Then, our shock effect scalars will be:

$$\begin{bmatrix} 1 \\ .9 \\ 1 \\ 1 \\ .7 \\ 1 \end{bmatrix}$$

Multiply these scalars by the current end-state values of the physical and service states. This product gives the new values of these variables after the shock.

Step 8

Continue the dynamics by repeating steps 2 through 5 for a specified period of time.

Step 9

Obtain graphs of the *P* and *S* variables over time. Analyze the changes over time in all the variables to determine the overall net effects. The graphical plot of each *P* and of each *S* variable over time enables the analyst to obtain the net effect. We can measure the effects of the shock on all *P* and *S* variables in our model.

Section 4: Data Elements and Metrics Used in the Model

All data elements for the physical and the first-level service layers are measured from existing data provided to Congress in reports and are transformed into per-week metrics and given initially as a percent level per week. We then normalized the values to obtain values between 0 and 1. For analyses to be utilized by decision makers, experts and validated data should be used. The variable list from which the primary and service variables are drawn is presented at the end of this section.

One of the key components in this model is the *Q* matrix, which measures the interactions among the variables. Class discussion in our defense analysis courses led to some of the values being used in the current *Q* matrix. It is recommended that experts be used to build the larger *Q* matrix.

We recommend that the *Q* matrix be a 30 × 30 matrix measuring the interactions between the physical layer, the service layers, and their components. We assume these values are non-time variant and stable. They are measured as correlations ranging from −1 to +1, where +1 implies a 100 percent positive increasing effect and −1 implies a 100 percent negative decreasing effect on the activities involved. Currently these correlations are subjective values and can be commander or nation dependent.

Positive values indicate that a variable affects the other variable in the positive direction—that is, producing an increasing result—and negative values indicate that a variable affects the other in a decreasing fashion.

Variables

Here we list the recommended variables (not an exhaustive list) for a first attempt at the larger model. The metrics for each variable can be expected values, actual values, or statistical distributions. Initial suggestions concerning the metric are provided where appropriate. Each of these variables can be handled by the model and Microsoft Excel with Oracle Crystal Ball.

Possible Primary Layer

Electrical power plants and substations: measured as percentage of demand met

Oil rigs and refineries: measured as percentage of target level (2.5 million barrels per day [mbd]). There is a distribution that could be used: as mean of 2.242857143 and a standard deviation (SD) of 0.1679481867; distribution not normal but assume normal

Water: direct measurements are not available, according to report to Congress; report says 30 percent have potable water

Hospitals: measured by ratio of facilities established (80) to number of facilities required (142), or 56.3 percent

Education: ratio of schools to students (data not currently found)

Transportation: –1 to 1 scale; currently rate subjectively at 0.5

Communications: –1 to 1 scale; currently rate subjectively at 0.5

Economy: measured by unemployment rate; currently listed as 17.6 percent with a 38.1 percent underemployment rate but listed as 30–40 percent in other articles

Security and justice: not available

Intelligence: level of accurate strategic intelligence

Police stations: measured in number of police stations per area; 397 police stations

Terrorist activity: 30.76 percent of all terrorist activity is in Iraq

Insurgents: number of insurgents estimated in Iraq as between 100,000 to 130,000; this value needs to be converted to an effectiveness value.

Civil war: ethno-sectarian violence, measured in weekly deaths in Iraq; estimated from Anthony Cordesman's report, "Pandora's Box: Iraqi Federalism, Separatism, 'Hard' Partitioning, and U.S. Policy" (Washington, DC: Center for Strategic and International Studies, October 9, 2007); mean = 1337.5, SD = 425.54, assume a normal distribution

Iraqi military: currently rated as 50 percent effective by U.S. generals

Iraqi police: 50 percent strength

U.S. military: 133,000 soldiers in country and about 65 percent effective

Possible Sublayer

Provide hours of power (percent per day): measured in hours; 12.7 out of 24

Produce oil: 1.71 mbd export: refineries at 5/7 production

Provide water (potable): 47 percent; mean = 29.925, assume a normal distribution, 6.7 of 8.4 million get potable water

Provide health services: 14,000 out of 24,000 doctors (10,000 doctors have left the country)

Provide education: 6,200 schools and 60,000 teachers
Enable transmission and receipt: 8 m cells
Facilitate movement of all items: 69/98 rails, as the percentage of usable rail lines in country
Provide jobs (unemployment): 30–40 percent
Impose justice: cannot measure at this time
Intelligence: level of accurate tactical intelligence
Provide law enforcement: see local security below
Degrade system components: measured by total Iraq improvised explosive device (IED) attacks 2006–2007: mean = 2,810.7, SD = 273.28, assume a normal distribution
Destabilize government in Iraq: measured by average weekly attacks; about 605 per week, SD = 198.42, distribution not normal
Discontent among tribes: measured by number of incidents/executions; incidents, mean = 645.5, SD = 286.63, distribution not normal
Provide national security: percentage of soldiers available for security
Provide local security: measured as percent of operations, currently at 21 percent; 17/22 police battalions ready (77.3 percent), brigades ready (8/9 = 88.9 percent), divisions ready (2 of 2), 88,000 police recruits (as of October 2006), 135,000 police, 24,400 national police=188,200 total
Casualties (U.S.): 4,048 U.S. soldiers killed, 29,395 wounded. Casualties, mean = 15.21 per week, SD = 9.67595; maximum = 67, minimum = 2; assume a normal distribution but not normal (<20: 0.299; 10–20: 0.4545; 20–30: 0.1666; 30–40: 0.0606; 40–50: 0.0037; 50–60: 0.0037, 60–70: 0.01136). Wounded, mean = 100.9375, SD = 48.51; assume a normal distribution

Section 5: Scenarios

Iraq Scenario 1: Small Scale

In this example, we consider only three physical and three service layers: “electrical power” and “provide hours of power”; “Iraqi police” and “provide local security”; and “terrorist activity” and “weekly attacks.” We watch the system dynamics operating until a shock hits the system directly at time period 6; in this case, car bombs are directed at police targets. This shock effect lowers the percentage levels of the police physical condition and their ability to provide local security directly, as we would expect. This outcome is reflected in the table A.5 showing a reduction over time of the police physical condition to less than 20 percent and provision of local security to less than 5 percent. The model shows the other effects as well: it predicts that the electrical power physical condition and provision of power are diminished by more than 10 percent and that the number of terrorist attacks increases by more than 20 percent. Analysis of these factors suggests that we need to monitor the electrical power system in Iraq and concentrate additional efforts to deter terrorist activities. If we consider options, we can measure their impact on the system to try to restore the system as quickly as possible and even improve it.

We hit the system with the following shock effect's vector at time 6.

Table A.4. System shock effects

Variable	Shock multiplier effect
Garbage trucks	1.0
Police cruisers	0.7
Roads and bridges	1.0
Trash removal	1.0
Enforcing laws	0.4
Safe, effective movement	1.0

We measure the effects of the shock on the effectiveness of our system (our scenario's variables) over time. We can easily see the change in effectiveness over time. To illustrate, see table A.5.

Table A.5. Summary of results for scenario 1

Time period	Electric power	Iraqi police	Terrorist activity	Provide hours of power	Provide local security	Weekly attacks
0	0.50	0.50	0.40	0.30	0.40	0.30
1	0.50	0.52	0.40	0.31	0.40	0.31
2	0.49	0.53	0.40	0.32	0.40	0.32
3	0.49	0.53	0.40	0.33	0.41	0.34
4	0.49	0.52	0.40	0.34	0.43	0.35

Table A.5. Continued

5	0.49	0.51	0.39	0.35	0.44	0.36
6	0.48	0.51	0.39	0.36	0.45	0.38
7	0.48	0.50	0.39	0.38	0.47	0.39
8	0.48	0.49	0.39	0.39	0.48	0.41
9	0.48	0.48	0.39	0.40	0.50	0.43
10	0.47	0.48	0.39	0.42	0.52	0.44
11	0.47	0.47	0.39	0.43	0.50	0.46
12	0.47	0.46	0.39	0.45	0.55	0.48

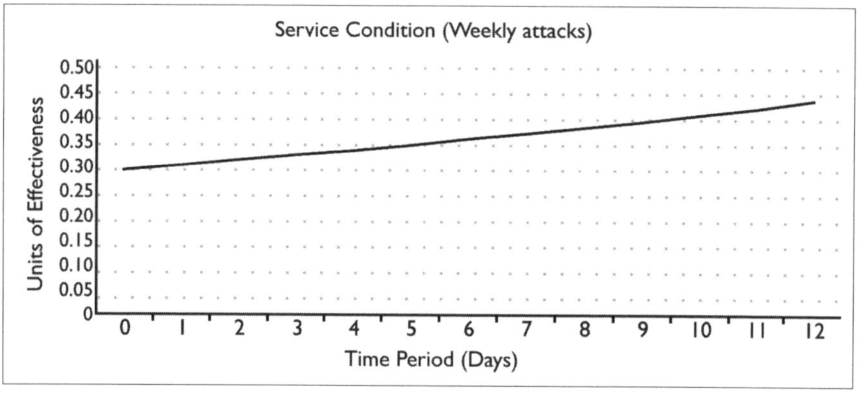

Note:

In the evolution of the model over time, reflected in table A.5, we assume that state condition levels' shocks and responses are applied in the period in which they occur. We also assume that it takes a complete cycle for the dynamics to change to those reflecting either the shock effects on interaction or the responsiveness. The dynamics are state dependent in that their level of intensity of effect (relative to 100 percent effect) depends on the percentage of "health" of the state condition level. In this manner, a state component that is degraded 30 percent from its maximum 100 percent induces an interaction of 70 percent of what it is capable of doing to other system elements.

Iraq Scenario 2: Small Scale

In this example, we consider only three physical and three service layers:

"economy" and "unemployment," "Iraqi police" and "provide local security," and "terrorist activity" and "destabilize government through weekly attacks." We watch the system dynamics operating until a shock hits the system directly at time period 6, and here again, car bombs are directed at police targets. This shock effect lowers the percentage levels of the police physical condition and their ability to provide local security directly, as we would expect. This outcome is reflected in table A.7, showing a reduction of the police physical condition to less than 20 percent and provision of local security to less than 5 percent. The model shows the other effects as well: it predicts that economy is decreased by about 10 percent, and provision of jobs is diminished by more than 15 percent while the number of terrorist attacks increases more than 18 percent. Analysis of these factors suggests that we need to monitor the economic system in Iraq and concentrate additional efforts to deter terrorist activities. If we consider options, we can measure their impact on the system to try to restore the system as quickly as possible and even improve it.

We set up the model with our new variables and the current levels of effectiveness. Again, we hit the system with a shock at time period 6 and measure the results over time. See table A.6.

Table A.6. System shock effects

Variable	Shock multiplier effect
Economy	1
Iraqi police	0.5
Insurgents	1
Unemployment rate	1
Provide local security	0.5
Destabilize government through attacks	1.0

We find that, for example, the economy fell from a high of 70 percent at the time of the attack to 54 percent, or about 16 percent. It fell a little over 10 percent from its original level of 65 percent. In table A.8, we illustrate the percent change for our variables.

Table A. 7. Summary of results for scenario 2

Time period	Economy	Iraqi police	Insurgents	Unemployment rate	Provide local security	Destabilize gov't through attacks
0	0.65	0.6	0.5	0.3	0.4	0.3
1	0.655590748	0.6327	0.4813	0.3012	0.3884	0.2886
2	0.662265645	0.6676	0.4628	0.303	0.3779	0.2771
3	0.67124833	0.6725	0.4415	0.3036	0.3789	0.266
4	0.680665093	0.6783	0.421	0.3045	0.3802	0.255
5	0.690557895	0.6848	0.4014	0.3059	0.3818	0.2441
6	0.700971974	0.3461	0.3824	0.3076	0.192	0.2334
7	0.688072909	0.361	0.3792	0.3212	0.1934	0.2253
8	0.676189538	0.3574	0.3742	0.3344	0.2	0.2193
9	0.66437667	0.177	0.3696	0.3479	0.1035	0.2135
10	0.652291752	0.1764	0.3643	0.3603	0.1073	0.2045
11	0.64027033	0.0875	0.3596	0.3727	0.055	0.1969
12	0.628190168	0.0873	0.3548	0.3844	0.0568	0.1904
13	0.616207138	0.0867	0.3504	0.396	0.0577	0.1846
14	0.60433204	0.0861	0.3464	0.4077	0.0587	0.1788
15	0.592566732	0.0854	0.3427	0.4194	0.0596	0.1731
16	0.58091536	0.0848	0.3393	0.431	0.0606	0.1674
17	0.569381904	0.0842	0.3362	0.4426	0.0616	0.1619
18	0.557970174	0.0835	0.3334	0.4541	0.0626	0.1565
19	0.546683803	0.0829	0.3308	0.4656	0.0637	0.1511
20	0.535526236	0.0823	0.3285	0.477	0.0647	0.1459

Table A.8. Change in variables

Variable	Percent change in effectiveness from original value
Economy	-10
Iraqi police	-52
Insurgents	-17
Unemployment rate	+18
Provide local security	-34
Destabilize government through attacks	-15

Iraq Scenario 3: Small Scale

In this example, we consider only four physical and four service layers: "U.S. military" and "casualty rate," "Iraqi police" and "provide local security," "insurgents" and "destabilize the government," and "civil war" and "discontent." We watch the system dynamics operating until a shock hits the system directly at time period 6. Here again, car bombs are directed at police targets. This shock effect lowers the percentage levels of the police physical condition and their ability to provide local security directly, as we would expect. This outcome is reflected in the illustrations of values showing a reduction of the police physical condition to less than 45 percent and provision of local security to less than 52.5 percent (see table A.10 and figure A.3). The model shows the other effects as well: it predicts that U.S. military effectiveness is decreased by about 17 percent and casualties increased by 150 percent. The insurgency, which becomes the object of all Coalition efforts, is temporarily decreased 72 percent and destabilization by only 10 percent. The civil war increases by 4 percent while discontent increases by 30 percent. Analysis of these factors suggests that we need to increase our efforts against the insurgents in order to stop the insurgents' activities and maintain our level of effectiveness in Iraq. We should also concentrate additional efforts in other areas to curb the increase in the population's discontent. If we consider options, we can measure their impact on the system to try to restore the system as quickly as possible and even improve it.

Shock multipliers in time period 6 are reflected in table A.9.

Table A.9. System shock effects

Variable	Shock multiplier effects
U.S. military	1
Iraqi police	0.5
Insurgents	1
Civil war	1
Casualty rate	1
Provide local security	0.5
Destabilize government through attacks	1
Discontent	1

The summary of results is illustrated in table A.10.

Figure A.3 shows that civil war increases under this scenario. Note the civil war initially declines and then it increases.

Figure A.3. Graph showing the effectiveness of civil war over time

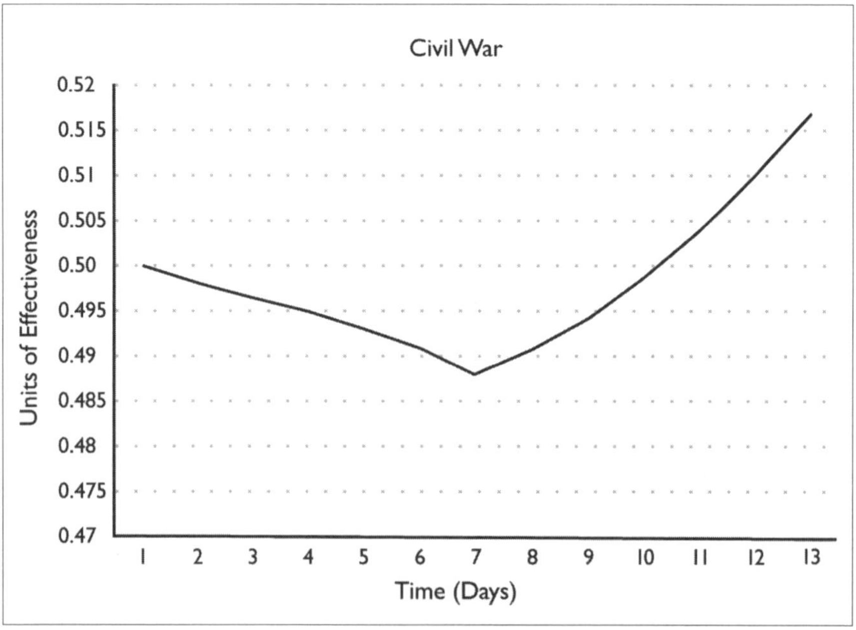

Table A.10. Summary of results for scenario 3

Time period	U.S. military	Iraqi police	Insurgents	Civil war	Casualty rate	Provide local security	Destablize gov't through weekly attacks	Discontent
0	0.650000	0.600000	0.500000	0.500000	0.300000	0.400000	0.300000	0.300000
1	0.640273	0.595677	0.465360	0.498000	0.307965	0.395770	0.299733	0.305907
2	0.631216	0.592561	0.432267	0.496709	0.317122	0.392926	0.299380	0.312605
3	0.622193	0.589840	0.401545	0.494998	0.326716	0.390183	0.298406	0.319495
4	0.613216	0.587472	0.372998	0.492940	0.336742	0.387540	0.296845	0.326584
5	0.604291	0.585423	0.346452	0.490601	0.347202	0.384997	0.294732	0.333880
6	0.595427	0.583662	0.321750	0.488043	0.358094	0.382554	0.292104	0.341391
7	0.586627	0.291081	0.291247	0.490621	0.373420	0.189456	0.288414	0.348787
8	0.577958	0.298097	0.262033	0.494182	0.388839	0.195869	0.284763	0.356284
9	0.569416	0.305569	0.242468	0.498711	0.404382	0.199997	0.282264	0.363883
10	0.561001	0.312536	0.223479	0.503943	0.420079	0.204427	0.279752	0.371592
11	0.552710	0.319017	0.205058	0.509877	0.435951	0.209152	0.277233	0.379413
12	0.544542	0.325034	0.187194	0.516515	0.452021	0.214166	0.274676	0.387348

A summary of all variable changes is reflected in table A.11.

Table A.11. Summary of variable changes

Variable	Percent change
U.S. military	-11
Iraqi police	-27
Insurgents	-31
Civil war	+2
Casualty rates	+15
Provide local security	-19
Destabilize government through attacks	-3
Discontent	+9

Iraq Scenario 4: Small Scale

In this example, we consider only four physical and four service layers: "U.S. military" and "casualty rate," "Iraqi military" and "provide security," "insurgents" and "destabilize the government," and "civil war" and "discontent." We watch the system dynamics operating until a shock hits the system directly at time period 6. In this case, the U.S. military withdraws substantial troops, and the Iraqi military gains minor improvement in overall effectiveness. This shock effect lowers the percentage levels of the effectiveness of the U.S. military and increases the casualty rate. The Iraqi military remains 93 percent effective, and its provision of security is at 85 percent. Both variables show slight decreases. Insurgents and their ability to create instability are both decreased by these shocks, and the civil war and discontent levels both increase.

Shock multipliers in time period 6 are reflected in table A.12. The summary of the results for scenario 4 is provided in table A.13.

Table A.12. System shock effects

Variable	Shock multiplier effects
U.S. military	0.50
Iraqi military	1.05
Insurgents	1.00

Civil war	1.00
Casualty rates	0.95
Provide local security	0.90
Destabilize government through attacks	1.00
Discontent	1.00

A summary of all variable changes is reflected in table A.14.

Table A.14. Summary of variable changes

Variable	Percent change
U.S. military	-37
Iraqi military	-4
Insurgents	-34
Civil war	+2
Casualty rates	+13
Provide local security	-6
Destabilize government through attacks	-3
Discontent	+9

Iraq Scenario 5: Stochastic Simulation

Inputs and Outputs

In this model, we allowed the state conditions of the variables to be uniform distributions with the means as the values in scenario 4. We also allowed the shock multipliers to be uniform distributions with the means as the values in scenario 4. We captured the *end state* as distributions using a thousand runs of the simulated model from scenario 4. In the simulated outputs below, in each case the expected value or mean is established, but a probability distribution is shown for all possible other output values.

Analysis:

The model results show the possible range of values and the probabilities of obtaining those values. Sensitivity analysis shows some typical and atypical results. The variability in the lowering of U.S. military effectiveness is a function of the force and its drawdown, which is typical. The same is true

Table A.13. Summary of results for scenario 4

Time period	U.S. military	Iraqi military	Insurgents	Civil war	Casualty rate	Provide local security	Destablize gov't through weekly attacks	Discontent
0	0.65	0.60	0.50	0.50	0.30	0.40	0.30	0.30
1	0.64	0.60	0.47	0.50	0.31	0.40	0.30	0.31
2	0.63	0.59	0.43	0.50	0.32	0.39	0.30	0.31
3	0.62	0.59	0.40	0.49	0.33	0.39	0.30	0.32
4	0.61	0.59	0.37	0.49	0.34	0.39	0.30	0.33
5	0.60	0.59	0.35	0.49	0.35	0.38	0.29	0.33
6	0.60	0.58	0.32	0.49	0.36	0.38	0.29	0.34
7	0.29	0.61	0.29	0.49	0.35	0.34	0.29	0.35
8	0.29	0.61	0.26	0.49	0.37	0.34	0.28	0.36
9	0.29	0.60	0.23	0.50	0.39	0.34	0.28	0.36
10	0.28	0.59	0.21	0.50	0.40	0.34	0.28	0.37
11	0.28	0.58	0.18	0.51	0.42	0.34	0.27	0.38
12	0.28	0.56	0.16	0.52	0.43	0.34	0.27	0.39

for the variable for the Iraqi military. The variability in the insurgency is atypical and is a function of the insurgency, but it is also 27.4 percent owing to the Iraqi military and 16.6 percent to civil war activities. The variability in the U.S. casualty rate is affected by the civil war and the effectiveness of the Iraqi military.

Comments:

In the following summary report, extracted from the full Crystal Ball simulation report, the following variables are defined:

AD11 = impact of shock multiplier effect on U.S. military
AD12 = impact of shock multiplier effect on Iraqi military
AD 13 = impact of shock multiplier effect on insurgency
AD14 = impact of shock multiplier effect on the civil war
AD15 = impact of shock multiplier effect on the casualty rate
AD16 = impact of shock multiplier effect on provide security
AD17 = impact of shock multiplier effect on destabilize government through weekly attacks
AD18 = impact of shock multiplier effect on discontent

Crystal Ball report extract

- number of trials run = 1,000
- precision control on confidence level = 95 percent
- running time = 7.88 sec

A summary of the output for the variables is provided in table A.15.

A summary of the graphical output from Crystal Ball is shown in figures A.4 through A.7. The change in effectiveness is no longer a point estimate as in scenarios 1 through 4; they are now distributions with statistics from table A.15.

Table A.15. Forecast values from Crystal Ball

Variable output	Civil war	Destabilize government	Discontent	Insurgents	Iraqi military	Provide security	U.S. military	Casualty rate
Mean	0.52	0.27	0.39	0.15	0.57	0.34	0.28	0.43
Median	0.52	0.27	0.39	0.15	0.57	0.34	0.28	0.43
Mode	—	—	—	—	—	—	—	—
St. Deviation	0.07	0.02	0.02	0.02	0.05	0.03	0.02	0.04
Variance	0.00	0.00	0.00	0.00	0.00	0.00	0.00	0.00
Skewness	-0.02	0.018	0.08	0.0351	0.09	0.184	0.211	0.1058
Kurtosis	1.87	2.13	2.05	2.56	2.45	2.63	2.56	2.63
Coeff. of Variability	0.13	0.066	0.06	0.1532	0.08	0.08	0.085	0.088
Minimum	0.39	0.23	0.34	0.08	0.45	0.27	0.22	0.34
Maximum	0.67	0.31	0.45	0.21	0.71	0.42	0.34	0.56
Mean St Error	0.00	0.00	0.00	0.00	0.00	0.00	0.00	0.00

Figure A.4. Graphical output from Crystal Ball for U.S. casualty rate

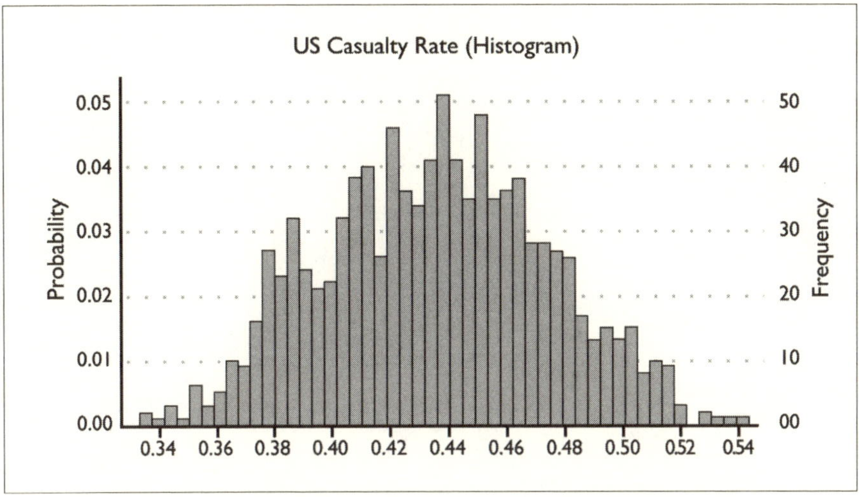

Figure A.5. Sensitivity analysis for U.S. casualty rate (percent)

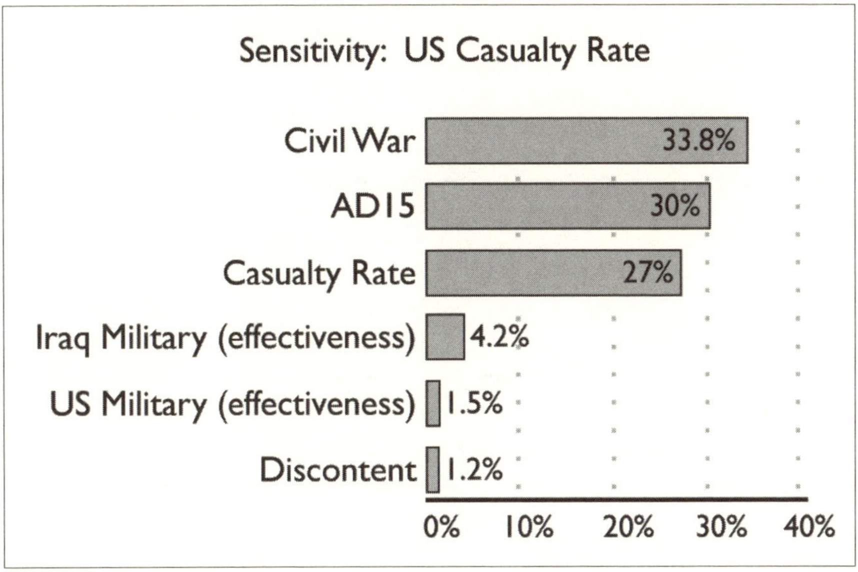

Figure A.6. Graphical output from Crystal Ball for insurgents

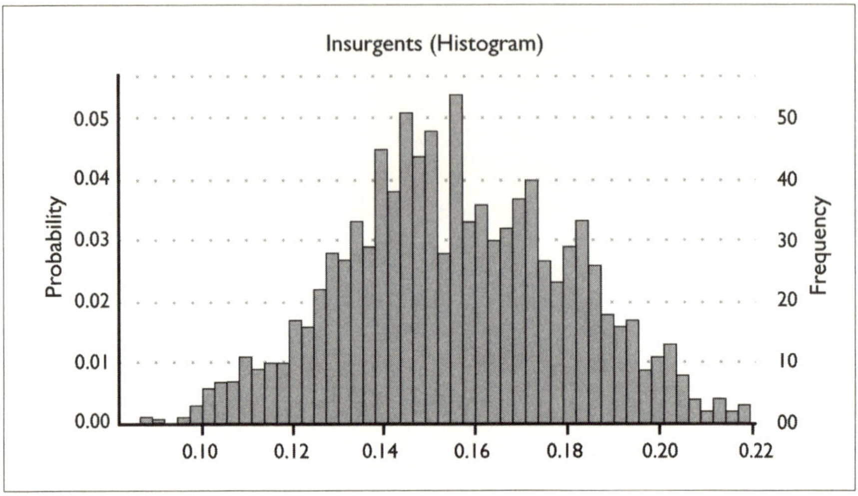

Figure A.7. Sensitivity analysis for insurgents (percent)

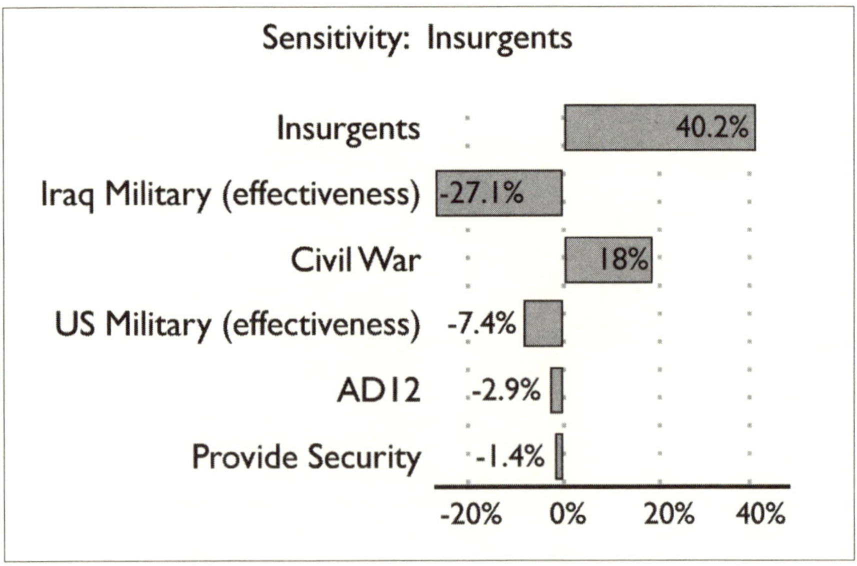

Recommended Readings

Articles

Anderson, Jon Lee. "Letter from Iraq: Inside the Surge." *New Yorker*, November 19, 2007.

Bakier, Abdul Hameed. "Forum Users Improve Electronic Jihad Technology." *Terrorism Focus* 4, no. 20 (June 26, 2007).

Baram, Amatzia. "Neo-Tribalism in Iraq: Saddam Husayn's Tribal Policies, 1991–1996." *International Journal of Middle Eastern Studies* 29, no. 1 (February 1997).

Best, Richard A., Jr. "What the Intelligence Community Got Right About Iraq." *Intelligence and National Security* 23, no. 3 (June 2008).

Chiarelli, Peter, and Patrick R. Michaelis. "Winning the Peace: The Requirement for Full-Spectrum Operations." *Military Review* 85, no. 4 (July–August 2005).

Coles, John P. "Incorporating Cultural Intelligence into Joint Doctrine." *IO Sphere,* Spring 2006.

Collins, Matthew. "Beyond the Van Riper Plan: How Are We Growing Intelligence Officers?" *Marine Corps Gazette* 90, no. 10 (August 2006).

Fearon, James D. "Iraq's Civil War." *Foreign Affairs* 86, no. 2 (March–April 2007).

Freedman, Lawrence. "War in Iraq: Selling the Threat." *Survival* 26, no. 2 (Summer 2004).

Gates, Robert M. "Guarding Against Politicization." *Studies in Intelligence* 36, no. 5 (1992).

"Hacking Manual by Jailed Jihadi Appears on Web." *Terrorism Focus* 5, no. 9 (March 4, 2008).

Hastedt, Glenn P. "Public Intelligence: Leaks as Policy Instruments—the Case of the Iraq War." *Intelligence and National Security* 20, no. 3 (September 2005).

Higgins, James L., Michelle L. Trusso, and Alfred B. Connable. "Marine Corps Intelligence." *Marine Corps Gazette* 89, no. 12 (December 2005).

Jinks, Derek. "The Applicability of the Geneva Conventions to the 'Global War on Terrorism'." *Virginia Journal of International Law* 46, no. 1 (Fall 2005).

Kagan, Kimberly. "How They Did It: Executing the Winning Strategy in Iraq." *Weekly Standard* 13, no. 10 (November 19, 2007).

Kimmons, John F. "Transforming Army Intelligence." *Military Review* 86, no. 6 (November–December 2006).

Kipp, Jacob, Lester Grau, Karl Prinslow, and Don Smith. "The Human Terrain System: A CORDS for the 21st Century." *Military Review* 86, no. 5 (September–October 2006).

Looney, Robert E. "The Business of Insurgency: The Expansion of Iraq's Shadow Economy" *National Interest* 81 (Fall 2005).

Lynn, John A. "Patterns of Insurgency and Counterinsurgency" *Military Review*, July–August 2005.

Malkasian, Carter. "A Thin Blue Line in the Sand." *Democracy: A Journal of Ideas* 5 (Summer 2007).

Packer, George. "The Lesson of Tal Afar." *New Yorker*, April 10, 2006.

Pascual, Carlso, and Kenneth M. Pollack. "The Critical Battles: Political Reconciliation and Reconstruction in Iraq." *Washington Quarterly* 30 (Summer 2007).

Pollack, Kenneth M. "After Saddam: Assessing the Reconstruction of Iraq." *Foreign Affairs*, January–February 2004.

Renzi, Fred. "Networks: Terra Incognita and the Case for Ethnographic Intelligence." *Military Review* 86, no. 5 (September–October 2006).

Sepp, Kalev I. "Best Practices in Counterinsurgency." *Military Review*, May–June 2005.

Teamey, Kyle, and Jonathan Sweet. "Organizing Intelligence for Counterinsurgency." *Military Review* 86, no. 5 (September–October 2006).

Wallace, David A. "The Law of Occupation and Post-Armed-Conflict Governance: Considerations for Future Conflicts." *Military Review*, November–December 2007.

West, F. J. Bing, "American Military Performance in Iraq." *Military Review* 86, no. 5 (September–October 2006).

Zeytoonian, Dan. "Intelligent Design: COIN Operations and Intelligence Collection and Analysis." *Military Review* 86, no. 5 (September–October 2006).

Books

Baker, James A., III; Lee H. Hamilton; Lawrence S. Eagleburger; Vernon E. Jordan, Jr.; Edwin Meese III; Sandra Day O'Connor; Leon E. Panetta; William J. Perry; Charles S. Robb; and Alan K. Simpson. *The Iraq Study Group Report: The Way Forward—a New Approach*. New York: Vintage Books, 2006.

Batatu, Hanna. *The Old Social Classes and the Revolutionary Movements of Iraq: A Study of Iraq's Old Landed and Commercial Classes and of Its Communists, Ba'thists, and Free Officers*. Princeton, NJ: Princeton University Press, 1978.

Bensahel, Nora; Olga Oliker; Keith Crane; Richard R. Brennan, Jr.; Heather S. Gregg; Thomas Sullivan; and Andrew Rathmell. *After Saddam: Prewar Planning and the Occupation of Iraq*. Santa Monica, CA: Rand, 2008.

Boardman, Anthony, David Greenberg, Aidan Vining, and David Weimer. *Cost-Benefit Analysis: Concepts and Practice*, 3rd ed. Upper Saddle River, NJ: Prentice Hall, 2006.

Cole, Juan. *Sacred Space and Holy War: The Politics, Culture, and History of Shi'ite Islam*. London: I. B. Tauris, 2002.

Collier, Paul, V. L. Elliott, Havard Hegre, Anke Hoeffler, Marta Reynal-Querol, and Nicholas Sambanis. *Breaking the Conflict Trap: Civil War and Development Policy*, World Bank Policy Research Report. Washington, DC: The World Bank and Oxford University Press, 2003.

DeForest, Orrin, and David Chanoff. *Slow Burn: The Rise and Bitter Fall of Intelligence in Vietnam*. New York: Simon & Schuster, 1990.

Dinstein, Yoram. *The Conduct of Hostilities Under the Law of International Armed Conflict*. Cambridge, UK: Cambridge University Press, 2004.

Dixit, Avinash K. *Lawlessness and Economics: Alternative Modes of Governance*. Princeton, NJ: Princeton University Press, 2004.

Eckstein, Harry, ed. *Internal War: Problems and Approaches*. New York: Free Press, 1964.

Fleck, Dieter, ed. *The Handbook of Humanitarian Law in Armed Conflicts*. New York: Oxford University Press, 1995.

Galula, David. *Counterinsurgency Warfare: Theory and Practice*. New York: Frederick A. Praeger, 1964.

Gartner, Scott Sigmund. *Strategic Assessment in War*. New Haven, CT: Yale University Press, 1997.

Giraldo, Jeanne, and Harold Trinkunas, eds. *Terrorism Financing and State Responses: A Comparative Perspective*. Stanford, CA: Stanford University Press, 2007.

Gompert, David C., John Gordon IV, Adam Grissom, David R. Frelinger, Seth G. Jones, Martin C. Libicki, Edward O'Connell, Brooke Stearns Lawson, and Robert E. Hunter. *War by Other Means: Building Complete and Balanced Capabilities for Counterinsurgency*. Santa Monica, CA: Rand, 2006.

Gordon, Michael R., and Gen. Bernard E. Trainor. *Cobra II: The Inside Story of the Invasion and Occupation of Iraq*. New York: Pantheon Books, 2006.

Gurr, Ted Robert. *Why Men Rebel*. Princeton, NJ: Princeton University Press, 1970.

Hall, Katharine, and Dale Stahl. *An Argument for Documenting Casualties: Violence Against Iraqi Civilians, 2006*. Santa Monica, CA: Rand, 2008.

Hashim, Ahmed S. *Insurgency and Counter-Insurgency in Iraq*. Ithaca, NY: Cornell University Press, 2006.

Keegan, John. *The Iraq War*. New York: Alfred A. Knopf, 2004.

Kimmage, Daniel, and Kathleen Ridolfo. *Iraqi Insurgent Media: The War of Images and Ideas*. Washington, DC: Radio Free Europe/Radio Liberty, June 2007.

Komer, Robert W. *Bureaucracy Does Its Thing: Institutional Constraints on U.S.-GVN Performance in Vietnam*. Santa Monica, CA: Rand, 1972.

Levitt, Steven D., and Stephen J. Dubner. *Freakonomics: A Rogue Economist Explores the Hidden Side of Everything*. New York: HarperCollins, 2005.

Malkasian, Carter. *Will Iraqization Work?* Alexandria, VA: Center for Naval Analysis, 2007.

Mao Tse-Tung. *On the Protracted War*. Beijing: Foreign Language Press, 1960.

Merom, Gil. *How Democracies Lose Small Wars: State, Society, and the Failures of France in Algeria, Israel in Lebanon, and the United States in Vietnam*. Cambridge, UK: Cambridge University Press, 2003.

Migdal, Joel S. *Strong Societies and Weak States: State-Society Relations and State Capabilities in the Third World*. Princeton, NJ: Princeton University Press, 1988.

Mill, John Stuart. *The Collected Works of John Stuart Mill*. Vol. 21, *Essays on Equality, Law, and Education*. Edited by John M. Robson. Toronto: University of Toronto Press, 1984.

Nakash, Yitzhak. *The Shi'is of Iraq*. Princeton, NJ: Princeton University Press, 1994.

Napoleoni, Loretta. *Insurgent Iraq: Al Zarqawi and the New Generation*. New York: Seven Stories Press, 2005.

Ricks, Thomas E. *Fiasco: The American Military Adventure in Iraq*. New York: Penguin, 2006.

Sageman, Marc. *Leaderless Jihad: Terror Networks in the Twenty-First Century*. Philadelphia: University of Pennsylvania Press, 2008.

Schuck, Peter H., and Richard J. Zeckhauser. *Targeting in Social Programs: Avoiding Bad Bets, Removing Bad Apples*. Washington, DC: Brookings Institution Press, 2006.

Snyder, Jack. *From Voting to Violence: Democratization and Nationalist Conflict*. New York: W. W. Norton, 2000.

Sterman, John D. *Business Dynamics: Systems Thinking and Modeling for a Complex World*. Boston: Irwin McGraw-Hill, 2000.

Venkatesh, Sudhir. *Gang Leader for a Day: A Rogue Sociologist Takes to the Streets*. New York: Penguin, 2008.

Walzer, Michael. *Arguing About War*. New Haven, CT: Yale University Press, 2004.

———. *Just and Unjust Wars: A Moral Argument with Historical Illustrations*. New York: Basic Books, 1977.

Weimann, Gabriel. *Terror on the Internet: The New Arena, the New Challenges*. Washington, DC: U.S. Institute of Peace Press, 2006.

Wright, Donald P., and Timothy R. Reese. *On Point II: Transition to the New Campaign*. Fort Leavenworth, KS: Combat Studies Institute Press, 2008.

U.S. Government and Military Documents

Department of the Army. *Field Manual 3-24: Counterinsurgency*. Washington, DC: Headquarters, Department of the Army, December 2006.

Office of the Director of National Intelligence. *National Intelligence Estimate: Prospects for Iraq's Stability: A Challenging Road Ahead*. Washington, DC, January 2007.

Rawcliffe, John, ed. *Operational Law Handbook*. Charlottesville, VA: International and Operational Law Department, Judge Advocate General's Legal Center and School, 2007. U.S. Congress. Senate. Select Committee on Intelligence. "Report on Prewar Intelligence Assessments About Postwar Iraq Together with Additional Views." 110th Cong., 1st sess., May 2007.

U.S. Department of Defense, "Measuring Stability and Security in Iraq," June 2008 Report to Congress in Accordance with the Department of Defense Appropriations Act 2006 (Section 9010), monthly.

Departments of the Army and the Air Force. *Field Manual 100-20/Air Force Pamphlet 3-20: Military Operations in Low-Intensity Conflict.* Washington, DC: Headquarters, Departments of the Army and the Air Force, 1990.

U.S. Department of State, Bureau of Political-Military Affairs. *Counterinsurgency for U.S. Government Policy Makers: A Work in Progress*, Publication 11456, October 2007.

The White House, *National Strategy for Combating Terrorism*. Washington, DC, 2006.

White House Office of Communications, "Strategy for Victory: Defeating the Terrorists and Training Iraqi Security Forces," March 2006.

Reports

Akcam, Bahadir K., and Victor Asal. "The Dynamics of Ethnic Terrorism." Unpublished manuscript, Rockefeller College of Public Policy and Administration, State University of New York at Albany, 2007.

Anderson, Edward G., Jr. "A Preliminary System Dynamics Model of Insurgency Management: The Anglo-Irish War of 1916–21 as a Case Study." Conference proceedings, 24th International Conference of the System Dynamics Society, Nijmegen, the Netherlands, July 23–27, 2006.

Bergen, Peter, Joseph Felter, Vahid Brown, and Jacob Shapiro. *Bombers, Bank Accounts, and Bleedout: Al-Qa'ida's Road In and Out of Iraq*. Edited by Brian Fishman. West Point, NY: Combating Terrorism Center at West Point, Harmony Project, 2008.

Center for American Progress. "Iraq Benchmark Report Card: One Year After the Surge," January 24, 2008.

Cilluffo, Frank, Gregory Saathoff, Jan Lane, Sharon Cardash, and Andrew Whitehead. *NETworked Radicalization: A Counter Strategy*. Washington, DC: George Washington University Homeland Security Policy Institute; Charlottesville, VA: University of Virginia Critical Incident Analysis Group, 2007.

Conetta, Carl. "Vicious Circle: The Dynamics of Occupation and Resistance in Iraq." Project on Defense Alternatives Monograph 10. Cambridge, MA: Commonwealth Institute, 2005.

Cordesman, Anthony H. "The Independent Commission on the Security Forces of Iraq: A Critique." Washington, DC: Center for Strategic and International Studies, September 6, 2007.

———. "Iraq's Evolving Insurgency: The Nature of Attacks and Patterns and Cycles in the Conflict." Working draft. Washington, DC: Center for Strategic and International Studies, February 2, 2006.

———. "Iraq's Sectarian and Ethnic Violence and Its Evolving Insurgency: Developments Through Spring 2007." With Emma Davies. Washington, DC: Center for Strategic and International Studies, April 2007.

———. "Pandora's Box: Iraqi Federalism, Separatism, 'Hard' Partitioning, and U.S. Policy." Working draft. Washington, DC: Center for Strategic and International Studies, October 9, 2007.

Hassan, Hussein D. "Iraq: Tribal Structure, Social, and Political Activities." Washington, DC: Congressional Research Service Report for Congress, March 15, 2007.

Hoffman, Bruce. *Insurgency and Counterinsurgency in Iraq*. Rand Occasional Paper. Santa Monica, CA: Rand Corporation, June 2004.

Initiative for an Open Arab Internet, "Implacable Adversaries: Arab Governments and the Internet," *Openarab.net,* "Iraq" page. Available at http://www.openarab.net/en/node/356.

Kimmage, Daniel. "The Al-Qaeda Media Nexus: The Virtual Network Behind the Message." Washington, DC: Radio Free Europe/Radio Liberty (RFE/RL), March 2008.

Martinage, Robert C. "The Global War on Terrorism: An Assessment." Washington, DC: Center for Strategic and Budgetary Assessments, 2008.

Mroz, J. Rami. "Countering Violent Extremism: Videopower and Cyberspace." Policy Paper 1/2008. New York: EastWest Institute, February 2008.

O'Hanlon, Michael E., and Jason H. Campbell. "Iraq Index: Tracking Variables of Reconstruction and Security in Post-Saddam Iraq." Washington, DC: Brookings Institution, 2007.

O'Hanlon, Michael E., and Ian Livingston. "Iraq Index: Tracking Reconstruction and Security in Post-Saddam Iraq." Washington, DC: Brookings Institution, Saban Center for Middle East Policy, November 17, 2003–ongoing.

Prados, Alfred B., and Christopher M. Blanchard. "Saudi Arabia: Terrorist Financing Issues." Washington, DC: Congressional Research Service, September 14, 2007.

Smith, James J. "U.S. Post-Conflict Integration Policy of Militias in Iraq." Thesis, Naval Postgraduate School, Monterey, California, March 2008.

Index

ABC News poll, 62
Abizaid, John, 48, 81
Abu Ghraib, 72
Abu Risha, Abdul Sattar, 184
Act Now to Stop War and End Racism (A.N.S.W.E.R.), 71
Additional Protocol I, 97–98
Advanced Encryption Standard (AES), 75
Afghanistan, 64, 206–207
aggrandizement, wars of, 104–105
aggressive wars, 104–105
al-Ahbab tribe, 14
Al Anbar, 14, 49, 50–52, 60, 183–184, 195
al-Askari Shrine bombing, 6, 29, 50, 128, 140, 182
Albu Mahal tribe, 51
Al Bu Nasir tribe, 14
Al-Fajr Media Center, 73
Al-Furqan Media Institute, 73
algorithms, 75, 148, 160, 217–220
al-Hakim, Abd al-Aziz, 16
al-Hakim, Ammar, 16
Alhurra, 168, 174
al-Iraqiya, 172–173, 174
Al Jazeera, 73, 168, 172
al-Jinan forum, 74
al-Maliki, Nouri, 12, 28–29, 52, 174
al-Obaidi, Abdul-Qadir, 52
al Qaeda, 5, 59, 69, 168. *See also* al Qaeda in Iraq (AQI)
al Qaeda in Iraq (AQI)
  al-Askari Shrine bombing, 29
  Anbar Province, 14, 195
  insurgency funding, 60, 63
  intelligence, 84
  Internet, 69–70, 72–77
  Iraqi Army, 49, 51
  strategy, 19–20, 174, 175, 181–184
  three circles of war, 13, 14–15, 154
Al Qa'im, 50–51
al-Sabah, 173–174
al-Sadr, Moqtada, 17–18, 19, 47, 61, 140, 195
al-Sahab media company, 72
al-Sahhaf, Mohammed Said, 72
Al-Sakinah campaign, 76–77
al-Sistani, Ali, 16, 27, 170
al-Zarqawi, Abu Musab, 73, 74, 175, 181–182
al-Zawahiri, Ayman, 72, 175, 182
anarchy, 36, 105
Anbar Awakening, 52, 189
Anbar Province, 14, 49–52, 60, 183–184, 189, 195
Ansar al-Islam, 19
A.N.S.W.E.R. (Act Now to Stop War and End Racism), 71
application of force, 92–93, 95
AQI. *See* al Qaeda in Iraq (AQI)
Army, Iraqi. *See* Iraqi Army
army field manuals, U.S., 84, 92, 96, 97, 175

assumptions for stability, 194–197
attacks, pattern and measurement of, 129–131, 140–141, 143–145
autonomy, Kurdish, 6, 19, 27
Awakening Councils, 184
'Azza, 13

Baath Party
  background, 12–15, 171
  de-Baathification, 19, 25, 26, 32, 127–128
  insurgency, 62, 174
  Shias and, 15, 47
  Syria, 170–171
Badr Brigades, 16, 140
Badrists, 16–17, 140. *See also* Shias
Baghdad, 12, 70, 147, 175, 183, 189
Baghdad Bob, 72
Baiji refinery, 60
Barzani, Massoud, 18
Barzani, Mustafa, 18
base-case simulation, 129–131
Bayan Jabr, 16
Beautiful Virgins, The, 170
Bensahel, Nora, 45
bin Laden, Osama, 72, 182
biological weapons, 79–80
black market, 36, 60, 63
blogs, 69, 71–72
Brigade Combat Teams (BCTs), 84, 183
Broadcasting Board of Governors (BBG), U.S., 168, 176
Brookings Institution, 141
Bush, George W., 139, 143, 153, 167
Bush administration, 81, 94, 113, 119

Caleb Temple, 61
Casey, George W., Jr., 48, 51, 138
casualties
  civilian, 105, 128, 139–140, 142–144, 182, 184
  coalition, 111, 143–144
  modeling, 106, 107, 150, 162–163, 227, 235
Central Intelligence Agency (CIA), 80–81
Chalabi, Ahmed, 28
charities, as source of insurgent funding, 61–65
chemical and biological weapons, 79–80
Chiarelli, Peter, 83
CIA (Central Intelligence Agency), 80–81
Cilluffo, Frank, 74
citizens
  Iraqi (*See* civilians, Iraqi)
  U.S., 108–109, 111, 205
civilians, Iraqi
  casualties, 105, 128, 139–140, 142–144, 182, 184
  counterinsurgency, 126–127
  intelligence, 82–83
  interstate war ethics, 104–105, 111–112
  law of war, 93, 95, 96–97
  political development, 31
  security, 46, 47, 52, 98
civil war
  background in Iraq, 6–7, 14–18, 20
  defined, 1, 2–3
  economic recovery, 38
  elections, 29
  ethics and, 105, 110
  exit strategies, 185–187
  insurgency funding, 65–66
  law of war, 95–99
  modeling, 154–155, 228
  question of in Iraq, 113
  security reconstruction, 52–53, 54
  strategic dimensions, 181–183
Clausewitz, Carl von, 137
CNN, 73
Coalition Provisional Authority (CPA), 6
  constitution and elections, 26–28
  de-Baathification and Iraqi Army disbandment, 26, 32
  law of war, 96, 97–98
  media, 173–174
collapse of Iraqi government, shock of, 200–203
collateral damage, 105, 184
Collier, Paul, 122
combatant distinctions, 92–93, 103–104, 110
combatant immunity, 93–94, 95, 104
combat-centric metrics, 140
Common Article 3, 94, 98–100
communications, strategic, 167–177
  local, 171–177
  overview, 167–168
  regional, 168–171
  U.S. institutions, 175–177
Concerned Local Citizens, 52, 184

conflict transformation, 138, 146, 148. *See also specific* sectors of
constitution, drafting of Iraqi, 26–28
contagions, social, 121–125, 133
conventional operations and irregular war, 81–84
Cordesman, Anthony H., 46–47, 52, 61
counterfeiting, 60, 64–65
counterinsurgency
  ethics, 110–112
  intelligence, 82–84
  Iraqi Army, 48–50
  law of war, 95
  security, 36–37, 45–46, 52
  strategic dimensions, 181, 184–185, 186
  system dynamics modeling, 125–126, 131
  U.S. strategy, 14, 144, 175
Counterinsurgency (FM 3-24), 92, 175
"Counterinsurgency Guidance," 144
coup d'état, 3
CPA (Coalition Provisional Authority). *See* Coalition Provisional Authority (CPA)
criminal activities and insurgency funding, 60–63, 64–65. *See also specific* crimes
Crocker, Ryan, 29–30, 137, 138
Crystal Ball application, 220, 233–236
customary international law, 94, 96–99, 195–196
cyber attacks, 69, 72, 74
cyber cafés, 70, 75
cyber intelligence, 71–74, 76, 77

data collection, 138, 147–148
data elements and metrics used in modeling, 160, 220–222
Dawa Party, 29
de-Baathification, 19, 25, 26, 32, 127–128
debating justice of war, 111
Defense Intelligence Agency (DIA), 80
democracy, achieving in Iraq, 12, 30–32, 169–170, 195, 206
denial of access to Internet, 75–76, 77
Department of Defense, U.S.
  communications strategy, 71, 171–172, 174
  initial planning of Iraqi conflict, 11, 19
  law of war, 92, 94
  progress measurement, 138, 139–140, 143, 146–147
  stability operations, 140
Department of Homeland Security model, 156–158
detention, 93–94, 95
DIA (Defense Intelligence Agency), 80
diffusion model, 121–124
diplomacy of the deed, 175–176
Di Rita, Larry, 172
displacement, citizen, 95
distinction of combatants, 92–93, 103–104, 110
Donovan, David, 147
drawdown of troops, 193, 194, 197–199, 202–203, 206–207
drug dealing, 63, 66
Dulaym, 13

economic crisis, global, 205, 207
economic reconstruction, 35–42
  background, 35–36
  exit strategies, 196–197
  localities strategy, 39, 41–42
  resource allocation, 39–42
  security, 36–37, 38–39, 42
  stabilization, 205–206, 207
  system dynamics modeling, 124, 132–133
  Washington Consensus, 37–38
effectiveness
  ethics, 103, 112
  Iraqi Army, 53
  measuring, 140, 142–143
  modeling, 162–163, 223, 227–228, 230–231
elections, Iraqi, 19, 25, 27–29, 30, 33, 206
El Salvador, 4, 53
e-mails, 69, 71, 74, 75
employment, 26, 124, 132–133, 205, 221–222, 225–227
encryption, 75
"Encyclopedia of Hacking the Zionist and Crusader Websites" (Tsouli), 74
engagement, rules of, 92, 100
engagement over the Internet, 76–77
equilibrium strategy, 156, 211–212
ethics, 103–112
  counterinsurgency, 110–112
  interstate war, 104–105

interventions, 105–110
stability assumptions, 195–196
ethnic cleansing, 15, 16, 18, 20, 83
ethnic identity. *See also specific* ethnic groups
elections, 25, 28–30, 206
grievances, 128
versus national identity, 26, 30, 31
political development, 30–31
security reconstruction, 46–48
ethno-sectarian violence, 66, 80, 121, 129, 140–141, 143, 182
evacuation, citizen, 95
evaluation
progress (*See* metrics and evaluation of progress)
project, 40–41, 42
exit strategies
assumptions for stability, 194–197
considerations, 185–187
courses of action, 197–200, 202–203
feedback loops and shocks, 200–202
Experiences in the Name of Jihad: Deception, 169
extortion, 60, 62–63, 64–65, 66, 68
extremists, Islamic. *See* jihadists

Fallujah, 51, 82, 96, 181
Fallujah Brigade, 48, 54
Farabundo Martí National Liberation Front (FMLN), 4
Fatah, 5
Fedayeen Saddam, 19, 62
feedback systems
metrics, 148
modeling, 117–118, 120–125, 127–128, 132–133
stability, 200–202
field manuals, U.S. Army, 84, 92, 96, 97, 175
filters, Internet, 75
financing, insurgent and terrorist, 59–66
sources and expenditures, 59–63
within the three circles of conflict, 64–66
vulnerabilities and countermeasures, 63–64
foreign support of insurgencies, 61, 62–65. *See also specific* countries
forums, Internet, 71–77
forward operating bases (FOBs), 181, 183, 185–186, 189, 197–199
Franks, Tommy, 139
free speech, 27, 75–76

game theory, 156, 209–212
GAO (U.S. General Accountability Office), 137, 140–141, 146–149
Garner, Jay, 172
Gartner, Scott, 142
Gates, Robert, 83
Geneva Conventions, 92–95, 97–99, 100
Global Islamic Media Front, 73
goal-seeking behavior, 119–120
goals in Iraq, U.S., 138
grievances, Sunni, 125–128, 132
guerrilla warfare, 3, 4

hacking, 71, 72, 74
Hague Regulations, 92
Hamas, 5
Hamdan v. Rumsfeld, 94, 100
Hamlet Evaluation System, 147
Harris Corporation/Lebanese Broadcasting Corporation (LBC)/Al Fawares group, 173
Hashemites, 12
hearts and minds, winning Arab, 65, 111, 112, 169, 216
Hezbollah, 59, 61, 64
Hi International, 169
Hobbes, Thomas, 36
Hobbesian imperative, 36–37, 42
humane treatment, 94, 146
Human Intelligence Collector Operations (FM 2-22.3), 92
human intelligence (HUMINT), 80, 84
Human Terrain System (HTS), 83, 84
Hussein, Qusay, 62
Hussein, Saddam, 13–14, 62, 132, 171, 174, 180, 182
Hussein regime
deposement, 2, 5, 26, 36
grievances, 6, 174
insurgency, 62
tribalism, 12–14, 36

ideas, war of, 167, 169–171, 175–177
identity politics, 11–20
background, 11–12

de-Baathification and disbanding Iraqi Army, 26
Kurds, 6, 18–19, 27
political stabilization, 30–32
Shias, 15–18
Sunnis, 12–15
U.S. appreciation of, 19–20
ideology, 14, 124, 132, 167, 169–170, 175–176
IEDs (improvised explosive devices), 59–60, 143–145, 222
IGC (Iraqi Governing Council), 27
immunity, 93–94, 95, 104
implementation, 146–147
improvised explosive devices (IEDs), 59–60, 143–145, 222
Indicators of Force Multipliers (INFORM) modeling. *See* INFORM modeling
infection rates, 121, 123–124, 130
information dissemination on Internet, 71–73
INFORM modeling, 153–163, 217–236
about, 153–155, 156–159, 163
algorithms, 160, 217–220
small scale scenario 1, 161, 222–224
small scale scenario 2, 161–162, 224–227
small scale scenario 3, 162, 227–230
small scale scenario 4, 162–163, 230–231
stochastic simulation and scenario 5, 163, 213–217, 231–236
using shocks, 159–160, 215, 219–220
variables and Q matrix, 160, 220–222
infrastructure
modeling, 129, 155–160, 213–216
providing, 31, 35–40
institution building, 25, 30–32, 47, 206
Instructions for the Government of Armies of the United States in the Field (Lieber), 91–92
insurgency in Iraq. *See also* counterinsurgency
Baath Party, 62, 174
background, 5–7, 14, 15, 16, 17–18, 19–20
causes, 26–27, 180–181
defined, 1, 3–5
elections, 25, 27, 29
ethics, 110–112
exit strategies, 185–187
foreign support, 59, 61–65, 197
funding (*See* financing, insurgent and terrorist)
intelligence, 81–84
law of war, 95–99
modeling, 118–121, 125–133, 154–155
pattern and measurement of attacks, 104–141, 129–131, 143–145, 236
recruiting, 123–124, 130–132
sectarianism, 29, 51, 65–66, 80, 127, 182–183
security reconstruction, 36–37, 48–53, 63, 171
Shias, 61, 182–183
strategy, 175, 181
Sunnis, 62–63, 122, 124–128, 182, 184
U.S. ability to counter, 45–46
intelligence, 79–86
cyber, 71–74, 76, 77
importance of, 50, 196
intelligence-policy dysfunction, 79–81
irregular war and, 81–84
policy relations, 79–81, 83, 85–86
politicization of, 80–81, 85
interactive forums, 71–77
international law, customary, 94, 96–99, 195–196
Internet, 69–77, 177
al Qaeda, 69–70, 72–77
background in Iraq, 69–70
interstate war, 71–72
Internet cafés, 70, 75
Internet World Stats, 69–70
interstate wars
background in Iraq, 5–7, 14, 16, 20
defined, 1–2
elections, 1–2
ethics, 104–105, 111–112
exit strategies, 185–187
insurgency funding, 65–66
Internet, 71–72
irregular warfare, 2, 3, 5, 180
law of war, 92–94
modeling, 153–155
strategic dimensions, 181, 182–183
interventions, 105–110

Iran
civil war, 6–7, 182
escalated conflict with, 202
insurgency support, 59, 61–65, 197
interference in Iraqi governance, 25, 30
interstate war, 6, 65–66, 154
Kurds, 19, 201
Shias, 15, 17, 20, 30, 63, 66, 182–183
Sunnis, 20, 66
television, 171
U.S. strategy, 170–171, 182–183, 185, 187, 206
Iranian Special Forces, 197
Iraqi Accord Front, 28
Iraqi Army
about, 17, 30–31, 196
assessment and formation, post-Saddam, 46–49, 53, 140, 196
disbandment, 26, 32, 168
identity, 30–31, 50, 53
insurgency, 50–51, 171
Iraqi Council of Representatives, 28
Iraqi Governing Council (IGC), 27
Iraqi Interim Government, 98
Iraqi Interior Ministry, 140
Iraqi Media Network (IMN), 171–174
Iraqi National List, 28–29
"Iraq Index" (Brookings Institution), 141
Iraqi Security Forces (ISF), 46–54. *See also* Iraqi Army; police force, Iraqi
assessment of, 46–47
attacks by, 6
early efforts to rebuild, post-Saddam, 17, 47–48
insurgency rise despite competence, 48–50
local forces, 47, 51, 53–54
reconstruction and three circles of war, 52
transition to Iraqi control, 147
Iraq Memory Foundation, 174
Iraq Study Group, 142–143
Irhabi 007, 74
irregular warfare
conventional operations, 81–84
interstate wars and, 2, 3, 5, 180
ISCI (Islamic Supreme Council of Iraq), 16–17, 28–29, 30
ISF (Iraqi Security Forces). *See* Iraqi Security Forces (ISF)
Islamic extremists. *See* jihadists
Islamic Revolutionary Corps-Quds Force, 61
Islamic Supreme Council of Iraq (ISCI), 16–17, 28–29, 30
Israel, 5, 64, 69
Israeli-Palestinian conflict, 5, 69

Jaburi tribe, 13
Jackson, Colin F., 82
jihadists
al Qaeda, 14–15
insurgency, 62
Internet, 72–77
Kurdish autonomy, 19
Syria, 171
television portrayals, 169–170
Joint IED Defeat Organization (JIEDDO), 143–144
Jones, James L., 46
Jones Report, 46, 52
Jordan, 62, 197
Just and Unjust Wars (Walzer), 103–104
justice of war, 103, 110–111

KDP (Kurdistan Democratic Party), 18–19
Keegan, John, 180
khams, 13
Khomeini, Ayatollah Ruholluah, 170
kidnapping and ransom activities, 60, 63, 64–65, 68
Kirkuk, 18, 29, 201
Kurdistan, 18–19, 201
Kurdistan Alliance, 28
Kurdistan Democratic Party (KDP), 18–19
Kurdistan Workers' Party (PKK), 19, 30, 186, 197
Kurds, 5
autonomy, 6, 19, 27
elections, 25, 28–29
identity politics, 13, 18–19
secession, 201
security reconstruction, 46–47, 48
Turkey, 30, 186, 197

law, customary international, 94, 96–99, 195–196

lawful combatants, 93, 95
Law of Land Warfare (FM 27-10), 92, 96, 97
law of war, 91–100
  insurgency and civil war, 95–99
  interstate war, 92–94
  overview, 91–92
  stability assumptions, 195–196
learning trap, 82–83
legal obligations of U.S. military. *See* law of war
legal transactions for insurgency funding, 61, 64–65
leverage, 131–133
Leviathan (Hobbes), 36
Lieber, Francis, 91
Lieber Code, 91–92
Light, 174
Lincoln, Abraham, 91
Lloyd George, David, 142
loyalty and security, 4, 11–12

Mahdi Army, 18, 47, 61, 140
manuals, U.S. Army field, 84, 92, 96, 97, 175
Martinage, Robert, 74
Measuring Progress in Conflict Environments (MPICE), 144–146
media. *See also specific* types
  local, 171–174
  regional, 168–171
  U.S. institutions, 176–177
metrics and evaluation of progress, 137–148
  data collection, 147–148
  early assessment problems, 138–139
  goals, 138
  indicators, 140–146
  treatment evaluation, 146–147, 148
mi2g, 71
military intervention and simulation-based models, 131, 133
military strategies. *See* strategic dimensions of Iraqi conflict
militias, local, 47, 50–51, 53–54, 196, 197
misconceptions, Arab, 169
MNF-I (Multi-National Force-Iraq), 48, 83
modeling. *See* INFORM modeling; system dynamics modeling
morality, 103, 111–112. *See also* ethics
Morocco, 63, 71
Mosul, 12, 60, 201
Mujahideen Secrets, 75
Mukhabarat, 62
Multi-National Force-Iraq (MNF-I), 48, 83
Muntafiq, 13
mutual reinforcement and three types of war, 155

Naqqash, Samir, 173
Nash equilibrium, 156, 211–212
national identity, Iraqi, 11, 26, 30–31, 66, 128, 195
National Intelligence Council (NIC), 80–81
National Intelligence Estimate (NIE) report, 59–61, 62, 64, 65–66
nationalist Sunnis, 13, 14, 15
National Security Council (NSC), 83, 172
"National Strategy for Combating Terrorism," 167
"National Strategy for Victory in Iraq," 139
nation-building paradigm, 38
newspapers, 70, 169, 173, 176–177
"New Way Forward in Iraq, The," plan, 143
New York Times, 61
NIC (National Intelligence Council), 80–81
non-combatants, 93, 95, 104
non-state actors, defined, 209
North Korea, 172

Obama, Barack, 199, 206
obligations to Iraq
  ethical, 105–110
  legal (*See* law of war)
occupying force obligations, 95–99, 195–196
Odierno, Ray, 144
Office of Management and Budget, 172
oil
  infrastructure, 37, 39
  Iraqi economy, 81, 196, 205–206
  smuggling, 60, 64–65
  wealth distribution, 31, 36
Operation Iraqi Freedom, 2, 167–168
Operation Iron Harvest, 183
Operation Kennesaw Dragon, 82

Operation Phantom Fury, 96
Operation Phantom Strike, 183
Operation Swarmer, 82
Operation Together Forward, 147
O'Sullivan, Meghan, 83
Ottoman Empire, 12
outposts and outreach strategy, 6, 183–187, 197–199

Palestinian-Israeli conflict, 5, 69
Patriotic Union of Kurdistan (PUK), 18–19
Pax, Salam, 72
Penal Code, Iraqi, 97
Perle, Richard, 81
Peshmerga, 47
Petraeus, David, 29–30, 61, 83, 137–139, 141–143, 175
physical infrastructure, 37–39
pirates, 105
PKK (Kurdistan Workers' Party), 19, 30, 186, 197
planning, U.S., 80–85
police force, Iraqi, 30–31. *See also* Iraqi Security Forces (ISF)
  assessment, 46, 140, 196
  economic reconstruction, 38–39
  law of war, 97
  modeling, 161–162, 215–216, 221–231
  security reconstruction, 51
  Shias, 16–17, 29, 140
  training, 30, 196
political intervention and simulation-based modeling, 132–134
political transition, Iraqi, 25–32
  correcting instability, 30–32
  events that shaped, 26–30
  overview, 25
politicization of intelligence, 80–81, 85
populace interactions, 93–94, 95–99
populace obligations, 94–99
print media, 70, 169, 173, 176–177
prisoners of war, 93, 105
problem identifications, 209
progress, metrics and evaluation of. *See* metrics and evaluation of progress
project evaluation, 40–41, 42
Provisional Irish Republican Army, 59
public
  Iraqi (*See* civilians, Iraqi)
  U.S., 108–109, 111, 205
PUK (Patriotic Union of Kurdistan), 18–19

qabila, 13
Q matrix and modeling, 160, 217, 220
quantitative and qualitative elements of strategy, 183–187, 199–200
Quds Brigade, 197

radio, 70, 168–169, 171, 173, 176–177
Radio Sawa, 168–169
Rand study, 143–144
ransom activities, 60, 63, 64–65
reconstruction, economic. *See* economic reconstruction
recruiting
  al Qaeda, 72, 73–76
  insurgency, 123–124, 130–132
  media, 172–173
relations, intelligence-policy, 79–81, 83, 85–86
Republican Guard, 62
resource allocation, 39–42
Roz, J. Rami, 74
RSA (Rivest, Shamir, Adleman) algorithm, 75
rules of engagement, 92, 100
Rumsfeld, Donald, 180

Sadrists, 11–12, 16, 17–18, 20, 28–29, 30
Sageman, Marc, 73, 74
Sanchez, Ricardo, 170
satellite television, 168, 171, 173, 174
Saudi Arabia, 197
  insurgency funding, 14, 61–66
  Internet, 76–77
  television, 169–170
Schuck, Peter, 39
Science Applications International Corporation (SAIC), 172
SCIRI (Supreme Council for Islamic Revolution in Iraq), 16, 28
secession, 29, 107, 198, 199, 200–201
sectarianism
  civil war, 52–53, 54
  elections, 28–30
  identity, 26, 31

- insurgency, 29, 51, 65–66, 80, 127, 182
- intelligence, 81, 85
- media, 172, 174
- modeling, 121, 128
- security, 46–47, 53–54, 196
- violence, 66, 80, 121, 129, 140–141, 143, 182

security, 45–54
- assessment of, 46–47
- democracy and, 31
- early efforts, post-Saddam, 47–48
- economic reconstruction, 35, 37, 38–39, 42
- exit strategies, 196
- identity and, 11–12
- insurgency, 48–50, 63
- law of war, 95, 97
- local forces, 47, 51, 53–54
- reconstruction and three circles of war, 52
- regional, 197
- standards for intelligence recruitment, 85

self-defense, 93, 95, 103–104, 105
Sewell, Sarah, 111
Shammar tribe, 13
Shias, 5–6
- constitution, 27
- elections, 25, 28–29
- identity politics, 11–12, 13, 14–18, 20
- insurgency, 61, 182–183
- Iran and Saudi Arabia, 66, 197
- media, 173
- security reconstruction, 46–47, 48, 50
- Sunni reconciliation, 132

Shinseki, Eric, 19
shocks, models and, 158–163, 200–202, 213–217, 219–225, 227–230, 233
signals intelligence (SIGINT), 84
Significant Activities (SIGACTS), 140–141
simulation-based models, 129–133, 163, 231–236
smuggling, 60–65
social contagions, 121–125, 133
social infrastructure, 37–38, 195, 206, 207
SOFA (status of forces agreement), 197–199, 206
software, 74, 75, 84
Somekh, Sasson, 173
South Korea, 172
sovereignty, Iraqi, 3, 96, 106, 109–110, 187, 197, 202
Spanish Civil War, 3
stability in Iraq. *See also specific* aspects of
- assumptions for, 194–197
- in hindsight, 19–20
- operations, 140–141, 146–147
- political, 30–31

State Department, U.S., 169, 174, 176
status of forces agreement (SOFA), 197–199, 206
stochastic dynamic systems modeling, 163, 213–220, 231–236
stock and flow modeling, insurgency, 119–121, 125–133
strategic dimensions of Iraqi conflict, 179–187
- civil war phase, 181–183
- communications (*See* communications, strategic)
- conventional war to insurgency phase, 181–182
- ethics and, 111–112
- exit considerations (*See* exit strategies)
- goal of U.S. in Iraq, 138, 153
- initial conflict phase, 180
- overview, 179–180
- performance measurement, 137, 142–144, 146, 148
- surge and swarm phase, 183–185

stuns of August, 181
subversion of Internet activities, 76, 77
Sumer, 173–174
Sunnis, 5–6
- de-Baathification and disbandment of Iraqi Army, 26
- elections, 25, 28–29
- grievances, 125–128, 132
- identity politics, 12–15, 19–20
- insurgency, 62–63, 122, 124–128, 182, 184
- Iran and Saudi Arabia, 66
- security reconstruction, 46–47, 48, 50–52
- Shia reconciliation, 132
- Sunni Awakening, 52, 189

Supreme Council for Islamic Revolution in Iraq (SCIRI), 16, 28

surge, troop, 138, 142, 143, 183–184, 193
susceptible-infected (SI) model, 121–124
Syria
 insurgency funding, 61, 62
 interference in Iraq, 25, 140, 170–171, 197, 201, 206
system dynamics modeling, 117–134, 153–163, 209–236
 about, 117–118
 building process, 155
 data elements and metrics, 220–222
 early conception of insurgency, 118–121
 game theory, 156, 209–212
 INFORM modeling (*See* INFORM modeling)
 insurgent reinforcing/creation loops, 125–128
 model behavior through computer simulation, 129–133
 problem identifications, 209–212
 scenarios (*See under* INFORM modeling)
 three circles of war, 121–125, 213–217

Tactical Ground Reporting System, 84
takfiri ideology, 175
Talabani, Jalal, 18
Tal Afar, 201
Tash ma Tash, 170
television, 70, 147, 168–174, 176–177
Territorial Forces Evaluation System, 147
terrorism, ethics and, 105
Terrorism in the Hands of Justice, 174
theory of the problem, 137, 139–140
threats to Iraq, 138–140
3-7 Iraqi Brigade, 50–51
training
 exit strategy, 186, 199, 206
 foreign, 61, 65–66, 182–183
 intelligence, 82, 84, 85
 Internet, 72
 Iraqi Security Forces, 30, 48–49, 51, 53, 138
Tranquility campaign, 76–77
Transitional Administrative Law, 27
treatment evaluation, 146–147, 148
tribal confederation, 13
tribal identity, 11–12, 13–14, 36. *See also* sectarianism
troop drawdown, 193, 194, 197–199, 202–203, 206–207
troop surge, 138, 142, 143, 183–184, 193
Tsouli, Younes, 74
Turkey, 6–7, 19, 30, 154, 185–187, 197, 201–202

Ubaydi tribe, 13
unemployment, 26, 124, 132–133, 205, 221–222, 225–227
United Arab Emirates, 62
United Iraqi Alliance, 28
United Nations headquarters bombing in Baghdad, 181
United Nations Security Council Resolutions, 13, 98–99
Unix Security Guards, 71
unlawful combatants, 93–94, 95
unmanned aerial vehicle (UAV), 84
Urban Sunni Nationalists, 13, 14, 15
U.S. Army Corps of Engineers, 144–146
U.S. Army Peacekeeping and Stability Operations Institute, 144–146
U.S. Civil War, 3, 5
U.S. General Accountability Office (GAO), 137, 140–141, 146–149
U.S. Information Agency (USIA), 176
U.S. Institute of Peace, 144
U.S. Marine Corps, 84, 146
U.S. Supreme Court, 94
use of force, 3, 100, 104–105, 175

variables, modeling, 160, 194–197. *See also specific* variables
Vieira de Mello, Sergio, 181
Vietnam War, 5, 141, 146, 147, 181
Voice of America (VOA), 168–169
volunteer organizations, 31

Walzer, Michael, 103–104, 110–111
war of ideas, 167, 169–171, 175–177
Washington Consensus, 37–38
wealth distribution, oil, 31, 36
web attacks, 71
websites, 71–77
winning Arab hearts and minds, 65, 111, 112, 169, 216

Zeckhauser, Richard, 39

About the Editors and Contributors

John Arquilla earned his degrees in international relations from Rosary College (BA 1975) and Stanford University (MA 1989, PhD 1991). He is a professor of defense analysis at the Naval Postgraduate School (NPS), where he has taught in the special operations curriculum since 1993. He also serves as the director of the Information Operations Center. His teaching interests revolve around the history of irregular warfare, terrorism, and the implications of the information age for society and security.

His books include: *Dubious Battles: Aggression, Defeat, and the International System* (Crane Russak, 1992); *From Troy to Entebbe: Special Operations in Ancient and Modern Times* (University Press of America, 1996), which was a featured alternate of the Military Book Club; (coeditor) *In Athena's Camp: Preparing for Conflict in the Information Age* (Rand, 1997); *Networks and Netwars:* (coeditor) *The Future of Terror, Crime, and Militancy* (Rand, 2001), named a notable book of the year by the American Library Association; *The Reagan Imprint: Ideas in American Foreign Policy from the Collapse of Communism to the War on Terror* (Ivan R. Dee, 2006); and *Worst Enemy: The Reluctant Transformation of the American Military* (Ivan R. Dee, 2008). His vision of "swarm tactics" was selected by the *New York Times* as one of the "big ideas" of 2001.

Heather S. Gregg is an assistant professor at the Naval Postgraduate School's Department of Defense Analysis. Prior to joining the faculty at NPS in 2006, she was an associate political scientist at the Rand Corporation. She earned her PhD in political science in 2003 from the Massachusetts Institute of Technology (MIT), where she focused on international relations and security studies. Dr. Gregg also holds a master's degree from Harvard Divinity School, where she studied Islam, and a bachelor's degree in cultural anthropology from the University of California, Santa Cruz. In addition to her academic experience, she has spent time in several regions of conflict, including Palestine/the West Bank (July 1998–July 1999) and Croatia and Bosnia (August 1994–March 1996). She most recently completed a three-month stint in Doha, Qatar, where she worked on postsecondary education reform for the Qatari government. Dr. Gregg is a contributing author of *Beyond Al Qaeda*, volumes 1 and 2 (Rand, 2006), and *After Saddam: Prewar Planning and the Occupation of Iraq* (Rand, 2008).

Hy S. Rothstein, senior lecturer in the Department of Defense Analysis at NPS, served in the U.S. Army as a Special Forces officer for more than twenty-six years prior to embarking on a teaching career. He spent many years in Latin America training and advising governments threatened by active insurgencies. Dr. Rothstein served as the director of plans and exercises of the Joint Special Operations Command (JSOC) for more than three years and helped develop and operate the first special operations battle lab immediately prior to his retirement in 1999. More recently, he has conducted research for both the Department of Defense and the Central Intelligence Agency.

Dr. Rothstein earned a degree in general engineering from the United States Military Academy; a military art and science degree from the U.S. Army Command and General Staff College; a master of arts in law and diplomacy from the Fletcher School, Tufts University; and a PhD in international relations from the Fletcher School, Tufts University. His book, *Afghanistan and the Troubled Future of Unconventional Warfare* was published in 2006 by the Naval Institute Press.

Tarek K. Abdel-Hamid has been a professor of information sciences and system dynamics at the Naval Postgraduate School since 1986. Dr. Abdel-Hamid received his PhD in management information systems and system dynamics at MIT and his master's in engineering economic systems at Stanford. Prior to joining NPS, he spent two and a half years at the Stanford Research Institute as a senior information technology (IT) consultant. Dr. Abdel-Hamid is the coauthor *of Software Project Dynamics: An Integrated Approach* (Prentice-Hall, 1991), which garnered the authors the 1994 Jay Wright Forrester Award. In addition to his book, he has authored or coauthored more than forty papers on system dynamics and its applications.

Douglas A. Borer serves as the Defense Analysis Department's associate chair for instruction at the Naval Postgraduate School. Dr. Borer received his BA in psychology from Ripon College in 1985, an MA in political science from the University of Montana in 1988, and his PhD in political science from Boston University in 1993. He has worked at a variety of academic postings, including the University of the South Pacific in Suva, Fiji; the University of Western Australia in Perth; Virginia Tech in Blacksburg, the Universiti Kebangsaan in Kuala Lumpur, Malaysia; and the U.S. Army War College in Carlisle Barracks, Pennsylvania. His scholarship focuses on the politics of legitimacy in times of war. He is the author of *Superpowers Defeated: Vietnam and Afghanistan Compared* (Frank Cass, 1999); and is co-editor with John Arquilla of *Information Strategy and War: A Guide to Theory and Practice* (Routledge, 2007).

Dorothy E. Denning is a professor of defense analysis at the Naval Postgraduate School. Her current research and teaching encompasses the areas of conflict and cyberspace, trust and influence, terrorism and crime, and information operations and security. She is author of *Information Warfare and Security* (Addison-Wesley, 1998) and more than 130 articles, and has testified before Congress on encryption policy and cyberterrorism. Dr. Denning has previously worked at Georgetown University, Digital Equipment Corporation, SRI International, and Purdue University. At Georgetown, she served as the Patricia and Patrick Callahan Family Professor of Computer Science, chair of the Computer Science Department, director of the Georgetown Institute for Information Assurance, and chair of the Computer and Network Task Force. She has also served as president of the International Association for Cryptologic Research, chair of the International Cryptography Institute, and chair of the National Research Council Forum on Rights and Responsibilities of Participants in Networked Communities.

Dr. Denning is an Association for Computing Machinery (ACM) Fellow and recipient of the Augusta Ada Lovelace Award, the Harold F. Tipton Award, the National Computer Systems Security Award, and several other security awards. She is an honorary certified information systems security professional (CISSP) and certified information security manager (CISM), and was a featured security innovator in *Time* magazine. She received her BA and MA degrees in mathematics from the University of Michigan and her PhD degree in computer science from Purdue University, which later awarded her a Distinguished Science Alumnus.

Christopher M. Ford is a major in the United States Army Judge Advocate General's (JAG) Corps currently serving as an assistant professor and executive officer in the Department of Law, United States Military Academy. He served in a variety of positions in the JAG Corps, including legal assistance attorney, administrative law attorney, and operational law attorney. From 2004 to 2005, he served as the 5th Brigade Combat Team, 1st Cavalry Division Command judge advocate in Baghdad, Iraq.

Major Ford received a bachelor of arts in political science from Furman University and a juris doctor from the University of South Carolina School of Law. Recently, he has published pieces in *Military Review, Parameters,* the *Tulane Law Review,* and the *Army Lawyer.*

William P. Fox is a professor in the department of defense analysis at the Naval Postgraduate School. Previously he was the chair of mathematics at Francis Marion University in Florence, South Carolina. He was also an academy professor and a professor of discipline in the mathematics department at the United States Military Academy.

Dr. William P. Fox received his BS degree from the United States Military Academy at West Point, New York; his MS from the Naval Postgraduate School; and his PhD from Clemson University. He served as an officer in the United States Army from 1973 to 1998.

He has coauthored several textbooks on mathematical modeling including: *Mathematical Modeling with Minitab* (Brooks/Cole, 1987), *A First Course in Mathematical Modeling* (Cengage, 2008), and *Mathematical Modeling with MAPLE* (forthcoming). He has prepared more than a hundred technical and educational articles, presentations, and workshop presentations. He serves as the associate contest director for the Consortium for Mathematics and Its Applications (COMAP) Collegiate Mathematical Contest in Modeling (MCM) and serves as contest director for the High School Mathematical Contest in Modeling (HiMCM).

Raymond E. Franck, Jr., joined the Naval Postgraduate School faculty in 2000, after thirty-three years of service in the U.S. Air Force (USAF). He graduated from the U.S. Air Force Academy in 1967 and received his graduate education (AM and PhD) in economics from Harvard University. His professional military education includes Air War College and the National Security Management course. Teaching assignments at NPS have included courses in economics plus systems and cost analysis. He has pursued research related to defense acquisition, military strategy, and military innovation. In addition, he has served on a number of faculty committees related to curriculum, personnel policy, and other matters. Finally, his faculty service has included the interim chairmanship of the Systems Engineering Department from July 2002 to September 2004.

Operational assignments in the air force included tours in B-57 and B-52 aircraft, as well as officer-in-charge of the air force element of the joint command center at Keflavik, Iceland. Brigadier General Franck is a command pilot with 2,300 hours' flying time. Staff assignments included tours with the Office of the Secretary of Defense and at Headquarters, Strategic Air Command. In addition, he was assigned to the USAF Academy as an instructor and later as a professor and head of the Department of Economics and Geography. He has also served with the faculty of the Joint Military Intelligence College as associate dean of the School of Intelligence Studies.

Michael E. Freeman is an assistant professor in the Department of Defense Analysis at the Naval Postgraduate School. His research interests focus on the causes of terrorism, the relationship between democracy and terrorism, and U.S. foreign policy. He has taught classes on international terrorism, terrorist financing, and homeland defense. He received a PhD from the University of Chicago in 2001 and is the author of *Freedom or Security: The Consequences for Democracies Using Emergency Powers to Fight Terror* (Praeger, 2003) as well as several journal articles on terrorism and democracy. Before joining NPS, he was a lecturer at the University of Chicago, a postdoctoral fellow at Dartmouth, and an analyst at the Central Intelligence Agency.

Karen Guttieri is an assistant professor at the Cebrowski Institute for Information Innovation and Superiority at the Naval Postgraduate School, Monterey, California, where she focuses on research relating to stabilization and reconstruction. She earned her PhD from the University of British Columbia in 1999. She is the coeditor of *Interim Governments: Institutional Bridges to Peace and Democracy?* (United States Institute of Peace Press, 2008).

Russell Muirhead, Jr., is the Robert Clements Professor of Democracy and Politics at Dartmouth College. Muirhead teaches contemporary political theory with a focus on American political thought, political ethics, and contemporary debates about justice. Prior to joining the faculty at Dartmouth, he taught at the University of Texas at Austin, and was on the faculty of Harvard University and Williams College. He is the author of *Just Work* (Harvard University Press, 2004) and is now at work on a book entitled *A Defense of Party Spirit.*

Robert Reilly is a senior fellow at the American Foreign Policy Council. Most recently, he has taught at the College of International Security Affairs at the National Defense University. In the Office of the Secretary of Defense, he served as senior advisor for information strategy (2002–2006). He also participated in Operation Iraqi Freedom in 2003, as senior advisor to the Iraqi Ministry of Information. Before that position, he was director of the Voice of America, where he had worked the prior decade. Reilly has served in the White House as a special assistant to the president (1983–1985) and in the U.S. Information Agency both in DC and abroad. In the private sector, he spent more than seven years with the Intercollegiate Studies Institute, as both national director and then president. He was on active duty as an armored cavalry officer for two years and attended Georgetown University and the Claremont Graduate University. He has published widely on foreign policy, "war of ideas" issues, and classical music. He has contributed chapters to ten books and authored two, the most recent of which is *The Closing of the Muslim Mind* (Intercollegiate Studies Institute, 2010).

Glenn E. Robinson is an associate professor in the Department of Defense Analysis and the codirector of the Center on Terrorism and Irregular Warfare at the Naval Postgraduate School. During 2007–2008 he was on leave at the Center for Middle East Studies at the University of California at Berkeley, where he was writing a book on Middle East politics and security issues. He is the author of *Building a Palestinian State: The Incomplete Revolution* (Indiana University Press, 1997).

Joshua Rovner is an assistant professor of strategy and policy at the U.S. Naval War College, Rhode Island. His research deals with a range of international security issues, including nuclear proliferation, deterrence theory, and the role of intelligence in national security affairs. Dr. Rovner earned his PhD in political science from the Massachusetts Institute of Technology, an MA from Boston College, and a BA from the University of California at San Diego. He is the author of *Fixing the Facts: National Security and the Politics of Intelligence* (Cornell University Press, forthcoming) and coauthor with Austin Long of "The Perils of Shallow Theory: Intelligence Reform and the 9/11 Commission," *International Journal of Intelligence and Counterintelligence*, 18, no. 4 (Winter 2005–2006): 609–637.